EUROPEAN CENTRAL BANK

Georg Christopher Schweiger

MINERVA PRESS
LONDON
MIAMI DELHI SYDNEY

EUROPEAN CENTRAL BANK
Copyright © Georg Christopher Schweiger 2000

All Rights Reserved

No part of this book may be reproduced in any form
by photocopying or by any electronic or mechanical means,
including information storage or retrieval systems,
without permission in writing from both the copyright
owner and the publisher of this book.

ISBN 0 75410 885 6

First published 2000 by
MINERVA PRESS
315–317 Regent Street
London W1R 7YB

Printed in Great Britain for Minerva Press

EUROPEAN CENTRAL BANK

Acknowledgements

I would like to thank Colin Bourn, Jeff Kenner, John Williams and Susan Thornton from the International Centre at the University of Leicester Faculty of Law for their support and guidance.

I am also grateful to my friends and colleagues at DG BANK Deutsche Genossenschaftsbank AG, London branch. Of enormous benefit to me has been the constructive criticism from a number of sources. In particular I would like to thank for their help and contribution the following: D.W. Bopp (Dallas), A.G. Garnett (Coventry), D. Gramlich (Bromley), W. Kantner and P. Wahl (Vienna), A. Legner (London) and H.J. Smith (Huntingdon).

The views expressed in this book are my own and I have attempted to make reference to the law as at December 1998 but it goes without saying that any mistakes and failures are my own.

I am grateful to the European Central Bank for permission to reproduce a number of information obtained from its official website www.ecb.int.

My thanks also have to be extended to the staff of Minerva Press for their patience and understanding in dealing with a forever changing manuscript and an impatient author.

Whilst every effort has been made to make clear reference to other sources and copyright material, I take this opportunity to offer my apologies to the holders of any such rights which I may have unwittingly infringed or any reference which has not been properly referenced or attributed.

Last but not least there is my family, who have lived with an increasingly distracted father and husband for a considerable period of time. It's over and I will not do it again – at least not until you are grown up.

Foreword

I do not believe that there exists a more effective description of the institutional arrangements surrounding the European Central Bank.

The author has managed to describe these arrangements and place them in their historical and political context with much clarity. Nor has he avoided controversy, such as the political autonomy question. However the approach is objective throughout.

There has been disappointingly little public debate within Europe on these issues. This book will both stimulate and inform such a debate. This is its lasting contribution.

Dr Rory F Knight
Dean Templeton College, Oxford

Contents

Abbreviations		xi
Introduction		xiii
I	Convergence Criteria	29
II	The European Monetary Institute	56
III	European Central Bank	63
	1. Establishment	63
	2. Organisation	67
	3. Structure	72
	4. Tasks and Objectives	95
	5. Powers	103
	6. Limits of Operational Independence	106
	7. Monetary Strategy	108
	8. National Central Banks	119
	9. Regulatory Role and Lender of Last Resort	123
	10. Reporting and Public Accountability	126
IV	Independence v. Accountability	132
	1. Political Interference	134
	2. Price Stability	140
	3. Market Credibility	162
	4. Conduct and Effectiveness of Monetary Policy	169
	5. Limits on Operational Independence	185
	6. National Central Banks	189
	7. Supervision of the ECB	191
	8. ECOFIN/ EURO X	192

	9. Role of The European Parliament	201
	10. Other EC Institutions	206
	11. Guardian of Banking System and Lender of Last Resort	207
V	Comparison with German Bundesbank	218
VI	Judicial Review	224
VII	Stability and Growth Pact	227
VIII	Legitimacy	241
IX	Risk of Failure and Possible Alternatives	247
X	The Opt-out of the United Kingdom	262
XI	Summary	269
Bibliography		276
Appendix I		305
Appendix II		321
Appendix III		328
Appendix IV		360
Appendix V		376
Appendix VI		380
Appendix VII		398

Abbreviations

BN	Billion
CFI	Court of First Instance
DM	Deutschmark
EBRD	European Bank for Reconstruction and Development
EC	European Community
ECB	European Central Bank
ECJ	European Court of Justice
ECOFIN	Economic and Financial Committee
ECSC	European Coal and Steel Community
ECU	European Currency Unit
EEA	European Economic Area
EEC	European Economic Community
EIB	European Investment Bank
EMI	European Monetary Institute
EMS	European Monetary System
EMU	European Monetary Union
EP	European Parliament
ERM	Exchange Rate Mechanism
ESCB	European System of Central Banks
EU	European Union
EUROSTAT	European Statistical Office
GDP	Gross domestic product
IMF	International Monetary Fund
IML	Institut Monetaire Luxembourgeois

OECD	Organisation for Economic Co-Operation and Development
SDR	Special Drawing Right

Introduction

The first manifestation of serious intent in Europe – or indeed anywhere according to some monetary historians[1] – to regulate exchange rates across national borders appears to have been the French dominated Latin Monetary Union, which was formed in 1865 as a venture in bimetallic (gold and silver) standard monetary co-operation between France, Italy, Belgium and Switzerland, later joined by several other countries including Greece and Spain.

European ideas for monetary integration and even a single currency (at least for a number of European States) find their roots in the increased trade between European countries during the nineteenth century and in the competing political and commercial interests of the historic European superpowers: the largely sterling-based United Kingdom with its almost global Commonwealth interests; the growing economic power of young Prussia with the introduction of the Reichsmark under Count Bismarck; and France with its colonies and dependencies in black Africa, Latin America and the Far East.

The French 'Latin Monetary Union' ceased after only eleven years in 1878 when its member states adopted the more common gold standard. Nevertheless, the Latin Monetary Union can be seen as a forerunner of the first EMU as it was treaty-based (previous pan-European projects from the Roman Empire to the Third Reich tended to be based on force of arms rather than on per-

---

[1] See K. Dyson, *Elusive Union: The Progress of Economic and Monetary Union in Europe*, Chapter 1.

suasion) and it tried to tackle problems associated with multiple currencies in an economically integrating and neighbouring group of countries. Its ultimate failure was not only attributed to the rise in the gold standard[2] that provided a common standard of value by a single commodity but also because it lacked a central institution and a single monetary policy.

Although under the gold standard where there was still no central monetary institution, participants tended to follow the Bank of England's policy lead and observed certain unwritten rules that allowed citizens to buy and sell unlimited amounts of their national currency against gold at their central banks. Britain's lead came largely from the fact that it been on a full legal gold standard since 1821; Germany adopted it after 1871 and the young United States in 1879.

Almost thirty years after the launching of its attempt for a modern single currency process by the Heads of States and Governments in December 1969, the European Union and all its citizens will witness over the next three years momentous decisions and events which will greatly affect their economic and political development, most likely on a permanent basis. Although the Werner Report[3] already provided for a clearly outlined plan to achieve economic and monetary union in Europe by 1980, extreme currency volatility caused by the first oil price crises effectively derailed its implementation. In all member states of the EU, citizens are confronted with the complete spectrum of political opinions and representations towards economic

---

[2] See M. Panic, *European Monetary Union: Lessons from the Classical Gold Standard*, Chapters 2 and 3.

[3] Report to the Council and the Commission on the Realisation by Stages of Economic and Monetary Union in the Community ('Werner Report'), Supplement to Bulletin II–1970 of the European Communities, Luxembourg, 1970.

and monetary union – from utter scepticism, mistrust and even outright opposition to wholehearted embrace and support every step of the way. It is too easy to forget that EMU is not just for financiers, central bankers and economists but it is a political undertaking and an integral part of further European integration. Even with a compelling economic rationale, EMU is not solely based on logic otherwise the new single currency would be to economics what Esperanto is to politics. Nevertheless, post-war experiences of many European states and the fall of communism between 1989 and 1991 have made it more and more logical and reasonable for an aggregation of otherwise conflicting national interests, especially as the EU no longer stands as a third force between the two superpowers.

At the centre of the programme towards economic and monetary union, which at its third stage introduces a single currency, there are a number of perceived advantages, e.g.:

1. Eliminating the variable nature of exchange rates will save hedging costs and will permit lower real interest rates (i.e. nominal interest rates less rate of inflation).
2. Savings from currency conversion and other transaction costs.
3. Improvements in the transparency of prices across a much larger market.
4. By eliminating exchange rate fluctuation between member states and lower real interest rates, commercial confidence and certainty is promoted.
5. Such stability should prove efficient and stimulate economic growth when backed by a collective and consistent monetary policy.
6. The efficacy of the Community's policy-making initiatives will be backed by a stable currency that is not susceptible to being undermined by the erratic economic behaviour of a single state.

7. A single currency can serve as a platform for global transactions and investments.
8. EMU should weaken the power of those who thrive on monetary chaos and financial speculation and more importantly their effect on the finances of member states.
9. The overwhelming powers of the global marketplace are better balanced and constrained by democratically decided economic and social priorities.

However, with every winner there will normally be a loser. Hence the above benefits might not be without costs but whether these costs turn out to be major will depend on the nature and extent of disturbances affecting individual member states and the effectiveness of other policies in securing adjustment in particular fiscal policy.

The benefits of monetary union will not only be linked to savings in currency conversion and other transaction costs for businesses and private individuals but also the dynamic gains for European economic development which could be considerable but impossible to quantify. As for the expected costs of monetary union, they are directly related to the scope and the measurable effectiveness of an independently conducted monetary policy, including the use of interest rates and the exchange rate, which will have to be abandoned in a single currency monetary union. No sensible calculation of the economic benefits of EMU is possible without giving some regard to the possible massive costs of failing to adopt the Euro.

Ever since the break up of Bretton Woods, economists[4] have asked the question whether countries would benefit

---

[4] R.A. Mundell in 'A Theory of Optimal Currency Area' in *American Economic Review*, 60(4), September 1961; R. I. McKinnon in 'Optimal Currency Areas' in *American Economic Review*, 53(4) September 1963; P.B.

from permanently locking their exchange rates and whether such a locking or single currency arrangement would constitute an 'optimal currency area'. Within such an area, labour (including potential social costs) and capital must be able to move freely between regions and across industries, there must be flexibility of prices and wages and economies must be fully open to trade and their output must have a diversified product range, however not necessarily in that order of preference. But which region in the world or group of countries could ever achieve the transition of such broad theoretical principles into actual operational and sustainable criteria?

This quickly destroys the argument that the present EU would ever represent an optimal currency area. Large member states such as Germany and possibly France together with the smaller economies clustered around them might show signs of a 'feasible' monetary union. As long as there are still considerable questions whether the United States can be deemed an optimal currency area, the long-term success and superiority of EMU cannot be guaranteed. This points again towards the fact that the motives behind EMU are essentially political in nature.

Critics, most of them politicians and other functionaries, in particular in the United Kingdom, are very reluctant to lose the tool of exchange rates as an adjustment mechanism in order to attract inward investment from overseas and to

---

Kenen in 'The Theory of Optimal Currency Areas: An Eclectic View' in *Monetary Problems of the International Economy*, University of Chicago Press, 1969; P.R. Krugman in 'Policy Problems of a Monetary Union' in *Currencies and Crises*, Cambridge, Mass., MIT Press, 1992; P. DeGrauwe in 'The Economics of Monetary Integration', *Oxford University Press*, 1992; L. Bini-Smaghi and S. Vori in 'Rating the EC as an Optimal Currency Area' in *Finance and the International Economy*, Oxford University Press, 1992 and W. M. Corden in 'European Monetary Union: The Intellectual Pre-History' in The Monetary Future of Europe, Centre for Economic Policy Research Discussion Paper, London, March 1993.

provide a counterbalance for otherwise painful, i.e. linked to job losses, measures for raising productivity. The costs in terms of potentially higher gross domestic product rates from lower investments and costs associated with productivity improvements will in my opinion be much smaller and essentially only opportunity profits than real savings from the replacement of a domestic currency with a high risk premium attached to its interest rates due to exchange rate uncertainty. Whether the loss of exchange rate as an adjustment mechanism would entail significant costs for some member states has in my opinion not been proven and often exaggerated by politicians. One should not forget that most member states, including the United Kingdom, have significant export volumes to regions such as North and South America as well as the fast growing economies of the Far East and with the Euro exchange rate against currencies such as the US dollar and the Japanese yen still being flexible, this will continue to offer some degree of flexibility and scope for adjustments.

Despite the above, one should not forget that the total cost of introducing the single currency will be considerable throughout the EC and can only be mitigated by the fact that they will be once-and-for-all costs. Estimates suggest that the actual conversion will take three to five years, not counting prior investigation and planning. Latest estimates put the total cost of conversion at 30,000 million Euros, equivalent to 2.5% of combined 1996 GDP of EU member states.

Economists have argued for a considerable period of time whether EMU will have any 'real' effects upon economic growth and more importantly jobs, or whether it would be a mere change in exchange rate regimes where EMU's economic sense would sooner rather than later become open to question. Savings on transactions and hedging costs alone are not sufficient reasons to change an

entire currency system. Lasting EMU must therefore be the catalyst for real economic changes fostering a positive dynamic impact from the interaction between the new single currency and the single European market.

Although the single European market already exists as a legal entity, at least since 1992, the supposed gains in efficiency and increased competition have not been realised to the extend envisaged since the signing of the Single European Act for a number of reasons. Most EU countries, in particular Germany as the motor for European growth, entered a protracted cyclical economic downturn. The demise of the ERM I and resultant currency realignments also distorted competitive forces. Crucially, consumers as well as producers (dominated in Europe by SMEs and not a small number of multinationals) did not behave as though they were in a single, borderless and open European marketplace.

EMU will not be without its problems generated by incentives which will be taken up by consumers and producers across the board as a reaction to almost total transparency of wages and costs. Consequently, EMU will:

1. Accelerate the move of industrial production even within the SME sector towards areas with the most cost-efficient processes.
2. Speed up the process of industrial transformation across an increasing number of industries.
3. Increase pressure for member states or regional governments continuing to support ailing or inefficient industries.
4. Highlight high redundancy costs as a key barrier for structural changes necessary for economies to cope with asymmetric shocks or deteriorating competitive standards.

5. Generally expose the interaction between microeconomics and politics leading to more transparency for the electorate.

Nevertheless, it is difficult to see how increased price transparency will drastically alter the behaviour of the European consumer, especially if he is already an experienced bargain hunter living near existing borders. A far bigger deterrence will remain with significant differences in consumer protection law throughout Europe even though plans for harmonisation are making painfully slow progress. The biggest advantage of EMU will not likely be in the form of increased price transparency at the retail end but with the Euro throwing light on the underlying factors which shape competitive forces and thus determine price levels within the Euro-zone. For example, the Euro might finally challenge the claims by car manufacturers that price differentials of up to 30% within Europe are caused by currency fluctuations.

If one listens to the people without the gloss and sensationalism that have become so often the trademarks of the popular media, one can detect that the citizens of Europe have a mixture of cold feet and unease about the new, and are often hindered by a lack of meaningful information and political guidance. Even the citizens of Germany and their memories of hyperinflation during the 1920s have started to question the need for replacing their trusted and 'strong' Deutschmark and its 'defender and guarantor' the Deutsche Bundesbank.

The initial credibility of the EMS and with it the increased stability of intra-ERM exchange rates was based on the downward convergence of inflation rates. How much can this convergence of inflation rates be attributed to the operation of the ERM? In truth, the link is virtually impossible to prove econometrically but instinct and some

circumstantial evidence might prove that participation in the ERM served, at least for a not inconsiderable part, as an additional weapon against inflation.

Why did a long period of stability for the EMS end in 1992–93, mainly at the hands of speculators? Resurgence of Euroscepticism in Denmark and the United Kingdom, the long and painful ratification process of the Maastricht Treaty, sceptical views on commitments solemnly undertaken by government leaders, excessive and overaggressive use of exchange rates by governments and central banks as an or the prime anti-inflationary instrument, the fact that national authorities had deprived themselves with the abolition of capital controls of a policy instrument to which they had frequently resorted in the past, and a fundamental asymmetry in the EMS on the back of the Deutschmark and the increasingly important role of the Deutschmark as an international reserve currency are just a few reasons.

Eurosceptics such as the EC insider Bernard Connolly who from 1989 to 1995 was responsible for analysis of the EMS and national and Community money policies alleges that the ERM and the 'glidepath' to EMU was not only inefficient but also undemocratic and for these reasons the demise of the ERM was simply what he called the 'market triumph of July 1993'.[5] The former Conservative Party Chairman Norman Tebbit once called the ERM 'Eternal Recession Mechanism'.

EMU is a major political issue because of its wider economic ramifications and also because it touches the very heart of national sovereignty. It can be argued without too much trouble that developments in this area will largely determine the future course of European integration and hence also the shape of the emerging new European

---

[5] Bernard Connolly, *The Rotten Heart of Europe*, London, Faber & Faber, 1995, p.xv.

architecture. Money and monetary policy has frequently been used as an instrument for wider political objectives, even though markets and economic fundamentals have not always obliged by adjusting themselves to the severity and peculiarities of politics. How important matters relating to EMU have become for political and financial British interests appear to have been confirmed when a renegade British spy claimed that MI6 spent vast sums of money since 1986 to obtain secret information from a highly placed informant inside the German Bundesbank, providing the British secret service with regular information ranging from sensitive matters such as planned interest rates movements (solely the prerogative of the German Bundesbank) to detailed information regarding the German Bundesbank's and the German government's position relating to the single currency and the negotiations of the Maastricht Treaty.[6]

The member states of the European Union have committed themselves under the Maastricht Treaty to forming an economic and monetary union by the end of the century. This will mean locking their exchange rates together permanently, with the ultimate aim of merging them into a single currency as soon as possible. Although the establishment of a single currency has its origins in the political will of now fifteen EU member states, the faithful implementation of the single currency according to the Treaty of Rome, as amended by the Single European Act and the Maastricht Treaty, is based on the rule of law and sanctity of treaty obligations. When EMU was challenged in the courts, the German Federal Constitutional Court in

---

[6] 'Spy claims MI6 has spy in Bundesbank' in *The Sunday Times*, 20th September 1998.

Karlsruhe declared that the Maastricht Treaty and with it EMU as a whole was a '...community based on stability'.[7]

The Delors Report[8] proposed that economic and monetary union should be achieved in three discreet evolutionary steps:

Stage One: The initiation of the process of creating an economic and monetary union with greater convergence of economic performance through the strengthening of economic and monetary policy co-operation within the existing institutional framework.

Stage Two: Transition to the third and final stage and setting up of basic organs and structure of economic and monetary union.

Stage Three: Movement to irrevocably locked exchange rates and introduction of a single currency to replace national currencies with ESCB becoming responsible for the formulation and implementation of monetary policy, exchange rate and reserve management, and the maintenance of a properly functioning payment system.

At its Madrid meeting in December 1996, the European Council confirmed that Stage Three will start on 1st January 1999, and agreed to name the European currency unit to be introduced at the start of Stage Three the 'Euro'. With doubters constantly challenging[9] the start of EMU on

---

[7] Brunner v. European Union Treaty (1994) 1 CMLR 57, 101.

[8] Study of Committee for the Study of Economic and Monetary Union (so-called Delors Committee) entitled 'Report on Economic and Monetary Union in the European Community', Luxembourg, 1989, p.38.

[9] Brunner v. European Union Treaty (1994) 1 CMLR 57, 99.

1st January 1999, even questioning the binding force of the Maastricht Treaty, any delay would have amounted to nothing more than short-sighted political opportunism ignoring the monetary timetable agreed in Maastricht and established as a legally binding instrument.

The report published by the European Commission in May 1995 and entitled 'Green Paper on the practical arrangements for the introduction of the single currency' proposes to introduce the Euro in three phases within Stage Three:

Phase A: Began with the decision in March 1998 about which countries form part of the first wave on 1st January 1999. By May 1998 most legislation had been enacted to give the Euro legal status and the ECB became formally established in June 1998.

Phase B: Begins on 1st January 1999 when the Euro becomes a currency in its own right with irrevocably fixed conversion rates for local currencies of participating countries. The ECU ceases to exist. Gradual changeover for the public and private non-bank operators.

Phase C: Starts on 1st January 2002 at the latest and will last six months at most. Will see the introduction of Euro denominated notes and coins and decommissioning of participating national currencies.

Eurosceptics and central banks (notably the Bank of England as a messenger for the British Government and the Deutsche Bundesbank under its President Karl Otto Poehl) were not hotly in favour of the early proposals for EMU after the exchange rate turbulence of the previous eighteen

months had pinned their hopes on the hard-headedness of the central bankers on the Delors Committee to stop the 'Trojan Horse of Eurofederalism'.[10] Instead of trying to block the monetary union plans in the Delors Committee altogether, Karl Otto Poehl as the representative of the Deutsche Bundesbank insisted instead on the fulfilment of certain conditions for the creation of a ECB. The conditions tabled by the Bundesbank called in essence for no ECB funding for governments in financial difficulties.[11] This included rescue finance, tight limits on the size of budget deficits for countries aspiring to participate in monetary union, and a totally independent status for all national central banks as a precondition to EMU.

Even the Governor of the Bank of England at the time, Robin Leigh-Pemberton, signed the report 'on the lame excuse that he did not want to be the odd one out' but in the full knowledge that this would enrage his ultimate boss, Margaret Thatcher.[12]

According to the Maastricht Treaty, the second stage of EMU was supposed to start on 1st January 1994; and officially it did so even though the old system of fixed but adjustable intra-EC exchange rates under the EMS, with narrow margins of fluctuations, had suffered a number of severe blows in 1992 and 1993. These developments have largely been underestimated as they severely undermined public confidence in the new treaty and the process of integration in general, causing a resurgence of 'Europessimism'. Despite the adverse economic environment, the decline in popular support for European integration and

---

[10] Bernard Connolly, *The Rotten Heart of Europe*, London, Faber & Faber, 1995, p.xx.

[11] Ibid., p.79

[12] Ibid., p.79. The Delors Committee had only advisory character and the Governor had no right to veto its findings unlike Mrs Thatcher in the Council of Ministers.

the problems experienced with the ratification of the new treaty, the Union seemed hardly to have lost its attraction in the outside world. A further enlargement took place in January 1995 with Austria, Finland and Sweden becoming full members of the European Community.

Credibility and permanence are to be achieved by pooling monetary sovereignty in a new ECB, constituted with the full legal force of the Treaty of Rome. As the blueprint for the ECB resembles in many respects a 'European Bundesbank', I will attempt to show that the ECB has been set up according to the principles of effectiveness, accountability, transparency, continuity and consistency and will be secure from undue political interference but accountable to the people of Europe. Only hindsight will tell whether this bold statement will prove to be that of a learned man or that of an utter fool.

Not all member states will join the project of EMU from 1st January 1999. A few might never do so. But the commitment has now firmly been made to introduce a single currency, the Euro, the effect if not initially the form, throughout much of the Community by around the year 2000. Throughout the EU, politicians, bankers, journalists and many other observers have started to use the term 'Euroland' to describe the territory in which the Euro will be used. Even the ECB has started to accept and use the term 'Euroland' both when using the German and English language. The term Euroland, however, has not found acceptance by the policy makers in France as it implies, so they claim, that the member states participating in the single currency would already have merged to form a single country. The French, whose purity of their language is protected since 1634 by the Académie Francaise, officially refer to the eleven member states participating in the single currency as 'zone monétaire européenne' and have reluctantly accepted the term 'Euro-zone'. In the true spirit of

European compromise, the term Euroland might carry the day but with the French adding an additional letter e for the use of the term Euroland in their native language to create 'Eurolande'.[13]

With national currencies being replaced by the Euro what will happen to the national postage stamp, for so long a symbol of national sovereignty and identity? But in many EU member states, the postage stamp was also the outward representation of many bastions of state or privatised monopolies. The central questions will be sooner rather than later when the monopoly for letters falls in many member states and all stamps will be denominated in Euro. Should member states still issue postage stamps at all?

---

[13] As reported in *Le Figaro* and German *Handelsblatt*, 13th August 1998.

Chapter I
Convergence Criteria

Crucial factors which had to be resolved in the run up of Stage Three – the conversion to the single currency – were whether member states met the convergence criteria. Problems were the ECB's apparent weak accountability and the potential conflict created by the separation of monetary and fiscal policy. Some remedies for what are seen as defects in the blueprint will be offered in this book but as with any uncharted terrain doubts will remain. The European Council meeting in December 1997 in Luxembourg provided the blueprint and necessary commitment[1] from each EU member state for economic policy co-ordination in the run up and during Stage Three as well as confirming that '…the Euro will be a reality, marking the end of a process culminating in the fulfilment of the economic conditions necessary for its successful launch.'[2]

The convergence criteria served to define the 'economically correct' behaviour for members in the final stage of EMU and represented a unique 'fitness and stabilisation programme' for Europe before the turn of the millennium in order to ensure that Europe will have a role as a global player in the twenty-first century. This part of the treaty is a clear reflection of the new economic orthodoxy: monetary policy will only serve as an anti-inflationary instrument in

---

[1] Resolution of the Luxembourg European Council of 12th–13th December 1997 on economic policy co-ordination in Stage Three of EMU and on Treaty articles 109 and 109b.
[2] Art. 1 of Declaration by the ECOFIN Council of 3rd May 1998.

the hands of independent central bankers, since it is no longer considered to have any long-standing effect on output and employment, while fiscal deficits and the accumulated debt will come under strict multilateral control. There was no provision made for an active macro-economic policy at the European level. Notable Eurosceptics such as Bill Cash, Conservative MP, endorse that 'the Bundesbank's record on monetary control is not better and no worse than that of many traditional dependent central banks [...] and that Germany's solid record on low inflation and of a strong and stable currency is a function [...] of the strengths of its political economy of its tradition of high skills, technical perfection, long-term corporate financing through universal banks, consensual industrial relations and above all of its trading structures, exporting high-value goods and importing lower added-value goods.'[3]

The heavy reliance on fiscal and monetary convergence instead of lasting economic convergence made some commentators[4] speculate whether 'the hand of Machiavelli could be detected in the drafting of the Maastricht criteria, but if not it was somebody just as cunning...' as the Maastricht criteria could be influenced by member states either by genuine means or by a little creative accounting and more than just a little fudging. The Maastricht Treaty set specific numerical reference values for government deficits and overall debt levels and tried to impose a common accounting framework for measuring each member state's compliance with the target figures. Some

---

[3] *Maastricht: The Case Against Economic & Monetary Union* by Ian Milne, Nelson & Pollard, June 1993, p.12.

[4] See 'The Euro is born: now comes the hard part' in *The Financial Times*, 3rd May 1998.

experts[5] have criticised the fact that Maastricht opted to set numerical targets in the domain of fiscal policy, whilst at the same time setting procedural rules in the field of monetary policy, mainly on national central banks during Stage Two of EMU. The benefit of hindsight however has shown that increased transparency and comparability of budget figures among a diverse group of EU member states and procedural requirements in connection with the transfer of monetary policy from national central banks to the new ECB during Stage Three changed the incentive structure in the field of fiscal policies for most EU member states and secured significant levels of budgetary consolidation in all EU member states irrespective of their initial participation in the new single currency or not. Whether such incentive structures have achieved fiscal discipline in all EU member states as a permanent feature of Stage Three of EMU has yet to be seen and secured within the terms of the Stability and Growth Pact.

Nevertheless, governments and political parties of most mainstream persuasions throughout the EU have started to realise that strong political bias and short-term political considerations lie at the root of excessive deficits and high public debt. This means that deliberate or unexpected deficits during periods of economic hardship are not sufficiently counterbalanced by budgetary improvements during periods of economic growth and prosperity. The Stability and Growth Pact represents hard evidence for such realisation where governments voluntarily limit their own fiscal misbehaviours and where penalties will be imposed on those not adhering to the necessary budgetary disciplines.

---

[5] See Barry Eichengreen's 'Saving Europe's Automatic Stabilisers' in *National Institute Economic Review*, 159, 1997, pp.92 – 98.

Research[6] undertaken in the recent past has shown a number of reasons why budget balances are essentially used as buffers between the political aspirations of a sitting government and economic activity. According to the 'fiscal illusion' theory, voters and even markets tend to underestimate the dangers of poor budgetary policies where benefits of government spending are overestimated (i.e. spending ministers enjoy large negotiating margins for spending decisions) and costs of future taxation are typically underestimated thereby never allowing surpluses during periods of economic expansion to offset deficits accrued during recessions, especially when governments tend to adopt for political reasons expansionary policies and/or increased deficits during election years. Economists, sociologists and other experts, however, have failed to explain why voters have not learnt from past experiences and seen through such obvious politically motivated government behaviour.

The various convergence criteria and the ability of individual member states to fulfil them have been assessed in the official convergence report published by the European Monetary Institute in March 1998.

1. Inflation Rate

All member states wishing to participate in EMU had to achieve an inflation rate of less than 1.5% above the average of the three best performing states.[7] The headline inflation

---

[6] See A. Alesina and R. Perotti 'The Political Economy of Budget Deficits' in IFM Staff Papers 42, 1995, pp.1–31 and 'Fiscal Discipline and the Budget Process' by the same authors in *American Economic Review Papers and Proceedings* No. 86, 1996, pp.401–407.

[7] European Monetary Institute, Convergence Report, March 1998. The criterion for price stability focused on the performance of member states over a twelve month period ending January 1998 as published by the

rate for each member state is adjusted by EUROSTAT into HICPs (Harmonised Indices of Consumer Prices) to iron out differences of national definitions for consumer price indices.

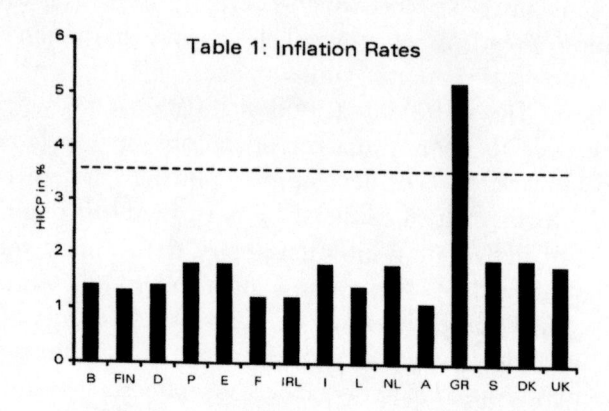

Table 1: Inflation Rates

It appears that most member states benefited during 1997 from low pressures on wage and unit labour costs often associated with a widened output gap and adverse labour market conditions affected by cyclically high rates of unemployment. Large stable European exchange rates and no significant development in the US dollar have also helped to keep down pressures on imported inflation.

Euro-wide interest rates together with economic convergence will not lead by themselves to the elimination or significant reduction of inflation but it will cause ongoing, even growing, divergence in regional inflation which will

---

European Commission and by using the unweighted arithmetic average for each member state and for the three best performing countries to which the reference criterion of 1.5% (as per Art. 1 of Protocol No. 6 on the convergence criteria referred to in Art. 109j of the treaty establishing the European Community as attached to the EC Treaty, OJ C191) was added.

be very difficult to control within the narrow remit of monetary policy and thus under the control and guidance of the ECB. Hence the ECB will not only have to pursue a monetary policy under which inflation up to 2% may well represent price stability but at even greater cost avert deflation down to a regional level and its potentially devastating real economic consequences.

The ECB will inherited modest inflation rates when it commences its money market operations on 1st January 1999. However, recent developments in the Far East have added a further threat to the stability of EMU through the import of deflation. Whilst temporary deflationary forces may not make the ECB economic planners unduly worried, the regained competitiveness of many Far Eastern economies and the resultant problems for many European economies could have considerable effects on inward investments and with it on Europe's already high unemployment. Differences in wage costs, unit labour costs and productivity throughout Europe would allow some member states to compete with such deflationary forces but EMU is generally expected to reduce productivity differentials within the Euro-zone.

Convergence in unit labour costs however is unlikely to be achieved with wages actually falling in high-cost countries. Labour market rigidities and a general lack of political pressure from left or left of centre governments in the majority of EU member states will create an environment where only different rates of wage inflation will eventually lead to a narrowing of wage differentials across Europe. Some economists fear that when deflationary pressures hit EMU and Europe is unable to compete with wage flexibility and labour mobility then 'with fiscal policy largely locked down by high public debt and the restrictions of the

EMU stability pact, governments in the core countries would have few tools to deal with the problem.[8]

Table 2: Unit Labour Costs 1990, 1993 - 1997

Hourly compensation costs in US$ for production workers in manufacturir
Source: US Department of Labor, Washington DC.

With labour market flexibility only a distant prospect, increased inflationary pressures from accelerating wage increases across parts of Europe might force the ECB to act in its pursuit of price stability. The intriguing question is going to be what impact these wage increases are likely to have across Europe and at what point the ECB will intervene with its Euro-zone measurements and monetary policy instruments to counterbalance these developments.

Fresh in the minds of some European central bankers will be the developments and actions of the German Bundesbank after the unification of the two former Germanys. With the benefit of hindsight, the Bundesbank now admits that their policies left room for improvement and concluded that 'even moderate rates of inflation are a very costly economic option'.[9] It is not certain whether the ECB will adopt such a hard line, at least during the early

---

[8] Bronwyn Curtis, chief economist at the Nomura Research Institute in 'Asian crisis creates risks for EMU', July 1998.
[9] Karl Heinz Tödter and Gerhard Ziebarth in *'Preisstabilität oder geringe Inflation'*, Deutsche Bundesbank, discussion paper 3/1997.

phases of EMU, but the necessity for the ECB to achieve credibility and the claim[10] that a permanent reduction of 2% in the rate of inflation could yield as much as 1.4% growth in GDP will be a heavy burden for the ECB decision makers. Limited inflationary pressures within the Eurozone mean that deflationary shocks from Far East Asia must not be underestimated as such pressures could indirectly lead to even higher unemployment in Europe with the ECB and its pursuit of achieving price stability acting as a catalyst for more job losses.

2. Long-term Interest Rates

Long-term interest rates in member states wishing to participate in EMU should over the twelve month reference period ending January 1998 not have been more than 2% above the long-term interest rates of the three best performing states not in terms of their HICP inflation rate.[11]

The reference value for the long term interest rates criteria was calculated based on the benchmark yields for Austria, France and Ireland as they had the lowest rates of HICP inflation. To their average of 5.8% p.a., the convergence criteria of 2% was added, generating a

---

[10] Joachim Fels in 'Is inflation too low? Discuss', Morgan Stanley Dean Witter, weekly briefing on Euro monetary policy, 30th July 1998.

[11] European Monetary Institute, Convergence Report, March 1998. The criterion for convergence of long-term interest rates focused on the performance of specific long-term benchmark interest rates in all member states over a twelve-month period ending January 1998 as published by the European Commission and by using the unweighted arithmetic average of the long-term interest rates in the three member states with the best performance in terms of HICP inflation, to which the reference criterion of 2% (as per Art. 4 of Protocol No. 6 on the convergence criteria referred to in Art. 109j of the treaty establishing the European Community as attached to the EC Treaty) was added.

qualifying reference value of 7.8% p.a. If the benchmark long-term interest rates of the three member states with the

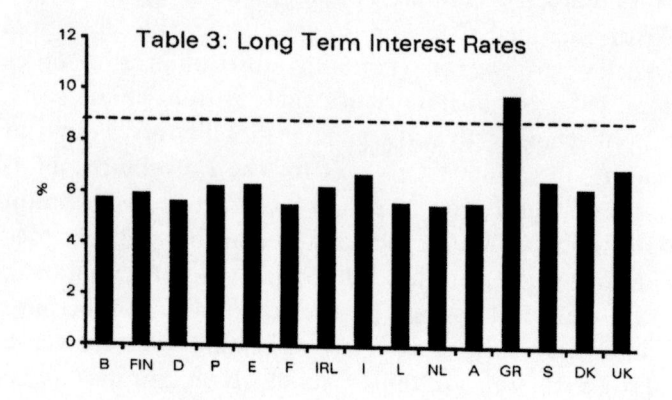

Table 3: Long Term Interest Rates

lowest rates of interest would have been used, the average rates of France, the Netherlands and Germany would have calculated a reference value of 7.5% p.a. Even with this possible adjustment, all member states with the exception of Greece would have qualified.

Improvements in inflation rates have not only facilitated a general reduction in long-term interest rates, especially in former high yield currencies, they have also aided government budgetary positions of many member states by reducing the cost of serving the national debt relative to GDP.

A single Euro interest rate has so far been preceded by a convergence of long-term interest rates, at least for those countries joining on 1st January 1999. This convergence has taken place in some countries somewhat divorced from their relative economic cycle, i.e. different growth rates. This could put the monetary policy of the ECB in a dilemma, as a single Euro interest rate no longer allows measures on a country by country basis. Higher Euro interest rates in Holland, Italy, Ireland, Spain and Portugal

would be the correct response to fast, credit driven growth whilst increased interest rates may not be suitable at present for the subdued economies of France and Germany.

With member states no longer being able to adjust currencies to correct economic disequilibrium, other factors will grow in importance such as unit labour costs, fiscal policy and with it the general mobility of labour and capital. A single interest rate set for the Euro by the ECB may cause overheating in parts of Europe or even within areas of member states. This may be an inevitable consequence of a single currency but did the French central bank set a different interest rate for the south of France because the north-east showed signs of overheating? The answer is no. True to the spirit of the Treaty of Rome, Europe will be a Europe of regions and not a Europe of participating and non-participating member states.

3. Government Budget Deficits

In order to qualify for EMU membership, member states should have achieved or maintained budgetary deficit positions at or less than 3% of national GDP.[12] Against the background of capital market rates having converged at very low levels, in some member states historic low levels, and many EU member states having achieved inflation rates well below the qualifying rate of 2.7%, the degree of convergence achieved by member states in terms of fiscal policy is much poorer.

During 1997, three member states (Denmark, Ireland and Luxembourg) recorded fiscal surpluses of between

---

[12] European Monetary Institute, Convergence Report, March 1998. The criterion for an actual or planned budget deficit of a member state at or below 3% of its gross domestic product at market prices was set in Art. 104c(2)(a) EC Treaty and Art. 1 of Protocol No. 5 on the excessive deficit procedure attached to the EC Treaty (OJ C191).

0.7% and 1.7% of GDP. The EMI is nevertheless cautious in its convergence report and points out that some of the measures undertaken by a number of member states to reduce their fiscal deficit may only have had 'a temporary effect'[13] and it estimates that these measures could have been as large as 1% in some countries.

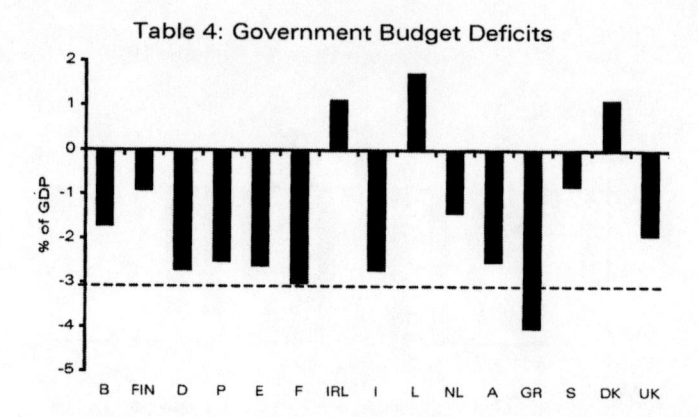

Table 4: Government Budget Deficits

Such creative accounting by governments of member states can normally only produce one-off shifts and the impact of such measures will reduce over time, just when member states will be forced to adhere to the strict financial disciplines imposed on them under the terms of the Stability and Growth Pact from 1999 onwards. If Euro-zone member states will not make efforts to achieve a balanced budget or if possible a surplus their deficit positions will rise in times of a cyclical economic downturn beyond the tough limits set by the Stability and Growth Pact.

As Art. 104c of the EC Treaty looks under the excessive deficit procedure not only at the actual government deficit for 1997 but also the planned deficit position of each member state for 1998 and beyond and whether under the

---

[13] European Monetary Institute, Convergence Report, March 1998, p.5.

terms of the EC Treaty 'the ratio has declined substantially and continuously and reached a level that comes close to the reference value', the European Commission provided projections for the general government surplus/deficits for each member state in its spring 1998 forecast so that they could be considered in the formal convergence report.

Table 5: Government Budget Deficits 1998

Even the fiscal deficit of the Greek government is expected to fall during 1998 below the required level. Although having qualified on an one-off basis for participation in the single currency, most of the eleven member states participating in the single currency are far away from achieving a balanced budget or even achieve a surplus.

4. General Government Debt Positions

In addition to their annual budgetary positions as a ratio of GDP, the convergence criteria for each member state also included a ceiling on public debt[14] of no more than 60% of

---

[14] General government gross debt as a percentage of GDP but adjusted by Council Regulation 3605/93.

national GDP.[15]

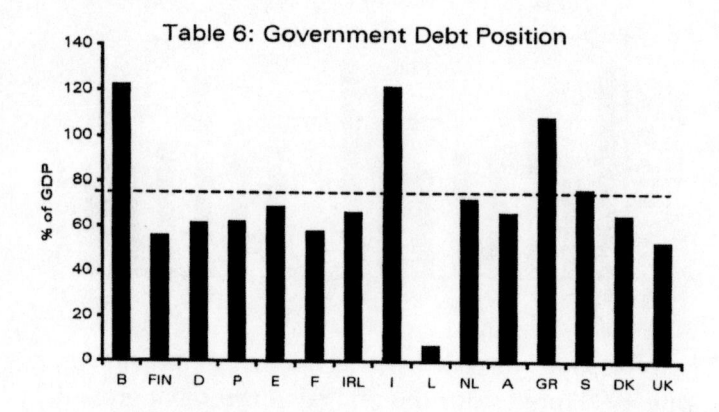

Table 6: Government Debt Position

% of GDP on y-axis (0 to 140); countries on x-axis: B, FIN, D, P, E, F, IRL, I, L, NL, A, GR, S, DK, UK

Although considerable and sustained progress has been made in a number of member states to reduce their respective public debt mountains, eleven of the fifteen member states still did not comply with the tough debt to GDP ratio.

Similar to the general budgetary position of each member state government, Art. 104c of the EC Treaty provides for due consideration to be given to the projected overall debt position of each member state for 1998 and beyond and in particular whether 'the ratio is sufficiently diminishing and approaching the reference value at a satisfactory pace'.

---

[15] European Monetary Institute, Convergence Report, March 1998. The criterion for a member state not maintaining gross government debt in excess of 60% of its gross domestic product at market prices was set in Art. 104c(2)(b) EC Treaty and Art. 2 of Protocol No. 6 on the excessive deficit procedure attached to the EC Treaty.

Table 7: Government Debt Position 1998

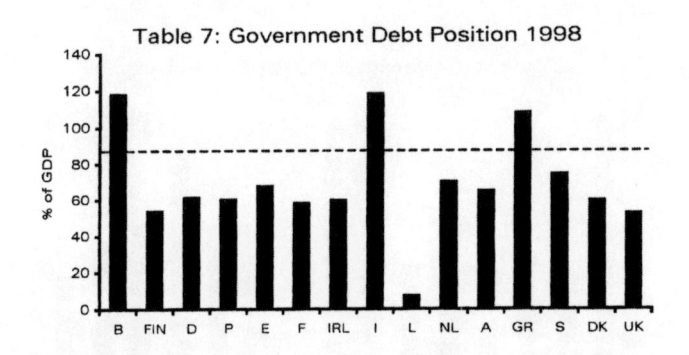

[Bar chart showing % of GDP for countries: B (~118), FIN (~55), D (~61), P (~60), E (~68), F (~58), IRL (~60), I (~118), L (~8), NL (~70), A (~66), GR (~108), S (~76), DK (~60), UK (~55), with dashed reference line at ~85%]

The projections provided by European Commission in its spring 1998 forecast for the general government gross debt for each member state showed further signs of improvement with three additional member states falling below the required 60% ceiling.

As can be seen above, the wording of Art. 104c of the EC Treaty for the ratio of public debt as a percentage of national GDP left a considerable margin for manoeuvre. It allowed for high deficits as long as they have been declining 'substantially and continuously' or are considered to be 'exceptional and temporary'. The same article allowed for higher government debt on the condition that the latter is 'sufficiently diminishing and approaching the reference value at a satisfactory pace'. The wording was thus vague enough to allow room for interpretation. Trying to clarify any uncertainties and to answer charges of Eurosceptics and opponents of the single currency, the European Council session in Dublin in December 1996 stated that 'as a matter of principle, continuity and equal treatment among all

member states with respect to the fulfilment of the convergence criteria... need to be ensured.'[16]

The EMI pointed out in its convergence report that a number of member states 'have benefited in part from a number of financial operations and transactions, such as privatisations' and 'such transactions are expected to continue to play a role in several member states.'[17]

Problems towards reaching convergence criteria have indeed been fudged allowing countries with lax fiscal policies into EMU before they were able to meet the EC Treaty's strict convergence criteria, thus promoting price instability throughout the EC. Some creative accounting undertaken in various member states in order to reach the necessary convergence criteria have dented public faith and received criticism both from the press and academic circles. Such measures included a generous re-estimation of Italy's black economy in calculating GDP, the French government receiving a substantial payment from the pension fund of the state owned France Telecom in exchange for taking over certain pension liabilities, German deduction of state hospitals from its deficit and the public row between the German government and the Bundesbank for the revaluation of the currency and gold reserves of the Bundesbank. When Brussels allowed France the inclusion of a FFR 37,500 million transfer from the France Telecom pension fund as treasury receipts, this reduced France's deficit equivalent to 0.5% of GDP. These adjustments, together

---

[16] See monetary and exchange rate policy co-operation between the Euro-area and other EU-countries – Report to the European Council session in Dublin on 13th–14th December 1996 contained in a report by the EMI entitled 'The Single Monetary Policy in Stage Three Specification of the operational framework', p.67.

[17] European Monetary institute, Convergence Report, March 1998, p.7. Transfers to and from the EC budget are not taken into account by the EMI when assessing the budgetary positions of member states.

with other factors such as consistently high level of unemployment, heavy burdens on future public expenditure or simply a change in the political landscape of Europe, could threaten the financial disciplines that have underpinned post-war progress along with social and political stability in most parts of Europe.

Whether interest rates will be an effective policy instrument for the ECB will not only be dependent on public and private indebtedness, the balance between public and private debt, but also the impact of changes in interest rates in aggregate across the public and private sector. In particular, changes in interest rates may slow private sector consumption at different rates across Europe and may have profoundly different impacts for the government sector and a member state's attempts to comply with the terms of the Stability Pact.

Pursuant to the terms of Art. 104b(1) of the EC Treaty, there will be no joint and several liability of the Euro countries for the debts of individual member states, hence budget consolidation will remain firmly on the shoulders of each member state. EMU will not even warrant any special financial transfers amongst member states.

5. Exchange Rate Stability

Member states wishing to qualify for EMU must also show national currency stability evidenced by membership in the ERM of the EMS and without significant fluctuation margins and without having been devalued during the previous two years against the currency of any other member state.

Although short-term interest rate developments and corresponding volatilities in exchange rates between the thirteen currently participating in the ERM have provided some strains on the EMS, the European Commission and

the EMI were satisfied in the convergence report that following the re-entry of the Greek drachma in the EMS and the moderate devaluation of the Irish punt 'relatively calm conditions'[18] occurred over the last two years within the ERM of the EMS. Denmark confirmed[19] that it will become a member of ERM II from 1st January 1999, probably in a narrow band above or below the Euro. Only the Swedish krone and the pound sterling now remain outside the ERM.

The establishment of a new Exchange Rate Mechanism (ERM II) at the 1996 Dublin summit was an essential feature and convergence barometer for future monetary and exchange rate policy co-operation between the Euro area and non-participating member states and was an important and successful response to the currency turmoils of 1992–93.

6. Other Factors

Art. 109j(1) of the EC Treaty provides that besides the above core convergence criteria, the regular progress reports of the EMI and the European Commission should also take into account and comment on:

1. The development of the ECU (mainly as a basket exchange rate and ECU as an accepted market instrument)
2. The results of the integration of the markets (concentrating on varying degrees to which legal obstacles to integration remain and measurements relating to trade flows, foreign investment and levels of taxation)

---

[18] European Monetary Institute, Convergence Report, March 1998, p.8.
[19] Report published by Danish Ministry of Economic Affairs and the Danish Central Bank entitled 'Denmark Outside the Euro', March 1998.

3. The situation and development of the balances of payments on current account (mainly as a cause or directly related to governmental budgetary positions, exchange rate stability and inflationary pressures)
4. An examination of the development of unit labour costs and other price indices (closely related to price stability and sustainability however, more recently also in connection with labour mobility and structural unemployment)

In its final convergence report, the EMI appeared to be largely satisfied with the overall development of the relevant price indices of member states as they have tended to follow the satisfactory trend of the HICP. The positive development of unit labour costs in almost all member states and healthy current account balances in a large majority of EU countries pointed at the time towards positive economic developments throughout most parts of the EU. The convergence report however did not mention whether these developments would have, at least partially, occurred without the EU convergence programmes. The report criticised that the public procurement sector maintained the highest technical barriers relating to the completion of the internal market and that taxation still lacked proper harmonisation both in terms of direct and indirect taxation partly delaying without harmonised capital income taxation the integration of financial markets.

The question arises whether governments of member states having successfully passed through the gateway of convergence will continue to work on national policies in order to deal with high unemployment, structural problems and high levels of public debt. A possible trade-off between unemployment and renewed inflationary pressures both in the short and long run must not be underestimated both in

terms of costs of currency union and potential shocks to the system. With most member states showing signs of 'natural' inflation rates, i.e. the rate at which there is no tendency for inflation to change, these rates might shift considerable following EMU and will depend to a large degree on whether markets are convinced that governments of member states will resist politically motivated desires to expand their economies and hence not only disturb the delicate equilibrium between wages and prices but also generally undermine their overall policy credibility.

The undoubted challenges for sustainable convergence and non-inflationary growth must be high and often persistent levels of unemployment, the unfunded or severely underfunded public pension system in most member states and the heavy burden on public expenditure associated with it.

Levels of unemployment (based on latest figures from the European Statistical Office[20]) are as follows:

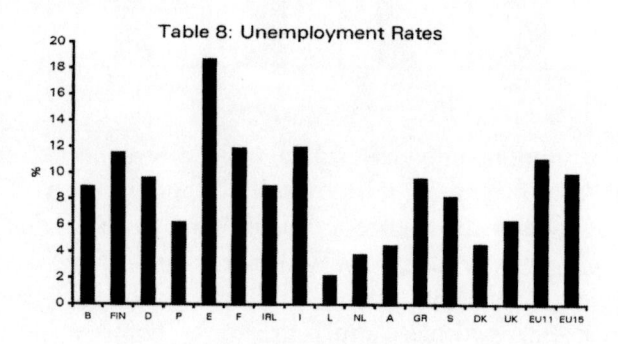

Table 8: Unemployment Rates

The development of unemployment within the Euro-zone and the EU as a whole shows no significant developments over the last three years although against the background of

---

[20] EUROSTAT Press Office Publication No. 9498, 7th December 1998.

strengthening economic growth during 1997 and 1998, employment has increased marginally. Unemployment in the EU, measured on a comparable basis, is more than twice that in the US and in Japan.

It is very difficult to assess for each member state post-EMU natural unemployment rates and what are sustainable levels of unemployment within the EU, especially with acute and widespread structural labour market problems and persistently poor external competitiveness in a significant number of member states.

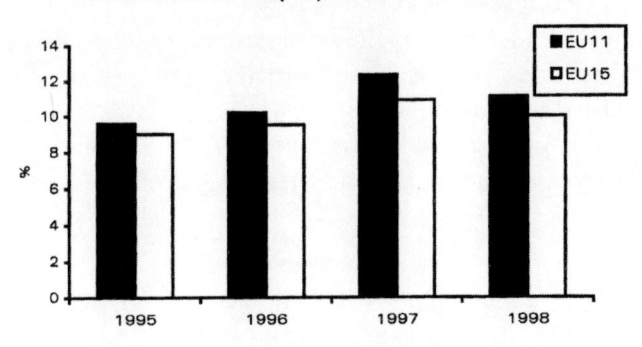

Table 9: EU Unemployment 1995 - 1998

Europe undoubtedly has still a wide divergence of unit labour costs both in terms of direct and indirect costs. Some of this divergence can continue to exist due to differentials in productivity. Whilst fixed and in due course a single exchange rate as well as uniform European levels of interest rates will place much greater emphasis on labour costs and productivity, it will be the elimination of uncertainties of conducting business and with it decisions on future investments that will be the key drivers for regional convergence or divergence within Europe and its neighbouring states. This unleashing of competitive forces across Europe must lead ultimately to a significant price and wage

convergence which will prove in aggregate disinflationary. However, for these competitive forces to work freely the ECB will have to take special care when it sets monetary policy, i.e. with interest rate levels set on the basis what is best for countries with the lowest levels of inflation and leaving countries with higher inflation rates exposed to their own and often home-made problems together with the forces of the market.

Although the former German Chancellor Helmut Kohl accepted the plan for EMU with some enthusiasm and the new German government continues to stress Germany's positive role in building a European Union for the people of Europe, many German citizens are still sceptical or indeed opposed to a single currency. This is partly due to the fear of seeing the trusted Deutschmark, that symbol of post-war German stability and success, being replaced by an unknown 'quantity' and the obvious and sometimes even public tensions between the German government and its lofty political aim to promote European Union which is quite obviously in conflict with the more prosaic concern of the bankers at the Bundesbank and their constitutional task to protect the monetary bedrock of the German economy.

What might be right for the German people might not be right for the rest of Europe. The dissatisfaction with the dependence (until its effective disintegration in 1992) of the EMS on the DM, which meant that the Bundesbank had become an unofficial EC central bank, convinced the majority of member states of the need to renew their pursuit of monetary union but the creation of a ESCB, effectively a 'Eurofed' with an independent mandate to promote price stability and set interest rates for the European Currency, did not find universal support, in particular in the United Kingdom which was dogmatically

opposed to the surrender of any more sovereignty to Europe.

If EMU is to succeed than the ECB must be strong and independent. The ECB and EMU will also need to be rock solid to cope with future enlargement of the EC, especially with only weaker economies (except Norway or Switzerland) applying to sign up.

What the politicians fudged to get the present eleven and future member states to join the single currency, the bankers of the ECB will have to rescue later on to achieve and more importantly maintain price stability. However their key tool, interest rates, could cause job losses and recession in many parts of the European Union, putting even more pressure on the institutions of Europe to bring influence to bear on the central bankers of Europe – a vicious circle. In pure economic terms the social market economies of France and Germany are currently more likely to succeed with monetary union (despite recent problems with high levels of unemployment) than the United Kingdom with her history of boom and bust cycles often driven by inflationary wage growth.

The Council in its composition of Heads of State or government and acting under Art. 109j(4) of the EC Treaty 'confirmed' rather than 'decided' on 2nd May 1998 which member states fulfilled the necessary conditions for the adoption of a single currency.[21] However, with the term 'necessary conditions' not clearly defined, the legendary European compromise allowed eleven member states to join an exclusive club. Nevertheless, the precedence of the December 1996 governmental conference in Dublin correctly suggested that the necessary conditions are the same as those assessed in the reports of the EMI and the European Commission as outlined above. But if the

---

[21] EC Council Decision 317/98 of 3rd May 1998.

Council in the composition of Heads of State or government acting under Art. 109j(4) of the EC Treaty merely endorsed the decision taken by the Council of Ministers (acting by qualified majority) under Art. 109j(2) of the EC Treaty, who actually decided which member state was ready for the adoption of the single currency? The wording of Art. 109j(2) and (4) of the EC Treaty suggests that the Council of Ministers decided which member states fulfilled the necessary conditions for the adoption of a single currency but the Council of Heads of State or government was able to depart from a strict application of the convergence criteria so as to allow member states not satisfying the strict letter of sustainable convergence requirements nevertheless to move to Stage Three.

Well ahead of the historic meeting in May 1998, it was clear that only France, Finland and Luxembourg would meet all convergence criteria but strictly speaking Luxembourg did not have a proper central bank. It is not clear whether this was in fact the most perfect form of central bank independence or a breach of the Maastricht criteria. Nevertheless, both the statutes of the EMI and of the ESCB carry provisions that the Institute Monetaire Luxembourgeois shall be regarded as the central bank of Luxembourg. In any case, Luxembourg has since decided to amend with Law No. 3862 the monetary status of Luxembourg and rename the IML to the 'Central Bank of Luxembourg'.

The European legislative process has never been noted for its simplicity or even transparency and with each treaty revision, the process has become more complicated and cumbersome. Provisions for the British opt-out from parts of the Treaty did not help matters. Whilst there is a requirement that national legislation should be compatible with the EC Treaty and the Statutes of the ESCB, in practice it will mean more likely an adjustment of national

laws to the requirements of the EC Treaty and the Statutes of the ESCB rather than the harmonisation of national law throughout member states.[22]

The provisions made for the creation of EMU were by far the most specific and far reaching and will in a historic context become the single most important milestone for achieving a peoples' Europe.

7. Fixed Rates of Exchange

The final stage of EMU will involve the replacement of the irrevocable fixity of intra-European Community exchange rates, the adoption of a single currency, and the establishment of a federal system of central banks, with the ECB being responsible for the conduct of monetary policy and exchange rate policy for the union as a whole. In accordance with Art. 109l(4) of the EC Treaty, the irrevocable rates for the conversion of participating member states' local currency into Euro will be adopted on 1st January 1999 after final consultation with the ECB.

To give the markets guidance in the run up to Stage Three, the member states adopting the Euro[23] as their single currency at the start of Stage Three agreed at their meeting on 2nd May 1998 in Birmingham the method for determining the irrevocable conversion rates of exchange for the Euro. The conversion rates were agreed by the governors of the central banks participating in round one after a formal proposal from the European Commission and guidance from the EMI.

When determining the irrevocable conversion rates for the Euro, the ERM bilateral central rates were used of those currencies of the member states joining on 1st January

---

[22] European Monetary Institute 1994 Annual Report, pp.100–106.
[23] Council Decision (EC) 974/98 of 3rd May 1998.

1999. Until that date, all central banks of the member states adopting the Euro had to ensure through intervention in the marketplace and other market techniques at their disposal that on 31st December 1998, the market exchange rates used for the calculation of the daily exchange rates of the official ECU would be equal to the ERM bilateral central rates agreed on 2nd May 1998 in Birmingham and set out below. This methodology[24] may appear to be cumbersome and difficult to reconcile, but the irrevocable conversion rates for the Euro had to deal with the replacement of the ECU by the Euro on a 1:1 basis on 1st January 1999.[25]

Complications in relation to the Euro conversion rates have principally arisen from the fact that only eleven of the fifteen member states and their respective national currencies making up the current ECU basket will join Stage Three from the start. The Danish krone, the Greek drachma and the British pound sterling are members of the ECU currency basket but will not be part of the conversion process to the Euro. At the same time, Art. 109l(4) of the EC Treaty stipulates that the Euro shall by itself not modify the external value of its predecessor, the official ECU.

The final official ECU exchange rates calculated on 31st December 1998 was formally proposed by the European Commission for adoption by the Council of Ministers on the first day of Stage Three, i.e. on 1st January 1999, as the irrevocable conversion rates for the Euro for the participating currencies. Once these irrevocable conversion rates had been adopted was it possible to convert either way

---

[24] To avoid minor arithmetical inconsistencies from inverse calculations, the conversion rates set only one bilateral rate for each pair of participating currencies will be used.

[25] Art. 2 of the Council Regulation of 17th June 1997 also stipulates that every reference in a legal instrument to the official ECU shall be replaced by a reference to the Euro on a rate of one ECU to one Euro.

between the Euro and the national currencies and between national currency units participating in the Euro.

The below initial bilateral central rates of the ERM were used in determining the irrevocable conversion rates for the Euro.[26]

---

[26] Deutsche Bundesbank, Monthly Report, May 1998.

	DEM	BEF/LUF	ESP	FRF	IR£	ITL	NLG	ATS	PTE
Germany: DEM	-								
Belgium/Lux: BEF/LUF	2,062.5500	-							
Spain: ESP	8,507.2200	412.4620	-						
France: FRF	335.3900	16.2608	3.9424	-					
Ireland: IR£	40.2676	1.9523	0.4733	12.0063	-				
Italy: ITL	99,000.2000	4,700.900	1,163.7200	29,518.3000	2,458.5600	-			
Netherlands: NLG	112.6740	5.4629	1.3245	33.5953	2.7981	1.1381	-		
Austria: ATS	703.5520	34.1108	8.2700	209.77740	17.4719	7.1066	624.4150	-	
Portugal: PTE	10,250.5000	496.9840	120.4920	3,056.3400	254.5600	103.5410	9,097.5300	1,456.9700	-
Finland: FIM	304.0010	14.7391	3.5735	90.6420	7.5495	3.0707	269.8060	43.2094	2.9657

INITIAL BILATERAL CENTRAL RATES OF THE ERM

Chapter II
The European Monetary Institute

Stage Two of the Delors Report[1] was ambitious, recommending a medium-term framework for monetary policy which would facilitate 'intervening when significant deviations occurred' and the establishment of the ESCB with policy functions which 'would gradually evolve as experience was gained'. In the event its plans for an embryo central bank in Stage Two with a policy co-ordinating role were not accepted.

The EMI, with its seat in Frankfurt[2], came into being on 1st January 1994 (although from the outset with a limited life only). It had its legal basis in Article 109f of the EC Treaty and its own Statutes (see Appendix I attached hereto). The treaty provisions and the Statutes were supplemented by the EMI's Rules of Procedures (see Appendix II). The EMI was a separate legal entity with its own legal persona and capacity but it was only a forerunner and not the ECB which was not established until June 1998.

---

[1] Study of Committee for the Study of Economic and Monetary Union (so-called Delors Committee) entitled 'Report on Economic and Monetary Union in the European Community', Luxembourg, 1989, p.38.
[2] Art 1. of EC Council Decision on 29th October 1998, OJ C323.

The function of the EMI was to make possible the monetary unification according to the procedure laid down in the treaty and in this respect its two main tasks had been:

1. To contribute to the fulfilment of the conditions necessary to reach Stage Three, in particular the convergence of the main macroeconomic indicators.
2. To make the preparations required for the establishment of the ESCB and the conduct of single monetary policy and for the creation of a single currency in the third stage.

The EMI had no responsibility for the conduct of monetary policy in the EU – this remained firmly the preserve of the national authorities – nor had it any competence for carrying out foreign exchange intervention. The EMI mainly acted through regular consultations and through the formulation of non-legally binding opinions or recommendations to national governments and central banks.

One of the key activities of the EMI was the preparation of the necessary regulatory, organisational and logistical framework for the ESCB to perform its tasks with a deadline of 31st December 1996.[3] This part was critical to the framework of the ECB as the Statute of the ESCB does not define the manner, principles and framework in which the single monetary policy is to be conducted in Stage Three. For a range of operations of the ESCB/ECB the rules also needed to be elaborated ranging from collateralised lending operations with credit institutions and the efficiency of cross-border payments, to the future holding and managing the official reserves of the member states.

---

[3] Article 4.2 Statute of the EMI.

Possibly the most visible part of the EMI's work was to prepare the new coins and bank notes for the Euro.[4]

To explore questions and aspects relating to the ECB's future operational and political independence and the issue of accountability, one could attempt to investigate whether a few lessons or even a few conclusions could be drawn from the workings of the EMI during the three years of its existence. The EMI had a vested interest in seeing Stage Three start on schedule but it must have had in mind the process of convergence and could not have ignored the macroeconomic environment in which the ECB will have to take its first steps in ensuring price stability.

The EMI was a formal organisation of the EU, with its own legal personality and with the central banks of the member states as its members. It was directed and managed by a council composed of the President of the EMI and the governors of the central banks of the member states.[5] Thus with the presence of governors from the central banks of member states, the EMI had a mixture of council members with varying degrees of autonomy and accountability ranging from Hans Tietmeyer, President of the fiercely independent Deutsche Bundesbank, to the politically appointed and controlled Eddie George, Governor of the Bank of England.[6]

An indication as to the EMI's former operational independence can be found in Article 8 of the Protocol on the Statute of the EMI which was added to the Treaty of

---

[4] The final design of the new Euro bank notes was agreed at the Amsterdam meeting in October 1997.

[5] Article 109f(1) of the EC Treaty.

[6] Changes introduced by the new Labour administration soon after their election victory and the new Bank of England Act which came into force on 1st June 1998 would indicate a reduced amount of control but these could be reversed without too much difficulty and are too fresh to suggest they have withstood the test of time or the markets.

Rome by the Treaty on EU, signed on 7th February 1992 in Maastricht. In this Article, the Community institutions and bodies, as well as the governments of the member states, 'undertake to respect this [principle of independence] and not to seek to influence the Council of the EMI in the performance of its tasks'.

One would have liked to see the words 'directly or indirectly' or 'in any way' added after the word 'influence' in Article 8 to ensure that no indirect influence could have been gained through politically controlled central bank governors but Article 8 also states that Council members of the EMI 'act on their own responsibility' thus ensuring a certain degree of independence.

The first President of the EMI was Baron Alexandre Lamfalussy, a Belgian and formerly the General Manager of the Bank for International Settlements (which already provided technical support for the setting up of the EMI) and largely acknowledged as a politically independent and experienced central banker.

The President of the EMI from 1st July 1997 until its winding up was the former President of De Nederlandsche Bank, Dr. Willem F. Duisenberg, who was appointed in May 1998 as the first President of the new ECB. Although Wim Duisenberg was always tipped as the hot favourite for the Presidency of the ECB, the rumours that the French agreed to the ECB being located in Frankfurt in exchange for assurances from the Germans that the first President of the ECB might be French or that the French might follow their own political agenda regardless proved only too true.

As early as 14th November 1995, the EMI released to the press a report entitled 'The changeover to the single currency' which provided for a chronological sequence of events with the following four critical benchmark dates which were later confirmed by the Council of Ministers and the Commission:

1. As soon as possible in 1998, the Council, meeting in the composition of the Heads of State or of Government, would confirm which member states fulfil the necessary conditions to participate in the Euro area and agree the irrevocably exchange rates between them.
2. As early as possible thereafter, the ECB and the ESCB would be established and would prepare for their operation at the start of Stage Three of EMU.
3. On 1st January 1999, the starting date of Stage Three, the currencies of participating member states' currencies would be replaced with irrevocably locked conversion rates and amongst other things the ESCB would start conducting its single monetary policy in the Euro.
4. By 1st January 2002 at the latest, the ECB would put Euro bank notes into circulation and start exchanging the national bank notes and coins against them.

The EMI's principal role had been to help strengthen the co-operation between national central banks and the co-ordination of monetary policies, thus preparing the ground for the final big step – a very big step indeed. The manner in which the single monetary policy is to be conducted in Stage Three is not defined in the statute of the ESCB and fell on the EMI to be developed and elaborated. This task also included the definition of intermediate objectives and the instruments of the single monetary policy.

Compared to the operation of the EMS, the creation of the EMI in 1994 made a real difference with the analytical work and the technical preparations needed for the final stage. Furthermore, through the publication of annual reports and the monitoring over the previous three years of the economic performance of member states, the EMI had started invaluable work on the operation of a common monetary and exchange rate policy, on reliable statistics and

properly functioning payments systems as well as the harmonisation of accounting rules of participating national banks and a host of other technical matters and legal questions. However, the most important decision – which monetary policy instrument(s) will be accepted by the ECB – was not made by the EMI but by the Governing Council of the ECB based on extensive analysis and studies undertaken by the EMI.

The list of options and potential candidate strategies for monetary policy in Stage Three had been under the work carried out by the EMI reduced from five original possible strategies (exchange rate targeting, interest rate pegging, nominal income targeting, monetary targeting and direct inflation targeting) to a final two: monetary targeting and direct inflation targeting. Whilst the exchange rate targeting was considered by the EMI as inappropriate due to the size of the Euro area, the use of interest rate as the ECB's primary monetary policy instrument was also ruled out. Experiences gained in various member states and the uncertainties surrounding the transmission process, together with monetary targeting being both easily observable and under the direct control of the ECB, make monetary targeting and direct inflation targeting within a wide set of economic and financial variables and indicators the most suitable monetary policy instruments which can be consistently and directly linked to prospective price behaviour.

The EMI started to go into liquidation in June 1998 when the ECB was established and its tasks were taken over seamlessly by the ECB.[7] Together with the national central banks, the ECB will constitute the ESCB that will assume

---

[7] Art. 109l(2) of the EC Treaty, Art. 23 Statute of the EMI and Art. 44 Statute of the ESCB.

responsibility for monetary policy in the third and final stage of EMU.

The primary objective of the ESCB will be to maintain price stability, which in the opinion of most economists, monetarists[8] and even the ECB[9] means 0–2% inflation. Practically all economists and monetarists now agree that relative price stability is obtained when the inflation rate is within a band of 0–2% p.a. John Redwood, leading UK Eurosceptic, argues that price stability for the ECB must be much tougher, i.e. zero inflation, than the policies currently being pursued in order for the member states to qualify for convergence, as the convergence criteria only call for relative price stability in relation to other member states.

To advise the Commission and the Council of Ministers until the third stage of EMU, the EC Treaty set up a Monetary Committee consisting of two members from each member state and the Commission. Its function shall be advisory only to the Commission and the Council of Ministers. It shall keep under review the monetary and financial situations of the member states and the Community and report to the Commission and the Council. It shall deliver opinions on request and help to prepare the Council of Ministers' decisions. When the Community has reached Stage Three, the Monetary Committee shall be replaced by a new body the Economic and Financial Committee (see Chapter III).

---

[8] See John Redwood in *Our Currency – Our Country*, Penguin, 1997, p.71.
[9] As announced by Wim Duisenberg on 13th October 1998.

Chapter III
European Central Bank

1. Establishment

The ESCB that the Delors Report proposed for Stage Three now finds a great deal of resemblance in the EC Treaty and Statute of the ESCB.[1] The Delors Report went further than the Werner Report[2] when it called for a single currency and for binding rules on fiscal policy and financing in Stage Three, including 'effective upper limits on budget deficits' and no monetary financings.[3]

Art. 107 of the EC Treaty as well as the accompanying protocol on the statute of the ESCB and the ECB (see Appendix III) refer in no uncertain terms to the independence of the new institution. Measures in the same direction will also have to be introduced for national central banks that have been until now with the exception of the German Bundesbank and its small sister the Oesterreichische Nationalbank, more or less under the tutelage of their political masters. Essentially the ECB will have a singleness of purpose and independence from political inference second to none in the world. With the Maastricht Treaty

---

[1] 'Report on Economic and Monetary Union in the European Community', Luxembourg, 1989.

[2] 'Report to the Council and the Commission on the Realisation by Stages of Economic and Monetary Union in the Community' published as a Supplement to Bulletin II–1970 by the European Commission, Luxembourg.

[3] 'Report on Economic and Monetary Union in the European Community', Luxembourg, 1989, p.28.

and the Stability and Growth Pact providing specific normative mechanisms for guaranteeing price stability, it places the ECB and its role in formulating and carrying out monetary policy into uncharted terrain which is historically without precedent.[4]

The 'Committee for the Study of Economic and Monetary Union', chaired by Jacques Delors, consisted apart from M. Delors and a fellow European Commission colleagues of the twelve EC national central bank governors, Alexandre Lamfalussy, then head of the Bank for International Settlements and later first President of the EMI; Miguel Boyer, former Finance Minister of Spain; and Niels Thygesen, a Danish academic. Hence central bankers constituted a large majority and the governors appeared only too keen to stress the full economic and institutional implications of EMU to their political masters. Much emphasis was placed on the independence of the new institution which would be in charge of monetary policy for the union. This consensus on the question of the independence of the ECB reflected not only the composition of the committee but also the leadership and prestige enjoyed by the German Bundesbank which had provided the role model. Doubters I am sure existed, but they largely kept a low profile and preferred to concentrate on specific problems and areas of contention instead of challenging the main principles and objectives of the whole project. After all, it was difficult to adopt a high moral stand as much of the work had already been done by committees of experts.

The Delors Report did not spell out what the common European monetary policy would look like in detail and how it would work in practice, what tools would be used to

---

[4] 'Price Stability and Budgetary Restrains in the Economic and Monetary Union: the Law as Guardian of Economic Wisdom' by Matthias Herdegen, 1998, 35 CMLR 9.

implement and administer it and how responsibility for its execution would be divided between national central banks and a central monetary institution. This would have gone too far for many central bankers already fearful of their jobs and would have more resembled Machiavellian ideas rather than closer economic integration. It is undisputed that the creation of the new single currency is one of the most momentous economic events in recent European history, created out of political will and not economic necessity. It was also the political will of the previous governments which negotiated the Maastricht Treaty and with it the legal foundations for EMU and the single currency which ensures that the single currency project survived various potential crises in recent years and that the majority of member states are ready on 1st January 1999. The same governments which acted as midwives for the new single currency could not fully separate the evil twins of politics from economics however, and it is doubtful whether one could ever separate the two completely. Compared to the economic model in the United States, the Euro is much more exposed to political and economic asymmetry where monetary policy is now the sole prerogative of the ECB, albeit with ECOFIN generating political input in some aspects of monetary policy. Fiscal policy, i.e. taxation and spending clearly remains under the control of national governments. The Stability and Growth Pact is attempting to reconcile economic and political interests essentially by depoliticising monetary and fiscal policy.

With the new balance of power in Europe, the ECB appears to be in a no win situation and criticism seems assured whatever the ECB does. For Wim Duisenberg and his colleagues, this will mean that the ECB will not have too many friends and will have to rely heavily on the Maastricht Treaty to protect itself from political manoeuvres. Not unlike the Bundesbank and the Federal Reserve

Bank in the US, the ECB will have to fast grow a thick skin, gain the trust of the people and plan for the long term.

The ECB formally replaced in June 1998 the EMI and began together with the ESCB with the important task of conducting single monetary policy in the Euro. The ECB has commenced its operations at a time when restructuring of the banking sector is taking a more pan-European dimension partly driven by the opportunities opened by EMU and partly by the global forces emanating from the consolidation of the banking sector in the United States and the fallout from the financial crisis in Asia which is spilling over into the banking sector.

Even before the ECB will become fully operational on 1st January 1999, a new wind is blowing through Europe threatening the stability of economic and monetary union. Europe is under new management and has not only abandoned fiscal orthodoxy and protection of the infant Euro, but appears to have fallen in parts back to 1970s-style demand management with state intervention to raise public spending, create growth and most important create employment. One of the new captains of Europe, Oscar Lafontaine, Germany's finance minister, has swiftly started to change course heading straight into confrontation with the Bundesbank and the nascent ECB almost ignoring that the seas are not only rough off the coasts of Europe but also around the rest of the world. Feeling committed to their election promises, the new government in Germany in alliance with France and a hesitant United Kingdom has started to abandon the supply-side reforms of the last decade and is turning to public spending as a shortcut to growth and employment. With such shortcuts intended to bypass fiscal prudence and the dangers of future inflation, the Bundesbank and the infant ECB have started to deliver warning messages. The most alarming feature of the new balance of power in Europe is not its inability to deal with

constructive criticism from the guardians of the one of the world's future leading currencies but their intent to rewrite the rule book and with an amendment to the Maastricht Treaty make the ECB and the national central banks more pliable. For the United Kingdom '[o]ne rusting iron chancellor is enough without having Herr[en] Schröder and Lafontaine on [its] backs.'[5]

2. Organisation

According to the provisions of the EC Treaty and its statutes, the ECB will be an independent institution and as such it may not seek but what is more important not take instructions from Community institutions, from any government of a member state or any other body. The Statutes of the ECB go even further and actively, one could even say pre-emptively, call on the member states to respect the independence of the ECB and the national central banks free from influence of any other EC institution and governments of member states.[6]

Despite the aforesaid, can EC institutions and bodies or member states exert such pressure or conduct such a campaign against individual members, including the President of the ECB, that he will be forced to resign from the Executive Board of the ECB? Experiences from the political arena suggest that the answer is probably yes. However, even if such a campaign would have been successful, the 'victim' would be replaced reasonably soon by a 'person of recognised standing and professional experience in monetary or banking matters'[7] on the Executive Board of the ECB. Furthermore, the strength and

---

[5] 'Trouble in Euroland', *The Sunday Times*, 1st November 1998.

[6] Art. 107 of the EC Treaty and Art. 7 Statute of ESCB.

[7] Art. 109a (2)(b) of the EC Treaty and Art. 11.2 Statute of ESCB.

independence of the ECB is such that it is very doubtful whether it would or even could alter its chosen course of monetary policy in order to achieve its objectives as defined in the EC Treaty.

The ECB's seventeen-strong Governing Council which consists of the six-member Executive Board and the heads of the first eleven founder member state central banks will have key responsibilities within the Organisation of the ESCB. It will adopt the general guidelines and make the necessary decisions to ensure that the ESCB can perform its tasks as set out in the EC Treaty and the Statutes of the ESCB. At the same time, it will be the key body to formulate the monetary policy within the EC including the setting of intermediary monetary policy objectives, key interest rates and the supply of reserves in the ESCB. This number however will increase with every new member state joining the single currency.

In the meantime, the ECB will have with a General Council a separate board of governors consisting of the six members of the ECB's Executive Board and the fifteen governors of all EU member states. Although the Governing Council will be the key decision making body, the General Council will have a role to play in issues such as EU-wide banking supervision. The General Council will also contribute to the collection of Community-wide statistical information, the preparation of the ECB's important quarterly and annual reports together with weekly consolidated financial statements of the ESCB. It already played a key role in relation to the establishment of the precise key and the initial share of the ECB's paid up

The European System of Central Banks

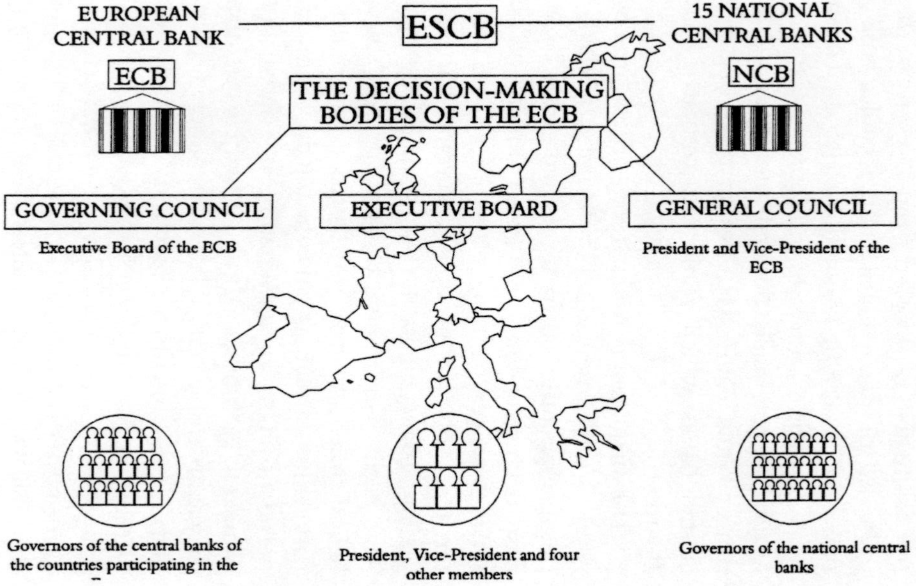

EUROPEAN CENTRAL BANK — ECB

ESCB

15 NATIONAL CENTRAL BANKS — NCB

THE DECISION-MAKING BODIES OF THE ECB

GOVERNING COUNCIL
Executive Board of the ECB

Governors of the central banks of the countries participating in the

EXECUTIVE BOARD
President, Vice-President and four other members

GENERAL COUNCIL
President and Vice-President of the ECB

Governors of the national central banks

capital subscription as well as laying down the terms and conditions of employment for the ECB staff.

Critics have argued that the six members of the Executive Board will be exposed from the start to the continued influence of the national central banks both within the powerful Governing Council but also the General Council whereby national interests will sooner or later be too strong leading to potentially destabilising situations. The biggest danger could come from voting pacts of several national central banks which could outmanoeuvre the Executive Board.

The first lessons have already been learnt by the ECB, when Wim Duisenberg admitted that it was a mistake to put the Executive Board at one end of the table during the first meeting of the Governing Council and governors of the national central banks at the other. 'And in the course of the day, you saw groupings develop.'[1] In response, the seating arrangements for subsequent Council meetings have been changed with every participant sitting in alphabetical order and with no reference to Council members' nationalities. 'There is only one big disadvantage... it means presidents Hans Tietmeyer and Jean-Claude Trichet always sit next to each other. Although there is one man, one vote, they are both big central banks, so although their vote is not bigger, it is sometimes louder.'[2] With Hans Tietmeyer due to retire in August 1999, seating arrangements will change again. With governors of eleven member states serving five-year terms and longer, seating arrangements would theoretically have to be altered every six months, thereby mitigating the risk of any voting blocs developing.

---

[1] 'Builder of the euro team spirit', *The Financial Times*, 7th December 1998.
[2] Ibid.

Perhaps the most important position, almost equal in importance to the President, is the board member in charge of the economics department. Otmar Issing, former chief economist of the German Bundesbank and ECB Executive Board member, will control economic research and with this control of such vital information comes real power as the person in charge of economic policy is likely to set the overall tone of the ECB's core policies.

Whether the ECB will be able to deliver its central policy objective will require experienced and skilled ECB politics and power play executed behind closed doors between the ECB's head office in Frankfurt and the national central banks. In terms of staff numbers, the ECB's 500 employees are a fraction of the 10,000 and more staff currently employed by the Bundesbank and the Bank of France each. The comparison must however take into account the large number of staff at national central bank levels which are involved in areas ranging from local administration to logistical services. Nevertheless, by having significant numbers of staff at their disposal and with no plans to scale down their research, statistics and economics departments, national central banks will continue to be powerful institutions in their own right. The comparatively small number of staff at the ECB could be seen as a weak centre and too highly decentralised to be a potent force on the world stage. One immediate solution for the ECB would be change in its employment practices with less staff being seconded from national central banks and more staff being recruited on a permanent basis.

With the European Union likely to expand in the not too distant future, this expansion could also lead to tensions within the European Community machinery as new member states joining will seek representation within the officials of the Community institutions. The danger for the ECB will be that the likely sizes of the Governing Council

and the General Council of the ECB will simply become too big with a corresponding fall in efficiency and effectiveness.

3. Structure

The key task of member states (without derogation) when dealing with the launch of the ECB was to appoint the President, Vice-President and four other members of the Executive Board of the ECB for a non-renewable period in office of up to eight years[3] provided that the persons so appointed are not political appointees. Even if that were so, they must be men and women of 'recognised standing and professional experience in monetary or banking matters.'[4] By not allowing members to be elected for more than one term of office and by appointing the first members of the Executive Board for different periods of office, the ECB will be able to evolve. The true European spirit is expected to be preserved within the Executive Board of the ECB with acceptance of a Portuguese proposal that Executive Board members will be rotated to come from all member states participating in the single currency.

At the Birmingham summit in May 1998, the member states approved[5] the appointment of the following members of the ECB's Executive Board effective from 1st June 1998:

---

[3] Art. 109l of the EC Treaty and Art. 50 Statute of ESCB. This period of office is longer than that of the members of the Commission, the EP, the Courts of Justice and the Court of Auditors.

[4] Art. 109a of the EC Treaty and Art. 50 Statue of ESCB.

[5] Decision (98/345/EC) of the government of the member states of 26th May 1998 on the appointment of the President, the Vice-President and the other members of the Executive Board of the European Central Bank.

1. Willem Frederik Duisenberg, born 1935, elected President of ECB for a term of eight[6] years, formerly President of EMI and Governor of Dutch Central Bank, an economist by profession and a former Dutch finance minister.
2. Christian Noyer, born 1950, elected Vice-President of ECB for a term of four years, a career civil servant whose last job was Director of the Ministry for Economic Affairs, Finance and Industry working on various assignments related to the banking reform after having served for two years as chief of staff to Jean Arthuis, France's former Minister for Economic Affairs and Finance.
3. Sirkka Aune-Marjatta Hämäläinen, born 1939, elected for a term of five years, an economist by profession and employed since 1961 by the Bank of Finland. Since 1992 Governor and Chairman of the Board of the Bank of Finland.
4. Otmar Issing, born 1936, elected for a term of eight years, formerly directorate member and chief economist of German Bundesbank. An economist by profession and has been professor of economics at various universities.
5. Tommasso Padoa-Schioppa, born 1940, elected for a term of seven years, former Deputy Director General of the Bank of Italy and chief regulator of Italian stock market. Also chaired the Basel Committee for banking supervision at the Bank for International Settlements.
6. Eugenio Domingo Solans, born 1945, elected for a term of six years, formerly Member of the Governing Council of the Executive Commission of Bank of Spain. An

---

[6] Elected for a period of eight years. Stated that he might retire early but also that he would stay at least until July 2002, possibly the full term of eight years.

economist by profession and professor of finance and monetary policy at various universities.

In a politically important but not legally binding vote, the EP approved on 13th May 1998 the appointment of the President, the Vice-President and their four fellow board members of the ECB. At the same time, the EP expressed its displeasure of any possible political deal relating to Wim Duisenberg's possible 'early retirement', and deputies acting through Christa Radzio-Plath, the EP's rapporteur on the ECB appointment, had tried to adopt an amendment that sought to obstruct Wim Duisenberg's declared intention to resign halfway through his eight-year term. The aim of the EP motion was to ensure that 'all candidates feel they are free from political pressure' and it was carried by a majority of one.[7] Original proposals contained in a draft report drawn up by Christa Radzio-Plath and approved by the EP's monetary affairs sub-committee on 18th March 1998 would have given the EP the power to veto appointments to the board of the ECB and effectively dismiss the President of the ECB should he persistently ignore to take into account the general economic conditions of the EU once the primary objective of price stability was assured. Introducing any motion of censure for any member of the ECB's Executive Board would have undermined the political independence of the ECB and the power to effectively dismiss the President of the ECB was deleted from the report before it was voted through.

The political haggling and deal-making over the appointment of the first President of the ECB undoubtedly dented the hitherto and carefully nurtured optimism surrounding EMU and left a stain on the potential strength

---

[7] 'Euro-MPs back Duisenberg but disapprove political deal' in *The Financial Times* on 14th May 1998.

of the Euro. The biggest damage related to the selection of the first President of the ECB was not caused by choices related to the possible incumbents Wim Duisenberg or Jean-Claude Trichet, but by laying bare a significant political and philosophical difference between the driving forces of European integration, Germany and France, and their expectations from the future monetary policy of the ECB. Whilst the former watched over the creation of the ECB essentially as a Bundesbank Mark II, independent, free from political interference and solely focused on price stability, the French government did not hide its expectations that the ECB should also assume responsibility for job creation or at least include it in its monetary policy objectives.

The terms and conditions of employment for the members of the Executive Board of the ECB, which must be nationals of member states without derogation[8], are subject to a contract fixed by the Governing Council on a proposal of a Committee comprising three members appointed by the Governing Council and three members appointed by the Council of Ministers.[9] Whether the EU goes as far as the US Congress and releases details concerning earnings[10] and contracts of employment of members of the Executive Board into the public domain remains highly doubtful but it would in my opinion do no harm and introduce an additional level of accountability at the very source of this ultimately very powerful institution.

A member of the Executive Board who fails to carry out his duty or is guilty of serious misconduct can be dismissed

---

[8] Art. 109a and 109k(1) of the EC Treaty and Art. 11.2 Statute of ESCB.

[9] Art. 11.3 Statute of ESCB.

[10] See comments by Wim Duisenberg admitting that he earns c. £160,000 p.a., a figure which has been set at 40% above the highest EU official for reference purposes. As reported in *The Daily Telegraph*, 16th July 1998.

by way of compulsory retirement by a decision of the ECJ. However, this can only be achieved following an application by the Governing Council or the Executive Board itself.[11] Even with the track records of national central banks and the EMI, no definition exists what constitutes failure to carry out his duties or serious misconduct for a member of the Executive Board. Hence such matters should be subject to a more detailed definition in the contracts of employment for members of the Executive Board as outlined above.

The Governing Council of the ECB comprising the members of the Executive Board and the governors of the national central banks without derogation will act according to democratic principles taking decisions by a simple majority, and if there is a tie the President has been given a casting vote.[12] The same will apply for the General Council in which all fifteen EU member states and the members of the Executive Board meet on a quarterly basis. Each member present will have in most cases one vote of equal value[13] unless otherwise provided in the Statute in specific circumstances and relating to specific matters.[14] In certain matters (the capital of the ECB, the transfer of foreign reserve assets to the ECB, the allocation of monetary income of national central banks and the allocation of net profits and losses of the ECB) decisions will be taken by a qualified majority according to the national central banks' shares in the subscribed capital of the ECB. A quorum of two thirds is required to achieve the ability to make decisions.[15] In principle only those present may vote but,

---

[11] Art. 11.4 Statute of ESCB.
[12] Art. 10.2 Statute of ESCB.
[13] Ibid.
[14] Art. 10.3 Statute of ESCB.
[15] Art. 10.2 Statute of ESCB.

exceptionally, the Statutes of the ECB allow votes to be cast by means of teleconferencing.[16] By opting in the large majority of matters to be discussed within the Governing and/or General Council of the ECB for a voting system of 'one country – one vote' did not follow the US model where only selected Federal Reserve Banks are represented and have the right to vote in the Federal Reserve Board.

The Executive Board of the ECB will have day-to-day responsibility for the operations of the ECB and the single currency[17] as from the starting date of the third stage in order to implement the monetary policy laid down through guidelines by the Governing Council of the ECB. As outlined above, they will be able to draw on all the preparatory work and the practical experiences gathered by the EMI. The most daunting challenge for the ECB will be psychological and its pan-European policy role where members of the Governing and General Councils but most importantly the six members of the Executive Board will have to make a mental transition from the nation state of Europe to a single Euro-zone as the overriding almost exclusive reference point for monetary policy.

To spread the burden of responsibility and to provide a broader policy base, the members of the Executive Board will be joined by the governors of the national central banks of member states without derogation to form the Governing Council of the ECB.[18] This extended body of experts will be the principal forum for the formulation of the monetary policy of member states which will be party to the single currency. Their tasks include, amongst others,

---

[16] Ibid.

[17] Art. 11.6 Statute of ESCB.

[18] Art. 109a(1) of the EC Treaty and Art. 10 Statute of ESCB.

intermediate monetary objectives, key interest rates and the supply of reserves.[19]

Contrary to the general principles of accountability, the proceedings of the meetings of the Governing Council and the General Council will be confidential unless the Governing Council and the General Council each agree to make matters public out of their own accord.[20] Given the often sensitive nature of their discussions and the well-established experiences that the smallest utterances of central banks and any of its members will be analysed and interpreted by the global financial community, the price of confidentiality will be stability.

The Governing Council will meet at least ten times a year[21] to discuss matters under its responsibility and to make decisions relating to the activities entrusted to the ECB. It will be the key decision-making body and its meetings will be chaired by the President or one of his Vice-Presidents.[22] The potential size of the Governing Council could be considered a possible point of weakness. With all present member states participating in EMU this would create a governing body composed of twenty-one persons. In addition, as the number of countries increases, the number of central bank Governors will tend to outweigh those of the Executive Board and this has already been considered as a possible danger for the independence of the ECB.[23] There are also indications that the relationship between the Executive Board and the Governing

---

[19] Art. 10 and 12 Statute of ESCB.
[20] Art. 10.4 Statute of ESCB.
[21] Art. 10.5 Statute of ESCB.
[22] Art. 13.1 Statute of ESCB.
[23] Charles Goodhart, Norman Sosnow Professor of Banking and Finance in 'The Draft Statutes of the European Central Bank', London School of Economics Special Paper No. 37, 1992.

Council may come under strain, especially during the early phase of EMU.

With national central bank governors representing national interests tainted by national political and economic interests such as growth and employment, the stage seems set for a possible power struggle within the Governing Council between the Executive Board and the national central bank governors. National central bank governors will continue to have extensive research staff at their disposal leaving the Executive Board vulnerable and open to criticism, even outright opposition, of their economic analysis and forecasts for the Euro-zone which are vital for a successful monetary policy strategy.

Given the decentralised nature of the ESCB, national central bank governors such as Antonio Fazio, Governor of the Bank of Italy, claim that the principle of subsidiarity should also be applied to the workings of the new ESCB and 'that the credibility and strength of the [governing] council derives from the credibility and strength of the national central banks themselves.'[24] Doubts can be expressed whether the strength and credibility of the Bank of Italy or any other national central banks with a somewhat shaky inflation record add much to the credibility of the future guardian of the single currency. This credit, if any, must clearly go to national central banks with a long-standing track record of price stability such as the German Bundesbank and national central banks which closely followed the monetary policy initiatives of the German national central bank. Attempts by governors of Euro-zone national central banks such as Antonio Fazio to hold on to their power do not come as a surprise given the nascent state of the ECB and the political fudge created by the

---

[24] 'Italy's bank chief hints at clash with ECB executive' and 'Hawk among the doves', *The Financial Times*, 10th November 1998.

principle of subsidiarity through the Maastricht Treaty. Experts have warned that if this possible power struggle is not resolved quickly, the ECB might well be afflicted with problems similar to those that crippled the Federal Reserve Bank System in the US during the first two decades after its establishment in 1913.

The ECB will have from the onset an operational capital of at least 5,000 million Euros[25] provided by the national central banks that shall be its sole subscribers and holders.[26] At its meeting on 3rd November 1998, the Governing Council of the ECB endorsed a recommendation presented by the ECB for a Council Regulation which would authorise the ECB to increase its capital from 5,000 million Euros to up to twice that amount. This compares with a share capital of the Deutsche Bundesbank as per 31st December 1997 of DM290 million[27] which equates to c.145 million Euros. To ensure independence at the shareholder level or any indirect control through legal or political means, Art. 28.5 of the Statute of the ESCB clearly states that 'the shares of the national central banks in the subscribed capital of the ECB may not be transferred, pledged or attached.' This feature is vital to achieve operational independence and to secure impartiality of the governor and his team at national level.

The provision of these non-redeemable crucial shareholders' funds of the ECB will be made according to a key (which also determines the weighting of the voting power as mentioned above) representing the size of the population and the share in the gross domestic product of each

---

[25] Art. 28.1 Statute of ESCB.
[26] Art. 28.2 Statute of ESCB.
[27] Deutsche Bundesbank 1997 Annual Report and Accounts.

participating member state.[28] Thus each national central bank shall be assigned a weighting equal to the sum of 50% of the share of its country in the population of the Community, and 50% of the share of its country in the gross domestic product at market prices of the Community.[29] To allow for future developments and changes within the population and the wealth of each member state, these weightings will be reviewed and if necessary adjusted in either direction every five years after the establishment of the ECB and the ESCB.[30]

To give it additional financial strength and the ability to act decisively and with sufficient muscle within the global foreign exchange and money markets, the ECB is to be provided by the national central banks not only with its above core capital but additionally with foreign reserve assets (other than any EU member states' own currencies) up to an amount equivalent to 50,000 million Euros.[31] Further calls beyond the limit of 50,000 million Euros are possible under Art. 30.4 Statute of ESCB but only with the two thirds approval of the Council of Ministers in accordance with Art. 106(6) of the EC Treaty. The Deutsche Bundesbank for example maintained according to its 1997 annual report and accounts reserves totalling DM13,309.5 million which at the convergence rates amounts to just over 6,800 million Euros.

There can be no question that if EMU is to succeed and the Euro is to be regarded in global terms as a major international currency with any reasonable degree of strength, than the ECB must also be strong financially. The

---

[28] European Council Decision 98/362/CE of 5th June 1998 on the statistical data to be used for the determination of the key for subscription of the capital of the European Central Bank.

[29] Art. 29.1 Statute of ESCB.

[30] Art. 29.3 Statute of ESCB.

[31] Art. 30.1 Statute of ESCB.

same applies to cope with future enlargement of the European Community, especially with mainly weaker economies applying to sign up.

The actual making available of such additional funds (by way of shareholder loans and not as non-repayable capital) from time to time or even on a more permanent basis, the denomination of such additional funding and what each national central bank will receive in return will be determined by the Governing Council of the ECB[32] making it almost a 'left pocket – right pocket' transaction without outside interference. The contribution of each national central bank to the foreign reserve assets will be arithmetically fixed in proportion to its share in the subscribed capital of the ECB.[33]

At its first meeting on 11th June 1998, the Governing Council of the ECB agreed under the terms of Art. 29 ESCB, and according to the size of the population and the share of the gross domestic product of each participating member state, the allocation of the share capital of the ECB. At its second meeting on 7th July 1998, the Governing Council of the ECB also agreed under the terms of Art. 30 ESCB the size and form of foreign reserve assets to be provided by national central banks to the ECB on 1st January 1999. It also decided that 15% of the reserves to be transferred by national central banks should be in the form of gold, with the remaining 85% in the form of foreign reserve assets as stipulated in the protocol on the statute of the ESCB and of the ECB attached to the EC Treaty.

Although the precise formalities have to be sorted out between the ECB and the national central banks prior to the start of Stage Three on 1st January 1999, the revised[34]

---

[32] Art. 30.3 Statute of ESCB.
[33] Art. 30.2 Statute of ESCB.
[34] ECB Press Release, 1st December 1998.

financial allocations shown in the table below will take place to provide the ECB with considerable financial means.

With Greece, Denmark, United Kingdom and Sweden not participating in Stage Three as from 1st January 1999 they would have not been required to provide the ECB with initial contributions to its share capital and foreign currency reserves. However, in order for all EU member states to support the operational costs of the ECB from day one, the General Council of the ECB agreed at their meeting on 1st September 1998 as a compromise solution that the national central banks of the four member states not participating in the single currency as from 1st January 1999 should provide 5% of their subscriptions to the capital of the ECB. The four national central banks concerned will not be asked to pay in their share in the capital contribution amounting to slightly over 52.7 million Euros as the amount due is less than they can expect to receive as their share in the proceeds from the liquidation of the EMI. Thus the ECB will have at the start of its operation a paid up share capital of 3,999.6 million Euros, but below the required 5,000 million Euros as per Art. 28.1. of the Statute of the ECB. It is likely that against the background of four member states not participating in the single currency from the start the Governing Council of the ECB decided that the initial transfer of foreign reserve assets to the ECB by the national central banks of those member states participating should be the maximum amount allowed under the statutes of the ESCB. This will give the ECB, together with its paid up share capital, total shareholder funds of 43,468.5 million Euros.

Country	Share in %	Subscribed share capital in Euro millions	Share in % to be paid up	Paid up share capital in Euro millions	Reserves in Euro millions
Belgium	2.8658	143.29	100	143.29	1432.90
Denmark	1.6709	8.545	5	4.17725	-
Germany	24.4935	1224.645	100	1224.675	12246.75
Greece	2.0564	102.82	5	5.141	-
Spain	8.8935	444.675	100	444.625	4446.75
France	16.8337	841.685	100	841.685	8416.85
Ireland	0.8496	42.48	100	42.48	424.80
Italy	14.8950	744.75	100	744.75	7447.50
Luxembourg	0.1492	7.46	100	7.46	74.60
Netherlands	4.2780	213.90	100	213.90	2139.00
Austria	2.3594	117.97	100	117.97	1179.70
Portugal	1.9232	96.16	100	96.16	961.60
Finland	1.3970	69.85	100	69.85	698.50
Sweden	2.6537	132.685	5	6.63425	-
United Kingdom	14.6811	734.055	5	36.70275	-
TOTAL	100.0000	5,000.000		3999.5502	39468.95

REVISED FINANCIAL ALLOCATIONS TO PROVIDE THE ECB WITH CONSIDERABLE FINANCIAL MEANS

The holdings of foreign currency reserves by the ECB will be significant even with only eleven out of fifteen member states participating from 1st January 1999.

	Population (millions)	GDP (billions)	Estimated net reserves excl. gold (billions)	GDP per inhabitant	Share of world trade
USA	267.9	US$7819.0	US$65	US$30200	19.6%
Japan	125.9	US$4223.0	US$215	US$24700	10.5%
EU11	290.4	US$6110.9	US$213	US$20929	
EU15	374.1	US$8093.7	US$280	US$20908	20.9%
All nations			US$1324		

OECD Secretariat, IMF – Annual Report 1997, Eurostat, UN Statistical Office

COMPARABLE FOREIGN CURRENCY RESERVES

Once former national currencies of participating member states have been netted by the ESCB, foreign currency reserves will be predominantly denominated in US dollars, an imbalance which the ECB will try to correct in favour of a more balanced foreign currency reserve portfolio over the coming years. Although a number of studies[35] have been undertaken as to the post EMU foreign currency reserves of the ESCB and ECB, most commentators[36] agree that there will be no immediate need for the ECB to reduce its US dollar holdings and when it decides to do so, there will be no significant or lasting effects on the Euro/US dollar exchange rate after EMU.

Whilst the national central banks will still be allowed to perform transactions in accordance with their existing and future obligations towards international organisations, all other operations in foreign reserve assets will be (above an agreed sum[37]) subject to the express approval by the ECB 'in order to ensure consistency with the exchange rate and monetary policy of the Community.'[38]

---

[35] 'One Market, One Money' an evaluation of the potential benefits and costs of forming an Economic and Monetary Union, published by the European Commission, October 1996. A good representative study of the various considerations can be found in 'Implications of the Future Evolution of the International Monetary System' by Barry Eichengreen, Jeffrey Frankel and M. Mussa, in J. Boughton and P. Isard, (eds.), *The Future of the SDR in Light of Changes in the International Financial System*, International Monetary Fund, Washington, 1996.

[36] See paper by Fabienne Ilzkovietz in 'Prospects for the Internationalization of the Euro', European Commission, DG-II, June 1996.

[37] To be agreed by the Governing Council of the ECB in accordance with Art. 31.3 Statute of ESCB. Such transactions will probably be restricted to amounts not exceeding 5 million Euros to 10 million Euros.

[38] Art. 31.2 Statute of ESCB.

Any discussions relating to the reserves held by the ECB and Euro-zone national central banks raises the question of the optimal reserve holdings and at how they should be divided among the ECB and the national central banks of the member states participating in the single currency.

Conventional macroeconomic wisdom suggests central banks should hold foreign exchange reserves as a means to intervene in the foreign exchange markets and to cover a certain volume of imports. The optimal level of reserves holdings will ultimately depend on size of the economic area, the level of imports denominated in foreign currency into the economic area, the need by the central bank to defend the local currency in the foreign exchange markets and the ability to raise funds in the international (non-domestic) capital markets.

Figures outlined below show that the eleven Euro-zone national central banks maintained in November 1996 reserves of US$404,557 million. However, this figure includes reserves held in national currencies of the Euro-zone member states estimated at c. US$80,000 million and those reserves will be converted into Euros. The actual figure of total reserves also has to adjusted due to the fact that some national central banks including the German Bundesbank are showing foreign currency and gold reserves at cost and not at market value. This could add US$20,000 million to US$40,000 million to the total reserves held by the eleven Euro-zone national central banks, i.e. c. US$345,000 million to US$365,000 million.

Under the terms of the Maastricht Treaty, the eleven national central banks participating in the Euro will hand over to the ECB foreign reserve assets (other than national currencies of Euro-zone member states) up to an amount equivalent to 50,000 million Euros (ca. US$58,500 million).

OFFICIAL RESERVES OF EU NATIONAL CENTRAL BANKS[1]

in US$million	Gold	Foreign Exchange[1]	SDRs	Reserve positions	Total	Average monthly imports[2]	Import cover in days
Austria	1,905	21,440	181	812	24,338	4,455	164
Belgium		16,001	500	1,080	17,581	11,255	47
Finland	334	8,646	341	584	9,906	2,553	116
France	31,851	23,246	985	2,711	58,793	20,436	86
Germany	8,922	78,917	1,932	5,501	95,272	31,255	91
Ireland	144	8,332	166	328	8,970	2,873	94
Italy	25,533	46,333	28	1,872	73,766	15,400	144
Luxembourg	17	29	11	34	91	see Belgium	
Netherlands	8,733	25,246	791	1,850	36,620	13,491	81
Portugal	5,190	15,211	99	463	20,963	2,964	212
Spain	4,221	54,396	453	1,611	60,681	8,400	217
Denmark	595	13,591	169	609	14,964	3,110	144
Greece	873	19,116	1	164	20,154	1,800	336
Sweden	243	20,918	349	652	22,162	4,564	146
UK	5,480	34,930	310	2,440	43,160	21,382	61

---

[1] IMF, International Financial Statistics, January 1997.

Euro 11	86,894	295,605	5,373	16,685	404,557	112,672	108
Euro 15	94,085	384,160	6,202	20,550	504,997	143,527	105
USA					65,000[4]	60,000	33
Japan	3,607	279,073			282,680[5]	51,000	165

1. A breakdown in individual currencies is not available. National central banks in countries other than Germany are expected to hold a considerable amount of DM as part of their foreign currency reserve holdings. The German Bundesbank only holds reserves denominated in US$.
2. Based on average for first five months of 1998 including imports from EU member states. Eurostat press release no.9098. Figures for USA based on 1997 data.
3. Belgium and Luxembourg.
4. Excluding gold reserves.
5. Bank of Japan monetary accounts 20th October 1998.

This would leave the Euro-zone national central banks with aggregate 'local' reserves of c. US$290,000 million, at market value in excess of US$310,000 million. But how much of these local reserves would be surplus to requirements?

For the Euro-zone member states to cover their imports from outside the EU at levels comparable with those of the United States or Japan, i.e. one month's trading, the respective national central banks would have to maintain aggregate foreign reserves of c. US$60,000 million. Apart from securing imports of Euro-zone member states, the ECB will require considerable resources to defend the value of the Euro on the foreign exchange markets. In order to be effective and provide credibility, ECB would not only have to be able to defend the Euro over the short term but also over long periods. The 50,000 million Euros (c. US$58,500 million) provided to the ECB under the terms of the EC Treaty of which 7,500 million Euros (c. US$8,750 million) would be in gold, appear to be sufficient for temporary intervention in the foreign exchange markets and if such intervention is accompanied by political agreement and with other major central banks. In the absence of such political agreement and the requirement to intervene over a longer period of time, the ECB would have to be able to call under the terms of Art. 30.4 Statute of the ESCB on further reserves of at least 50,000 million Euros (c. US$58,500 million). This prudent approach would reduce the amount of possible 'excess' reserves to c. US$175,000.

The gold holdings of the Euro-zone member states amounting to c. US$100,000 million if market values are taken into account, can only be considered as secondary reserves in connection with collateralised forms of lending, swap transaction or repurchase contracts. At the same time, the fragile nature of the world gold market and the massive

impact of even modest disposals by central banks on the gold price severely restricts the realisable value of this traditional form of reserve holdings. With the option of selling gold in the world markets on a large scale and at short notice not available to central banks, the ECB must be provided with sufficient currency reserves instead of gold holdings in order to carry out effective intervention in the foreign exchange markets.

Euro-zone member states experienced no difficulty in transferring the required foreign exchange and gold reserves to the ECB at the start of Stage Three. Prudent reserve management in support of international trade flows and the restricted realisable value of the gold holdings significantly reduce the level of 'excess' reserves to considerably less than US$100,000 million. At the same time, almost three quarters of all official gold holdings are in the hands of the central banks of France, Germany and Italy.

Proposals presented in September 1998 by the Italian government suggested that national central banks ought to be permitted to liquidate their excess reserves to finance European infrastructure projects, research and development. Any sale of foreign currency reserves by Euro-zone central banks above an amount yet to be agreed requires the approval[1] of the ECB. With the ECB totally opposed to such sales of surplus reserves and the Council of Ministers unlikely ever to agree to a change in the Statute of the ESCB, the Italian plans are never expected to get off the drawing board even though other member states such as France initially supported[2] the idea. Modest disposals of surplus reserves by national central banks conducted over

---

[1] Art. 31.2 Statute of ESCB.
[2] '*Paris begrüßt Roms Pläne für EZB-Reserven*', *Handelsblatt*, 7th October 1998.

the long term will be possible provided repercussions on exchange rates and the price of gold are avoided.

Also doomed to failure are Italian proposals to permit the ECB to purchase bonds issued by the EIB for its currency reserves. Even if such bonds would be denominated in major currencies such as US dollars or yen, such paper would essentially be illiquid and therefore not available to the ECB and the ESCB as an effective tool for intervening in the foreign currency markets. If such plans would ever succeed, this would represent a clear bypass of the Stability and Growth Pact as well as a breach of the spirit and the letter of the Treaty of Rome.[3] The damage to the credibility of the ECB would be immense and the external value of the Euro indefensible.

Over the medium to long term, the demand for the US dollar as an international resource currency is expected to decline, largely in favour of the Euro. With the US dollar and the Euro expected to represent well over 50% of global central banks' reserves and an even higher percentage in terms of global trade, the future US dollar/Euro exchange rate will gain significant monetary, economic and possibly even political importance. In terms of optimal central bank reserves, the development of US dollar holdings by the ESCB and Euro holdings by the Federal Reserve Bank could either resemble a Cold War build-up of foreign currency 'war chests' or lead to mutual recognition of common global financial interests leading to enhanced central bank credibility, policy co-ordination and lower yet prudent levels of foreign currency reserves related to economic activity and long term portfolio considerations.

To achieve operational fairness and a truer reflection of operational activities and financial performance of each national central bank, the income accruing for the account

---

[3] Art. 104 of the EC Treaty.

of each national central bank in the execution of the ESCB monetary policy will be redistributed according to a complex formula as outlined in the Statute of the ESCB.[4] The amount of monetary income for the ECB is expected to be substantial and when compared with the 1997 profits of the German Bundesbank of DM24,200 million could be well in excess of 10,000 million Euros. Differences between the amount of national currency in circulation (both within and outside) of each member state participating in the single currency in relation to their relative GDP and size of population and the allocation of monetary income according to the percentage shares held in the ECB's capital will result in significant changes in the amounts of monetary income received by the national central banks of the eleven participating member states. Member states whose share in the capital key is lower than its share in the banknote circulation of the whole Euro area will become losers under the new system and vice versa.[5] In order to achieve a fairer allocation of monetary income and to smooth the allocation of the monetary income of national central banks at the start of Stage Three, Art. 51 of ESCB Statue allows the Governing Council of the ECB to derogate for a period up to five years from the rules of Art. 32 on the distribution of monetary income. Should the application of Art. 32 of the ESCB Statute lead to major changes in the relative income positions of Euro-zone national central banks, the amount of monetary income which is pooled and redistributed according to the share of each member state's contribution to the ECB share capital may be reduced to by up to 60%. To relate this reduction back to the maximum period of derogation of five years, this reduction has to decrease by at least 12% p.a. At its meeting on 3rd November 1998, the

---

[4] Art. 32 Statute of ESCB.
[5] Losers are expected to be Germany, the Netherlands, Spain and Austria.

Governing Council of the ECB decided to allocate monetary income of the national central banks for the transmission years 1999 to 2001 by multiplying a defined liability base by a specified reference rate of interest. The sum of the monetary income of each Euro-zone central bank will be allocated to them in proportion to their share in the ECB's paid-up capital. The ECB will however, revisit this formula before the introduction of Euro bank notes in 2002.

Any profits and/or losses of the ECB will be, as with any commercial enterprise, directly or indirectly for the account of the shareholders either through a change in the reserve position of the ECB or under a worst case scenario with the national central banks having to inject further capital.[6] The Statute of the ESCB does not specifically cater for the eventuality of the reserves and the capital of the ECB ever becoming fully used up through losses. However, it is assumed that the Governing Council of the ECB may never let it come to that situation as any sustained losses will considerably undermine the credibility of the ESCB and possibly the entire system of EMU.

Beneficial for the ECB are the updated[7] terms of Art. 23 of the Protocol of 8th April 1965 on the Privileges and Immunities of the European Communities which provide amongst other that:

> The European Central Bank shall [...] be exempt from any form of taxation or imposition of a like nature on the occasion of any increase in its capital and from the various formalities which may be therewith [...] The activities of the Bank and of its organs accordance with the Statute of the European

---

[6] Art. 33 Statute of ESCB.
[7] Art. 9 of the Treaty of Amsterdam.

System of Central Banks and of the European Central Bank shall not be subject to any turnover tax.

Should the EC Treaty or the statutes of the ECB contain a statutory duty for the ECB to make a profit, or at least to avoid a loss? The answer must be a clear no, because this could and sooner or later would conflict with the ECB's prime responsibility of maintaining price stability even if the ECB would incur losses on the scale as the Bank of England did on 16th September 1992. The same would apply to the unwarranted argument that a substantial loss of the ECB should amount to an offence which would allow some or all of the management of the ECB to be fired on the grounds of incompetence as per Article 109a of the EC Treaty and/or under Article 50 of the statue of ESCB.

The German government has always been grateful for the considerable dividends paid (DM24,213 million from 1997 profits of DM24,228 million) by the German Bundesbank to the finance ministry. The 1997 annual result of the German Bundesbank was boosted by a substantial DM13,300 million gain from restating its foreign currency and SDR reserves closer to their actual market rates in order to be in line with future ECB policy. A further revaluation during 1998 to bring the foreign currency and SDR reserves up to their market value level should yield a further DM13,000 million to DM15,000 million with most of it again being paid by the German Bundesbank to the government.

These considerable profits/dividends could be a powerful incentive for the European institutions in favour of operational independence for the ESCB. Nevertheless, over the first couple of years the ECB will try and build up its reserve positions.

In order to assist the Executive Board, the Governing and the General Councils of the ECB and the ESCB in

general, the Governing Council approved in accordance with its own Rules of Procedure (see Appendix IV) a number of committees:[8]

- Accounting and Monetary Income Committee
- Banking Supervision Committee
- Banknote Committee
- Budget Committee
- External Communications Committee
- Information Technology Committee
- Internal Auditors Committee
- International Relations Committee
- Legal Committee
- Market Operations Committee
- Monetary Policy Committee
- Payment and Settlement Systems Committee
- Statistics Committee

4. Tasks and Objectives

A key task for the ESCB with the ECB at its helm will almost from day one be to defend the credibility of the fixity of the exchange rate between currencies of participating member states until the single currency is introduced.[9] It will be vital for the ECB to establish quickly direct substitutionality between the Euro and the local currency as well as set an independent objective for the money stock in the whole system and translate that into

---

[8] See Appendix IV.

[9] See comments by Wim Duisenberg, then President of the EMI, when he stated the future ECB's strong commitment and unquestionable ability to withstand expected market tensions between the time when agreement is reached on the fixity of exchange rates between participating countries and the introduction of the single currency on 1st January 1999. As reported in *The Times*, 23rd October 1997.

objectives for each national currency through the national central bank. Although this alone does not avoid the credibility problem, irrevocably fixed exchange rates can in theory survive without a common ECB, but a common currency cannot.

To provide a legal framework for the changeover to the Euro, the EU has passed two key regulations based on Art. 109l of the EC Treaty and Art. 235 of the EC Treaty. Council Regulation 1103/97 which took effect on 20th June 1997 and applies to all fifteen member states confirms the important legal principle of continuity of contract to ensure legal certainty for all matters relating to the new single currency at an early stage. The regulations also deal with the replacement of the ECU by the Euro on a 1:1 basis as well as conversion and rounding rules for converting Euro-zone national currencies into Euros. Council Regulation 974/98 was passed in May 1998 but will not come into effect until 1st January 1999 and will only apply to member states participating in the single currency. Key parts of this regulation determine the legal status of the Euro versus national currencies of Euro-zone member states during the transitional period phase until June 2002 at the latest when national currencies will cease to be legal tender and be irrevocably replaced by the Euro.

The ECB will have the main responsibility for controlling the new single currency. Art. 105 (1) of the EC Treaty establishes the ECB's primary objective as the maintenance of price stability, and Art. 105 (2) of the EC Treaty gives it certain tasks:

1. To define and implement the monetary policy of the member states that are party to the single currency.
2. To conduct foreign exchange operations.
3. To hold and manage the official foreign reserves of member states that are party to the single currency.

4. To promote the smooth operation of payment systems.

The member states without derogation and not the ECB will have to agree unanimously in the Council of Ministers on the precise conversion rates at which their individual currencies will at the starting date of the third stage be irrevocably fixed and at which irrevocably fixed rate the Euro will be substituted for their respective national currencies.[10] Together with the strict adherence to the fulfilment of the convergence criteria in order to determine which member state was permitted to participate in the single currency, the determination of the 'economically correct' exchange rate in May 1998 was vital for the future success of EMU. What the politician might have accepted as a compromise to get as many member states to the join the single currency, the bankers of the ECB will have had to rescue later on to achieve price stability with their principal tool – interest rates.

As already stated above, the prime responsibility of the ECB is to maintain price stability which implicitly and ambitiously excludes any departure from it. But how does one measure price stability or the value of money? The value of money can be defined in at least three ways:

1. The internal value or the purchasing power of money measured in terms of the general level of prices (where monetary stability and price stability coincide).
2. The external value of the currency usually expressed in terms of the exchange rate with other currencies (where monetary stability and price stability do not usually coincide in the short term).
3. The opportunity or intertemporal value of money, i.e. the rate of interest (where monetary and price stability

---

[10] Art. 109l(4) of the EC Treaty.

do not necessarily coincide as maintaining a stable rate of interest may lead to inflationary pressures).

The current provisions contained in the EC Treaty as amended by the Single European Act and the Maastricht Treaty as well as the blueprint for the Statute of the ESCB clearly envisage under EMU a total separation of monetary policy from other policies. Although this is well accepted in countries with a tradition of independent central banks such as Germany and Holland, other member states such as the UK or France have long-standing traditions where ultimate responsibility for all branches of macroeconomic policy is retained by the government of the day and hence subject to more frequent changes. Member states without independent central banks have also more often used currency exchange rates and controls over capital flows as part of their fiscal and monetary policy. Such policy decisions however tended to cater for and last only for shorter periods of time as overall economic forces which make currency exchange rates and relative rates of domestic inflation interdependent (provided there are no controls over cross border capital flows) and adjust each other over the longer term. In many member states such exchange rate policies often came into conflict with fiscal policies.

In a modern financial system and money economy, financial institutions and central banks play an active role which can facilitate the creation of productive capacity and the expansion of economic output. Thus the banking system carries a potential contribution to economic growth. When societies and people are fortunate to have a spirit of enterprise and when this spirit is shared by its financial institutions it may be a double blessing. Experiences during a recessionary environment however have taught us that it can also be a double curse. With the assistance of financial institutions, indirectly aided by national central banks and

governmental policy, enterprises may often be encouraged to use leverage, i.e. grow and accumulate wealth at a rate much higher than households within the economic area are planning savings. Conversely, at times of insecurity, financial institutions may actually magnify the rush to liquidate, often expressed as a 'credit crunch' and thereby accentuate slumps. It is into this industrial and financial circulation that the ECB must step both in terms of its monetary policy and its role as supervisor of the financial system and possible lender as a last resort.

Post World War Two economic performance has shown that there is no mechanism which automatically and in a self-regulating manner assures equality of the actual, warranted and natural rate of economic growth. A rational monetary policy to promote growth is therefore as important as price stability. Deliberate policies to limit the growth of the money supply and/or the onset of a credit crunch can quickly turn optimism into pessimism. Ultimately, the monetary policy of the ECB must be compatible with a socially desirable stable growth rate and a relatively stable level of prices. With strong social and political forces at work 'the control of the price level may pass beyond the power of the banking system.'[11] Monetary policy must be co-ordinated with fiscal policy which assures the proper balance of the real forces underlying aggregate demand and potential supply. In an economy where strong social and political forces have already gained control of the ever-rising money costs of production, the control of the domestic price level has passed beyond the power of the national central banks. The same applies for national central banks where political considerations outweigh monetary policy even if monetary policy alone cannot by itself prevent domestic inflation as it cannot directly influence

---

[11] John Maynard Keynes, *A Treatise on Money*, Vol. II, p.351.

the major costs of production of reproducible goods. The ECB with its statutory enshrined independence and primary objective of price stability will to a large degree be able to step outside politically inspired policies and have a central role to play in the establishment of a European environment of non-inflationary expectations. As in any modern capitalist society, there will be no Marxist control over the factors of production and the ECB will be acutely aware that its monetary policy has no safety net.

In a working paper published in May 1997[12], the IMF made public the results of various stochastic simulations[13] to explore the behaviour of European economies post-EMU and to analyse the effects of replacing their national currencies with the Euro. Figures[14] published by the European Commission for 1995 suggest that the five[15] main European currencies account to over 30% of external trade compared with 52% for the US dollar. The global share of the European currencies in the international bond market is with 37.1% already higher than the US dollar's share of 34.2%. The share of world private portfolio holdings has been increasing steadily but with 36.9% not yet overtaken the US dollar share of 39.8%. This compares well considering that the combined domestic market capitalisation of

---

[12] 'Characteristics of the Euro, the Demand for Reserves, and Policy Coordination Under EMU' by Paul R. Masson and Bart G. Turtelboom published by Research Department, International Monetary Fund, May 1997.

[13] The model used was the MULTEU version of MULTIMOD, the IMF's global macroeconomic model. Details of the model can be found in 'MULTIMOD Mark II: A Revised and Extended Model' published by Paul R. Masson, Steven Symansky and Guy Meredith in Occasional Paper No. 71 by International Monetary Fund, July 1990.

[14] See 'The implications of the introduction of the Euro for non-EU countries' by Peter Bekx, European Commission, Directorate General II – Economic and Foreign Affairs, No. 26, July 1998.

[15] DEM, FRF, GBP, ITL and NLG.

the member states' equity markets was in October 1998 around US$3,730 billion compared with well over US$9,680 billion for the New York and NASDAQ markets.

The models used by the IMF researchers tried to include predictions for monetary policy of the ECB when asymmetric monetary policy resulting from historic developments of various, often long established economic relationships, and shocks to consumption and investment across member states of the EU (relative to the size of their respective economies) will be replaced by a largely symmetric policy for developments across the Euro-zone as a whole. In its conclusion, the IMF expects that EMU in itself is likely 'to promote stability of major macroeconomic variables.[16] However, it also states that no simulation can predict the future credibility of the ECB and its possible effects on volatility within the Euro-zone and the foreign exchange markets.

The widespread existence of international money markets and the banking system of the various nations provide a potential source of Euro money holdings or potential Euro money supply that may be beyond the reach of the conventional policy actions of the ECB. Empirical studies[17] have shown that even with the Bretton Woods fixed exchange rate system, it was possible to maintain monetary policies independent of monetary events in other countries. But has the movement from the Bretton Woods fixed exchange rate system to more flexible rate systems enhanced the ability of central banks to control the domes-

---

[16] 'Characteristics of the Euro, the Demand for Reserves, and Policy Coordination Under EMU' by Paul R. Masson and Bart G. Turtelboom published by Research Department, International Monetary Fund, May 1997, p.9.

[17] 'The Monetary Approach to the Balance of Payments' by J. Frenkel and H. Johnson, 1977.

tic money supply and more efficiently execute monetary policy? Experiences of various European central banks and the ultimate demise of ERM I suggest that even though central banks no longer guarantee that two currencies are perfect substitutes, the private market still regards the two monies as having similar monetary characteristics and structures and adjust a diversified portfolio of monies as the relative risks of holding the monies change. This high degree of substitutionality will apply to the relationship of the Euro and the national currencies of the four member states not joining the single currency on 1st January 1999. The policy dilemma for the ECB will come right from the start of EMU, since the ECB will not be able to control the quantity of Euros in countries outside the Euro-zone and hence cannot control the quantity of Euros potentially available to residents in the Euro-zone.

The limitations on the ability of central banks to regulate where monies are substituted in demand has important implications for the Euro-zone and the proper world monetary system. Lessons from the crisis in the Far East suggest that co-operation and co-ordination are key elements for successful monetary policy without the loss of monetary independence. A world monetary system which emphasises totally independent policies would not only be less than optimal, but would be potentially destabilising and depressionary. As far as monetary policy is concerned, the introduction of the Euro may well be beginning of the end of the current regime of floating currencies. The development of currency blocs and the synchronisation of monetary policies could ultimately lead to the return to a fixed exchange rate system not too dissimilar to the ERM II except on almost a global basis between the major trading currencies.

5. Powers

It will be a requirement of Stage Three that not only the ECB, but also the national central banks, having almost become branches of the ECB, shall be independent of other Community institutions and bodies, as well as of national governments and any other body, when carrying out their functions under the Treaty.

The ECB will in addition to providing recommendations and opinions also be able to make regulations[18] and decisions about certain matters, and will have the power to impose fines or periodic penalty payments on undertakings that fail to comply with that legislation[19]. The scope of any legislative function of the ECB is clearly restricted and has been devised 'in order to carry out the tasks entrusted to the ESCB'.[20] Whilst recommendations and opinions will have no binding force[21], decisions by the ECB will be binding in their entirety upon those to whom they are addressed and regulations will have general application in all the member states. Although the ECB will be able to make legally binding regulations and decisions, these are subject to Articles 190 to 192 of the EC Treaty which imposes not only a requirement of reasoning (which could be held appropriate) but also deals with reference to any proposals or opinions which were required to be obtained pursuant to

---

[18] Applying Articles 190 and 191 of the EC Treaty, regulations are to state the reasons on which they are based and referring to any proposals or opinions required to be obtained and be published in the official journal of the EC.

[19] Art. 108a of the EC Treaty and Art. 34 of the Statute of the ESCB. See draft EU Council Regulation concerning the power of the ECB to impose sanctions in EMI report entitled 'The Single Monetary Policy in Stage Three – Specification of the operational framework', p.85 and in European Commission Euro Papers No. 25, July 1998.

[20] Art. 108a(1) of the EC Treaty and Art. 34.1 of the Statute of the ESCB.

[21] Art. 108a(2) of the EC Treaty and Art. 34.2 of the Statute of the ESCB.

the Treaty, i.e. formal consent or opinion of other Community institutions in order to act. This requirement to consult others must sooner or later clash with functional autonomy of the ECB. With ECB regulations and decisions being binding in their nature, they will be open to judicial review under Art. 173 of the EC Treaty.

Even with the ECB having no obligation to publish its decisions, recommendations and opinions, the ECB is expected to follow the established practice of publishing some of the documents in the official journal under the heading 'Acts whose publication is not obligatory'. This practice will not only foster transparency and accountability, but it can also serve as a powerful political weapon to put pressure on the addressee.

Whilst the EC Treaty does not grant a general legislative power to the Community institutions, the Commission is nearly always required to initiate the legislative process by making a proposal and there are no serious doubts that the Commission exercises this power with due diligence. The ECB however represents an exception to the Commission's right of initiative as some legislation can be passed by the Council on the recommendation of the ECB[22]. This will apply to certain provisions referred to in the Statute of the ESCB and to certain provisions on the relationship of the single currency with currencies of third countries.

Under the conditions laid down by the Council of Ministers, acting by a qualified majority on a proposal from the Commission and after consulting the ECB, or, acting on a recommendation from the ECB and after consulting the Commission and the EP, the ECB will be able to impose fines and periodic penalties on essentially national

---

[22] Art. 106(6) and 109 of the EC Treaty.

central banks for failures to comply with the ESCB regulations and decisions.[23]

Not underestimated should be Art. 109b(2) of the EC Treaty which provides that from the start of its operations, the President of the ECB must be invited to participate in Council meetings when the Council is discussing matters relating to the objectives and tasks of the ESCB. This will allow the ECB to manage monetary policy to a considerable degree on a proactive basis rather than on a reactive basis as its national counterparts currently have to do, often based on conflicting or incomplete economic data available after the event.

As a further plank to meaningful independence, Articles 178 and 215(2) of the EC Treaty state that the ECB shall be free from liability unless tough requirements as established by the ECJ have been fulfilled.[24] The ECJ has consistently held for liability to be established that:

1. The institution against which the action is brought must have acted unlawfully.
2. The person bringing the action must have suffered damage.
3. There must be a direct link in the chain of causality between the wrongful act and the damage complained of.

The ECB will under Art. 105a of the EC Treaty have the exclusive right to authorise the issue of bank notes both by the ECB and the national central banks within the member states that are party to the single currency.

---

[23] Art. 108(3) of the EC Treaty and Art. 34.3 Statute of ESCB.

[24] See cases such as Case C-146/91, KYDEP v. Council and Commission [1994] ECR I-4199, para. 19.

The ECB will have its own distinct legal personality[25] and in order to have independence as well as power it will enjoy in each of the member states the most extensive legal capacity accorded to legal persons under their laws. In particular it may acquire property and dispose of movable and immovable property and may be a party to legal proceedings.[26] The ESCB represents the ECB and its shareholder national central banks but the ESCB itself does not have a legal personality like the ECB.

In order to support full independence, the ECB has full financial autonomy as neither its income nor its expenditure falls under any Community budget. Matters related to the financial resources of the ECB are outlined in the Protocol attached to the EC Treaty. Following publication of the Rules of Procedure of the ECB's General and Governing Councils as per Art. 12.3 of the Statutes of the ESCB, it is the Governing Council upon a proposal from Executive Board of the ECB which approves the budget of the ECB[27]. However, the Executive Board will have drawn up the budget and it will be largely a formality for the Governing Council to approve it.

6. Limits of Operational Independence

Despite this operational freedom, the ECB will not be free to enter into agreements concerning monetary or foreign exchange matters between the Community and non-Community States or international organisations, for example the World Bank or the IMF. In derogation from the exercise of the treaty-making power regulated by Article 228 of the EC Treaty, such agreements will be negotiated

---

[25] Art. 106(2) of the EC Treaty.
[26] Art. 9.1 Statute of ESCB.
[27] Art. 15.1 Rules of Procedure of the Governing Council of the ECB.

and concluded by the Community according to arrangements laid down by the Council acting on a qualified majority and on a recommendation from the Commission.[28] According to the words of the EC Treaty: 'These arrangements shall ensure that the Community speaks with one voice on such occasions.' To give them universal application, agreements concluded according to such arrangements shall not only be binding on the ECB but also the other Community institutions and the member states.[29]

The exchange rate regime of the ECB is an important part of the ECB's monetary policy transmission process but for formal exchange rate agreements with non-Community currencies the ECB has its hands tied and therefore its independence curtailed. In order to safeguard any undue political motives for agreeing and participating in exchange rate systems with other currencies heavy emphasis has been placed in the EC Treaty on a requirement to reach consensus and the hurdle of unanimity has been set for the Council before any such agreements can be adopted.[30] Nevertheless, such agreements could be adopted, albeit requiring unanimity, even though they may be contrary to the opinions expressed by the ECB. Any critical opinions expressed by the ECB will clearly be picked up by the EP which must be consulted.[31]

Even with EMU bringing a lot of monetary policy matters into the competence of the ECB or under Community competence in general, the member states are still free to negotiate in their own right in international bodies and conclude international agreements such as bilateral trade agreements and export and inward invest-

---

[28] Art. 109(3) of the EC Treaty.
[29] Ibid.
[30] Art. 109(1) of the EC Treaty.
[31] Ibid.

ment support programmes.[32] However, such agreements will mainly be concluded with countries and bodies outside the EC.

7. Monetary Strategy

With the ECB and the EC Treaty as it now stands, the Community will have acquired for the first time an important macroeconomic dimension that will at least match the provisions for the creation of the common market contained in the original Treaty of Rome. As part of its preparatory work and by taking into account the above tasks, the EMI had developed and spelt out[33] early key elements for a corresponding monetary strategy to be pursued by the ECB:

1. A quantified definition of the final objective of price stability (to be made public to achieve credibility and in order to enhance transparency).
2. A quantified definition of the specific targets against which the ESCB can be assessed and its performance in terms of meeting the above objective (important for matters of accountability).
3. A communication policy for the ESCB to explain its strategy to the general public (important for enhancement of transparency and accountability not only to member states but for people of Europe as a whole).
4. The availability of a meaningful yet broad set of indicators in order to help assess risks to future price stability[34] (crucial to allow ESCB to pursue pre-emptive and forward looking policy decisions).

---

[32] Art. 109(5) of the EC Treaty.

[33] EMI 1996 Annual Report, p.62.

[34] See proposal by EMI for a draft EU Council Regulation concerning the collection of statistical information by the ECB as published in report

5. Detailed information on and a prominent role for EU wide money aggregates including publication of targets, regular updates and progress reports.
6. Tools to allow forecasts for inflation and other economic variables for the Euro area.

In practice all these elements and principles only when mixed together will constitute the operational framework of the ESCB. They will be interlinked and can be combined in different ways either against the background of a specific time horizon or a particular policy objective.

Based on the model followed by the Bundesbank, the ECB is likely to focus first on domestic rather than external targets and will not regard the Euro exchange rate as its principal target. Announcements and decisions made by the ECB suggest that the guiding policy tools for intermediate and long range targets are likely to include domestic monetary aggregates and broad moneys such as M3. The heavy reliance by the Bundesbank on M3 has since reunification showed signs of unreliability when measuring the relationship between M3 and inflation. Not only in the interest of market credibility, it is important for the ECB to give clear guidance to the markets on how it will conduct monetary policy according targets set in advance. What will be even more difficult to determine will be whether EMU will facilitate stronger competition within the financial sector and whether the development of active and liquid European capital markets will force the ECB to adopt

---

entitled 'The Single Monetary Policy in Stage Three – Specification of the operational framework', p.77. This new regulation will complement but later replace the current 'European System of National and Regional Accounts' (OJ No. L310 and 321). The United Kingdom apparently questions the need for a monthly balance of payments statistic for policy and operational reasons in the Euro area but it promised to review its position in 1998.

monetary policies more familiar to Anglo-Saxon central banks. In any case, the ECB is required by its statute to operate in accordance with 'the principle of an open market economy with free competition favouring an efficient allocation of resources.'[35]

When applying monetary and inflation targeting as its preferred choice of monetary policy instrument, the ECB can draw on 'Goodhart's Law', named after Charles Goodhart, Professor of Finance at the London School of Economics, who discovered in the 1980s that the relationship between the supply of money and the rate of inflation no longer holds as soon as policy-makers start to adopt money supply as their targeted policy variable. Hence, the reliance by the ECB on a single variable for monetary policy direction might either result in an unacceptable rise in unemployment or an increase in the rate of inflation. In both cases, this would seriously impair the hard to be earned credibility of the ECB. Robert Lucas, the 1995 Nobel Prize winner for economics, strikingly pointed out that a change in policy fundamentally alters the structure of econometric models. Whatever the economic policy, whatever the monetary policy instruments, economic theories and experiences since Bretton Woods have made it more and more apparent that interest rate decisions by the ECB are essentially judgement calls based on the instincts of central bankers, their collective experience mixed with thorough analysis of political and economic realities.

Some of the biggest threats for the credibility of the ECB do not necessarily come from its own action or inaction but from loose fiscal policies pursued by governments of member states with highly divergent economies and with different fiscal views and aims to tackle problems such as unemployment, budget deficits and high public

---

[35] Art. 2 Statute of ESCB.

debt. Past experience shows that the temptation can be just too great for governments to use what they describe as 'modest' inflation as a convenient mechanism to erode the value of its indebtedness. Prior to the stabilising forces of the Stability and Growth Pact taking effect, imprudently loose fiscal policy and the lack of early countermeasures by any member state participating in the single currency could lead to a rapid rise in its government indebtedness and with it spiralling budget deficits resulting from higher and higher debt servicing costs. Early countermeasures by the ECB such as increased interest rates would only add to a member state being pushed nearer and nearer a fiscal black hole or debt trap as experienced by many Latin American countries during the 1970s.

The dynamics of how a dept trap and its dangers for fiscal budgeting can develop within a single currency area have been demonstrated by economists through the following model:[36]

$$(D/Y)_t - (D/Y)_{t-1} = (P/Y)_t + ((r_t - g_t)/(1 + g_t)) \times (D/Y)_{t-1}$$

Where:

D_t is the net stock government debt (net of the government's financial assets)
P_t is the primary budget deficit (excluding net interest payments)
S_t is the secondary budget deficit (i.e. the net interest payments term)
r is the effective interest rate on the stock of debt
Y_t is nominal GDP
g_t is the growth rate of nominal GDP.

---

[36] See 'Fiscal policy in EMU' in *ABN Amro European Strategy & Economics*, Vol.5, No.13, April 1998, p.11.

The model shows that if the nominal rate of interest is greater than the nominal growth rate of the economy, the ratio of debt to GDP will rise unless it is offset by a primary budget surplus. On the other hand, if the budget surplus excluding net interest payments is not sufficient to cover the net interest payments on the government's interest-bearing indebtedness, then the ratio of debt relative to GDP will rise and indebtedness will start to rise at an ever faster pace. The ECB will sooner or later be forced to act with appropriate measures to protect its monetary policy objectives. The threat to the ECB's credibility will be serious in both cases, either through its failure to delivery price stability or by acting as a catalyst for higher budget deficits or a rapid build-up of indebtedness leading ultimately to a government defaulting on its debt obligations. The role of Euro X and ECOFIN as a bridge between the monetary policy objectives of the ECB and the fiscal policies of all member states will be crucial, especially during periods of economic downturns as experienced in most parts of Europe in the early 1980s and the late 1980s/early 1990s.

The size of the domestic market within the Euro-zone but indirectly across the entire EU will undoubtedly give the Euro in addition to its domestic role a much larger role as an international trading and reserve currency. EMU macroeconomic policy and monetary policy pursued by the ECB will have an impact on the external value of the Euro. At the same time, international demand patterns for the Euro could influence monetary policy considerations of the ECB as well as fiscal policies of EU member states, especially if the external value of the Euro would prove to be erratic. Volatile exchange rate patterns often fuelled by speculative forces could have a number of implications for EMU. The key consideration for the ECB will be likely

effects on general macroeconomic management and monetary aggregates, and whether targeted monetary aggregates would have to be questioned leading to over-reaction through the use of interest rates as the main policy driver. Innovative financial markets, their leverage effects and increasingly swifter movements of significant amounts of capital will make traditional monetary aggregates less reliable indicators for both domestic economy and inflation targets. Not underestimated for the avoidance of erratic exchange rate developments should be the credibility of the ECB and its ability to minimise uncertainty from the application of monetary policy tools to a policy of openness and transparency with the financial community and the public at large. Uncertainty arising from diverging fiscal policies will have to be addressed by the ECB and its ongoing dialogue with member states and its central banks. For this reason, there is a vital role to play for Euro X and ECOFIN.

In order to manage the liquidity situation in the market and to provide signals of its stance of monetary policy, the ECB will mainly use so-called open market operations and standing facilities. Open market operations will be the key tool for the purpose of steering interest rates via tender transactions[37] and bilateral procedures. The choice of monetary instruments and actual operating procedures should not influence the use by the ECB of intermediate and long range targets. The ECB intends to use the various instruments at its disposal, to steer through open market operations the money market rates within a target corridor sandwiched by two standing facilities.

---

[37] See proposal by EMI concerning technical features of the ESCB's tender operations as published in report entitled 'The Single Monetary Policy in Stage Three – Specification of the operational framework', p.53 and General documentation on ESCB monetary policy instruments and procedures, ECB, September 1998.

Limiting the volatility of short term market interest rates around the ECB's policy rate is expected to maximise its influence over market expectations and minimise the chances for the market to misinterpret policy. For this purpose, the ECB will be using the requirement for banks to maintain minimum reserves with the ESCB. The requirement for financial institutions to maintain minimum reserves throughout the years but calculated on a monthly basis has been referred to as 'reserve averaging'. Under this system given minimum levels of reserves have to be maintained at the ESCB provided on an average basis during the maintenance period, i.e. one month, the minimum sum required is maintained. Most central banks appear to operate a fairly wide interest corridor of c. 2% so that market rates can still fluctuate widely. Averaging reserves can significantly stabilise market rates of interest thereby reducing the volatility of market interest rates.

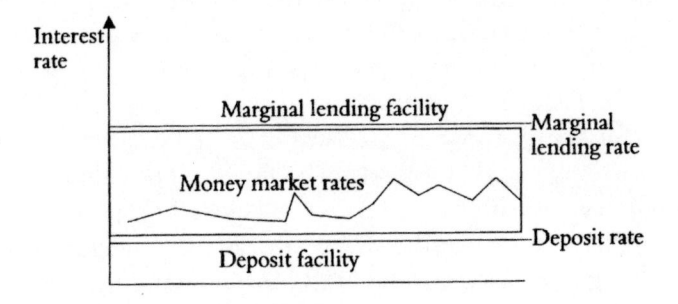

The drawback of averaging is that it allows banks to speculate if they expect a change in the ECB's interest rate during the maintenance period. This could however be avoided if the ECB would change its policy rates at the start of each maintenance period only and not during it. Given the contributory factors of reserve averaging to the reduc-

tion in the volatility of market interest rates, this should significantly reduce the frequency with which the ECB will have to change its policy rate. The ECB decision to pay interest on the average of the monthly market rates should also help to reduce speculation.

Based on preparatory work undertaken by the EMI[38], the ECB and the ESCB have decided and will be able to make use of the following open market operations:

Monetary policy operations	Type of transaction: Provision of liquidity	Type of transaction: Absorption of liquidity	Maturity	Frequency	Procedure
Main refinancing operations	Reverse transaction		Two weeks	Weekly	Standard tenders
Longer-term refinancing operations	Reverse transaction		Three months	Monthly	Standard tenders
Fine-tuning operations	Reverse transaction	Reverse transaction	Non-standardised	Non-regular	Quick tenders
	Foreign exchange swaps	Foreign exchange swaps			Bilateral procedures
		Collection of fixed-term deposits			
	Outright purchases	Outright sales		Non-regular	Bilateral procedures
Structural operations	Reverse transaction	Reverse transaction	Standardised/ non-standardised	Regular and non-regular	Standard tenders
	Outright purchases	Outright sales		Non-regular	Bilateral procedures

Open market operations will be central to the ESCB transmission process for conducting monetary policy for the purpose of steering interest rates, managing the liquidity situation in the market and most importantly setting signals for any changes in the ESCB's monetary policy stance. Weekly open market operations provide the bulk of

---

[38] EMI 1996 Annual Report, p.63 and General documentation on ESCB monetary policy instruments and procedures, ECB, September 1998, p.8.

refinancing to the financial sector in Europe and will serve as the main policy valve to manage liquidity. Longer-term refinancing transactions executed on a monthly basis will not by themselves set any signal to the market about changes in the ECB's monetary policy direction but the fact that the ESCB will be at all creating a monetary instrument with longer maturities creates an undiluted benchmark and thus an important signal of overall market conditions.

In addition to open market operations, the ECB can also avail itself of standing facilities mainly for the provision and absorption of overnight liquidity. Whilst open market operations will be primarily initiated by the ECB, standing facilities will be administered by the national central banks in the Euro-zone albeit with broad guidance by the ECB.

The ESCB has decided and will be able to make use of the following standing facilities:

Monetary policy operations	Type of transaction: Provision of liquidity	Type of transaction: Absorption of liquidity	Maturity	Frequency/ Procedure
Marginal lending facility	Reverse transaction		Overnight	Access at the discretion of the counterparties
Deposit facility		Deposits	Overnight	Access at the discretion of the counterparties

The monetary policy instruments proposed by the EMI and generally accepted by the ECB reflect the policy makers' strong desire to create a self-stabilising system counter-balancing ongoing and constantly changing volatilities in liquidity and interest rate development. The standing facilities of the ESCB will allow the creation of an effective interest corridor within which financial institutions can obtain (against eligible assets) as well as place short-dated, usually overnight liquidity. The width of this liquidity corridor coupled with the high amounts of liquidity

channelled through this system will allow standing facilities to become an additional instrument of monetary policy at the disposal of the ECB. Provided a financial institution has sufficient eligible assets, there will under normal circumstances be no upper credit limit or other restriction on how much liquidity may be obtained under the marginal lending facility. In turn there will under normal circumstances be no upper limit for a financial institution placing overnight liquidity with the national central bank. The short-dated nature of these instruments and the fast changing rates environment will mean that all market participants including the ESCB will have to develop a uniform and clear set of market signals in order to correctly interpret ongoing rate changes.

The ESCB will allow a wide range of assets to underlie its open market operations although all credit operations must be based on adequate collateral.[39] For largely internal purposes, the ESCB will make a distinction between two categories of assets:

1. 'Tier one' assets consist of marketable debt instruments which fulfil uniform eligibility criteria specified by the ECB throughout the Euro-zone.
2. 'Tier two' assets are marketable and non-marketable assets of importance for national financial markets and banking systems and for which eligibility criteria are established by national central banks however, with the approval of the ECB.

The private as well as public sector paper which can be used in collateralised[40] credit operations of the ESCB can be summarised as follows:

---

[39] Art. 18.1 Statute of ESCB.
[40] Ibid.

CRITERIA	TIER ONE	TIER TWO
Type of asset	ESCB debt certificates Other marketable financial obligations	Marketable financial obligations Non-marketable financial obligations Equities traded on a regulated market
Type of issuer	ESCB Public sector Private sector International institutions	Public sector Private sector
Financial soundness	The issuer must be deemed financially sound by the ECB.	The issuer/debtor must be deemed financially sound by the national central bank that included the assets in its tier two list.
Location of issuer	EEA except for international institutions	Euro area Location in other EEA countries can be accepted subject to ECB approval.
Location of asset	Euro area	Euro area Location in other EEA countries can be accepted subject to ECB approval.
Currency of denomination	Euro (or its national denominations)	Euro (or its national denominations) Other EEA or widely traded currencies can be accepted subject to ECB approval.

Although no distinction will be made between the two asset categories in terms of their quality and their eligibility for the various types of the ESCB monetary policy operations, tier two assets will normally not be used for outright transactions. In any case, strict control measures will be used to protect the ESCB against financial loss caused by a counterparty defaulting on its obligations. An incentive to create as many tier one assets as possible will be provided for national central banks by the fact that any losses from a defaulting tier one asset will be shared across the entire Euro-zone whilst any losses from tier two assets will be for the account of the national central bank only.

With fiscal sovereignty remaining in the hands of member states' governments this will create sizeable risks for EMU in form of a bias towards excessive expansionary fiscal policies, especially in member states set on improving or remedying structural problems exposed and magnified

by EMU. Constraints imposed upon member states by the Stability and Growth Pact will have their part to play. At the same time tight limits imposed on member states will also have to withstand the test of time as they could unduly constrain the ability of governments to deal with sizeable shocks and cycles to their respective economies with corresponding pressure on the ECB.

8. National Central Banks

In order to align its system with the ESCB each member state must ensure that its national legislation concerning the national central banks is compatible with that of the Treaty and the Protocol annexed to the Treaty[41] otherwise the system of central control and monetary policy setting at the ECB but local control and execution at the level of national central banks would have serious operational and legislative flaws. In particular the term of office of a governor of a national central bank must be not less than five years[42] but the Treaty and the Protocol of the ECB do allow, contrary to rules for members of the Executive Board of the ECB[43] renewal of office for central bank governors.

Similar to provisions governing the office of any member of the Executive Board of the ECB,[44] the governor of a national central bank may only be relieved from office on the grounds of serious misconduct or failure to perform his duties,[45] i.e. only extreme personal incapacity or misdemeanour. A decision to this effect enjoys added protection as it may be referred to the ECJ by the governor concerned or the Governing Council of the ECB.

---

[41] Art. 108 of the EC Treaty and Art. 14.1 Statute of ESCB.
[42] Art. 14.2 Statute of ESCB.
[43] Art. 109a of the EC Treaty and Art. 11.2 Statute of ESCB.
[44] Art. 11.4 Statute of ESCB.
[45] Art. 14.2 Statute of ESCB.

Despite this apparent protection, can member states or as we have even seen in the past, the press, exert such pressure or conduct such a campaign against individual governors, that he or she will be forced to resign? Experience suggests that the answer is probably yes. However, even if such a campaign should be successful, the ousted governor would be replaced reasonably soon by what the Protocol on the ESCB describes as a 'person of recognised standing and professional experience in monetary or banking matters' even if this precise definition does not specifically apply to governors of national central banks. Furthermore, the strength and independence of the ECB with its local national central banks forming the ESCB is such that it is very doubtful whether the 'enforced' replacement of a governor of a national central bank would or even could alter the overall course of monetary policy.

With national central banks being the extended arm and therefore an integral part of the ESCB, they are compelled to act in accordance with the guidelines, commitments and instructions of the ECB[46] free from any interference, instructions or pressure from local member states or any other body including any other Community institution as outlined above.[47] Compliance and the serious implications of non-compliance are not the sole prerogative of the Executive Board of the ECB but a matter for the Governing Council as a whole.[48]

As part of its convergence report ahead of the decisions taken in Birmingham in May 1998 the EMI reviewed the compatibility of national legislation with the EC Treaty in all EU member states, to identify areas where national legislation needed or still needs to be adapted to make

---

[46] Art. 14.3 Statute of ESCB.
[47] Art. 107 of the EC Treaty and Art. 7 Statute of ESCB.
[48] Art. 14.3 Statute of ESCB.

national legislation and statutes of national central banks compatible with the EC Treaty and the Statutes of the ECB. To safeguard the institutional and functional independence of national central banks from third parties such as governments and/or parliaments and as a prerequisite for the independence and credibility of not only the ECB but the EMU as a whole, the EMI differentiated in its review of national central bank legislation and statutes between three categories of central bank independence: institutional, personal and financial.

When focusing on institutional independence through the looking glass of Art. 107 of the EC Treaty and Art. 14.2 of the ESCB Statute, the EMI looked[49] at national central banks and their respective decision making bodies whether any national parties such as governments, parliaments, monetary/financial committees or even heads of state

1. had the right to give them instructions,
2. had the ability to approve, suspend, annul, defer any of their decisions,
3. had the right to censor any of their decisions on legal grounds,
4. had the right to participate in their decision making process with a right of vote; or
5. had the right to be consulted on any of their decisions.

If any such rights or abilities already existed, these might require adaptation or amendment for the national central bank with such changes becoming effective at the latest by the date of establishment of the ESCB.

Apart from institutional independence, the statutes of national central banks, in order to be held as compatible

---

[49] European Monetary Institute, Convergence Report, March 1998, pp.12–13.

with Art. 107 of the EC Treaty and Art. 14.2 of the ESCB Statute, must also provide for significant personal independence, in particular:

1. A minimum term of office for governors of five years.
2. Safeguards that a governor may not be dismissed for reasons other than those mentioned in the Statute of the ESCB (see above).
3. The same security of tenure as the governors for other members of the decision making bodies, provided they are involved in the performance of tasks related to the ESCB.
4. Assurances that no conflicts of interest will arise between the duties placed on member of the decision-making bodies of national central banks vis-à-vis their national central banks.
5. Safeguard that no conflicts of interest will arise for governors vis-à-vis the ECB.

Complete financial independence means that no third party (essentially governments) can use financial means, directly or indirectly, to influence the national central bank in their ability to fulfil their mandate. National central banks are not mere 'robots' for the ECB without any additional local activities. They are permitted to perform other functions such as banking supervision, local market regulation or numismatic activities at their own risk and for their own account, provided such operations have not been deemed contrary to the functions and responsibilities of the national central bank as outlined in the Statute of the ECB. For an activity to be declared incompatible or in interference with the objectives and the tasks of a national central bank within the overall ESCB requires the decision

of the Governing Council of the ECB with a clear majority of two thirds of the votes cast.[50]

Practical considerations will largely dictate whether the ECB or national central banks will participate in the financial markets. Such considerations suggest that the ECB rather than national central banks will conduct foreign-exchange operations since the onus will be on the ECB's ability to make fast decisions and a significant portion of the foreign exchange reserves of the ESCB will be held in the books of the ECB. Participation in the money market and the operation of minimum reserve requirements together with the provision of central bank clearing facilities will be best handled on a national level in compliance with the statutes of the ESCB which require the ECB to call on 'the national central banks [to the extent deemed possible and appropriate] to carry out the operations which form part of the tasks of the ESCB.'[51]

9. Regulatory Role and Lender of Last Resort

The exact monetary functions and operations of the ESCB are outlined by the Treaty and extensively documented in the Protocol on the Statute. These include provisions on the nature of accounts with the ECB and the national central banks,[52] open market and credit operations,[53] minimum reserves,[54] instruments on monetary control,[55] operations with public entities,[56] clearing and payment

---

[50] Art. 14.4 Statute of ESCB.
[51] Art. 12.1 Statute of ESCB.
[52] Art. 17 Statute of ESCB.
[53] Art. 18 Statute of ESCB.
[54] Art.19 Statute of ESCB.
[55] Art. 20 Statute of ESCB.
[56] Art. 21 Statute of ESCB.

systems,[57] and external operations.[58] In the latter context the ECB and the national central banks may: provide for clearing and payment systems in support of a smooth running of a pan-European settlement of single currency payments and for operational reasons and on a strictly independent and neutral basis establish relations with central banks and financial institutions in other countries and with international organisations; acquire and sell, spot and forward all types of foreign exchange assets which include securities and all other assets in currency of any country or units of accounts; and conduct all types of banking transactions in relations with third countries and international organisations, including borrowing and lending operations.

From a different angle, the ECB clearly requires as a prerequisite for a proper functioning monetary policy strong control over banking supervision throughout the EC but Art. 25.1 of the Statute of the ESCB merely provides that 'the ECB may offer advice […] relating to prudential supervision of credit institutions and to the stability of the financial system.' This weak provision clearly shows that subsidiarity in the field of banking supervision is not in the interest of the European financial markets. How can problems in payment systems be detected first and on time if the ECB does not participate in banking supervision? The ECB could mention in mitigation to any criticism that it is bound to receive sooner or later, when the expected and inevitable consolidation within the European banking market claims its first victim, that Art. 105 of the EC Treaty and Art. 3.1 of the Statute of the ESCB states that the ESCB should have at its basic task only 'to promote the smooth operation of payment systems.' There is no doubt

---

[57] Art. 22 Statute of ESCB.
[58] Art. 23 Statute of ESCB.

that there is a strong interdependence between a sound and consistent monetary policy and an efficient, competitive and stable financial system. Recent experiences with hedge funds in the US have shown that a financial sector vulnerable to disruption or systemic risks poses considerable risks to the entire monetary system and ultimately to the safety of the currency.

In legal terms there is a world of difference between the mere promotion and a legally binding obligation to ensure a smooth operation of payment systems, and the ECJ will not hesitate to make use of its prerogative to interpret the EC Treaty as it sees fit. Whether they like it or not the public at large will look at the ECB as a possible scapegoat for any major post EMU banking crisis and the ECB will find it very difficult to walk away from a serious bank failure without substantial damage to its own credibility.

As per the provisions of the Statute of the ECB, the institution may offer advice and be consulted by the Council of Ministers, the European Commission and even individual member states on the scope and implementation of Community legislation relating to the prudential supervision of credit institutions and to the stability of the financial system as a whole.[59] But what, if any, should the regulatory role of the ECB be? Should it not be better left at national level? Due to the increasingly global nature of financial markets, regulation at the national level or even the European level will always be subject to severe constraints. Although the EC Treaty allows under Art. 105(6) and Art. 25.2 of the Statute of the ESCB for specific tasks to be conferred upon the ECB with regards to supervision of credit institutions, the hurdle for it is a high one with a unanimous decision within the Council of Ministers and compliance with the assent procedure of the EP.

---

[59] Art. 25 Statute of ESCB.

The preparatory work undertaken by the EMI concerning banking supervision at this stage merely aims to identify possible ways in which Art. 105(5) of the EC Treaty and Art. 25(1) Statute of ESCB could be implemented under a joint umbrella of central bank and national central bank. A full assessment how the ECB will define its role in practise in respect of Art. 105(6) of the EC Treaty has not yet been made public. However, it is expected that supervision of the banking and financial sector will largely stay in the hands of national authorities in all fifteen EU member states thereby also admitting the four member states not participating in the single currency from 1st January 1999 to the workings of the ECB. A banking supervisory committee at the ECB is expected to act as a central body for co-ordinating supervision policy not only across the Euro-zone but across all fifteen EU member states.[60]

10. Reporting and Public Accountability

As part of a formalised method and legally enshrined obligation for public accountability, the ECB will be required to draw up and publish weekly consolidated financial statements[61] together with quarterly interim reports[62] and an annual report (for its financial year which runs from 1st January to 31st December[63]) on the activities

---

[60] As reported in *The Financial Times* on 10th September 1998 in 'UK to be given Euro-zone banking supervision role.' The UK is expected to be represented in the ECB banking and financial supervision committee by the Bank of England and the Financial Services Authority (FSA).
[61] Art. 15.2 Statute of ESCB.
[62] Art. 15.1 Statute of ESCB.
[63] Art. 26.1 Statute of ESCB.

of the ESCB and on the monetary policy.[64] The ECB is furthermore required to make such reports and statements available to interested parties free of charge.[65] The onus of drawing up annual accounts for the ECB and consolidated figures of the ESCB has been placed on the Executive Board according to principles and uniform practices established by the Governing Council and it is up to the Governing Council of the ECB to approve these accounts.[66] The precedent for form and substance of future reports and accounts of the ECB has largely been established by the three annual reports and accounts of the EMI for 1995, 1996 and 1997.

Accountability does not necessarily mean naked scrutiny but scrutiny within predetermined and agreed limits. For this purpose, the accounts of the ECB and the national central banks are subject to an independent external audit.[67] However, the audit role of the Community's Court of Auditors under Art. 188c of the EC Treaty has been limited with the ECB to an examination of the bank's operational efficiency of the management. The audit by the Court of Auditors does not extend to the financial performance of the ECB and the national central banks because it would clearly interfere with the bank's activities in the money and foreign exchange markets and other tasks entrusted to it under Art. 105 of the EC Treaty.

The most crucial function to ensure public accountability is the Treaty-based obligation of the ECB to address an annual report of its and the ESCB's activities to all principal institutions of the European Community, e.g. the

---

[64] Art. 109b(3) EC Treaty, Art. 15.3 Statute of ESCB and EP's Rules of Procedure (1994) Rule 39.
[65] Art. 15.4. Statute of ESCB.
[66] Art. 26 Statute of ESCB.
[67] Art. 27 Statute of ESCB.

Commission, the Council of Ministers and the EP.[68] To add a personal element of accountability to an institutional obligation, Art. 109b(3) of the EC Treaty requires the President of the ECB to present the annual report in person to the Council of Ministers and the EP. The latter may hold a general debate[69] on it that can be enhanced through the President of the ECB and members of the Executive Board, at the request of the EP or on their own initiative, being heard by the competent committees of the EP.[70] These procedures have already begun well with the President of the EMI giving full and detailed account of the EMI for the previous financial year as forerunner of the ECB. However, the independence of the ECB is and must be such that it can choose to ignore the views of the EP and its President and members of the Executive Board can refuse to answer particular questions from members of the committee responsible in the EP. Even when raised under the delicate point of public accountability, it would never be correct to suggest that the President of the ECB or any of his colleagues on the Executive Board should be answerable in any way to national governments. Within the governing system of the ECB, national central bank governors are represented on the General and/or Governing Council of the ECB. They are the sole links to national parliaments and only national central bank governors should be answerable to their respective national governments.

The President or his appointed nominee will be the only persons authorised to represent the ECB externally,[71] but

---

[68] Art. 109b(3) of the EC Treaty and Art. 15.3 Statute of ESCB.
[69] Art. 109b(3) of the EC Treaty and EP's Rules of Procedure (1994) Rule 39.
[70] Ibid.
[71] Art. 13.2 Statute of ESCB.

the ECB will be able to decide how the ESCB shall be represented in the field of international co-operation.[72] The above two principles will ensure that the ECB will be able to act independently within the global financial community, an ability which is absolutely essential, in particular when it comes to the management of the Euro exchange rate vis-à-vis other major trading currencies such as the US dollar and the Japanese yen.

Many observers have been encouraged by Wim Duisenberg's willingness to answer detailed questions put to him by the EP even if he would have had the right of refusal to answer questions such as details relating to his annual salary. This should help to establish a general culture of openness even though minutes of the board meetings of the ECB will not be published for a period of sixteen years. Despite the formal rules of confidentiality for the regular meetings of the Governing Council and the General Council of the ECB, the sheer number of people participating in those meetings and considerable national interests will ensure that national governments will know within a very short period of time what votes were taken during council meetings and what political forces affected or appeared to have affected votes. This will clearly give governments of member states participating in the single currency and their national 'insiders' on the Governing Council a considerable advantage over those bodies actually charged with the supervision of the ECB, in particular the EP, and over the governments and central banks of those member states not participating from the start. These leaks[73]

---

[72] Art. 6 Statute of ESCB.

[73] According to ECB insiders, the fact that the ECB would decide on a minimum reserve requirement and the ECB's gold reserves at their meeting on 7th July 1998 was apparently leaked through local central bank sources up to four weeks in advance of the meeting.

and open breaches of confidentiality could seriously undermine, even destroy any vestige of individual accountability of members of the ECB's Executive Board. This would undermine the ECB's ability to pursue difficult policies and long-term policy objectives. It would ultimately create a one-man show where individual accountability of members of the ECB's Executive Board would be converted through consensus pressure to a monopoly style of control for the President of the ECB over policy decision-making. When this happens, the unhappy experience of many central banks including the German Bundesbank shows that too much pressure for compromise sooner or later spills out into the open from leaked minutes and confidential press briefings to stage-managed press conferences. Nevertheless, the ECB is widely expected to run a cabinet-style system of governance with each member of the Executive Board having to share overall responsibility and represent the ECB's agreed line to the outside world.

The question remains whether a plausible argument can be made for the ECB to publish minutes of Governing Council and the General Council meetings. There are a number of advantages and disadvantages to be considered for releasing minutes or extracts into the public domain, some of them very practical.

ADVANTAGES	DISADVANTAGES
Insight into key facts and considerations for determining policy would enhance the ECB's credibility.	Detailed transcripts would substantially reduce participants' ability and willingness 'to speak their mind' during meetings.
Council members not being able to yield to national political pressures.	Open-minded and sometimes controversial discussions would be replaced with pre-agreed statements.
Creation of general culture of openness and public accountability.	'Real' discussions would move outside the forum of Council meetings.
Avoiding 'insider' knowledge for	

member states participating from the start of Stage Three.	
Replacing uninformed market speculation with considered and informed speculation.	

The President of the ECB made it clear that he does not intend to publish any minutes when he said: 'If we would do this, we would influence expectations of the markets ahead of the next meeting. We do not want to do this.'[74] Nevertheless, the ECB has accepted the need to communicate broad policy guidelines and decided for the President of the ECB to hold a news conference once a month although the Executive Board of the ECB will meet on a fortnightly basis from 1999, thereby again emulating the operations of the German Bundesbank. Current ECB policy appears to be that the minutes of Council meetings will not be published for a period of sixteen years. The question remains whether better and timely information provided by the ECB relating to the setting of monetary policy would over the short or longer term negatively impact on economic performance or the achievement of price stability. At the same time, those arguing for the publication of Council meetings would have to make a case whether considered and informed speculation is less damaging to financial markets than uninformed and blind speculation.

---

[74] As reported in the *Frankfurter Allgemeine Zeitung* on 29th June 1998.

Chapter IV
Independence v. Accountability

In its 1995 convergence report[1] the EMI set out a number of grounds for the independence of national central banks and the ECB as constituent parts of the ESCB:

1. Independence from political authorities would allow the ECB to define a monetary policy aimed at the statutory objective of price stability.
2. Independence would enable the ECB to possess the powers necessary for it to implement monetary policy decisions.
3. Central bank independence is a prerequisite for EMU in that the pooling of monetary powers in the ECB would not be acceptable if member states could influence the decisions taken by the governing bodies of the ECB.
4. Central bank independence is essential to the credibility of moving towards monetary union.
5. Independence of the ECB and national central banks must be achieved in institutional, personal, functional and financial terms.

This places the two most powerful and influential voices of post-war economic thinking – monetarist anti-inflationists and neo-Keynesian economic interventionists – more or less on a collision course, even though more interven-

---

[1] EMI report entitled 'Progress Towards Convergence' 1995, pp.91–92.

tionist-minded economists have started to accept a stronger role for monetary policy and hence blurred traditional principles and doctrines governing the relationship between the supply of money and its impact on inflation and growth. At stake is the role of the ECB either as a positive instrument of public policy or a truly independent guardian of monetary policy. Willem Buiter, Professor of International Macroeconomics at the University of Cambridge and Member of the Monetary Policy Committee of the Bank of England, recently went so far to describe the ECB as 'the latest offshoot of a central bank tradition that views central banking as a sacred, quasi-mystical vocation, a cult whose priests perform the holy sacraments far from the prying eyes of the non-initiates.'[2]

Even if full accountability according to democratic principles should not have found its way into the EC Treaty and the conventions and procedures of the ECB and its supervisory bodies, it is estimated that more than 500 permanent 'ECB watchers' have started to monitor, analyse interpret and even predict every aspect of the ECB's future existence. The pan-European group of academics and its working party entitled 'Monitoring the European Central Bank' organised by the Centre for Economic Policy Research (CEPR) in London, the German Zentrum für Europäische Integrationsforschung (ZEI) in Bonn, the Centre for Financial Studies (CFS) based in Frankfurt and the 'Macroeconomic Policy Group' organised by the Centre for European Policy Studies (CEPS) in Brussels are just one example of the constant expert scrutiny which the ECB will have to withstand in addition to general market forces testing every aspect of the ECB credibility.

---

[2] 'The UK and EMU' by Willem Buiter, EmuNet, 8th July 1998.

1. Political Interference

Eurosceptics still attempt to frighten, even shock, voters in most member states by claiming that with EMU all key economic decision would be taken by an unaccountable ECB sitting in Frankfurt, where bankers and technocrats will be solely responsible for monetary policy. But how shocking is this in reality? There was also cause for alarm in the possible interpretation of the Maastricht treaty and in particular the shape and influence of the ECB when President Mitterand outlined during a television conference that 'the technicians of the [European] Central Bank are charged with applying in the monetary domain the decisions of the European Council [...] One hears it said that the European Central Bank will be the master of the decisions. It's not true! Economic policy belongs to the European Council and the application of monetary policy is the task of the [European] Central Bank in the framework of the decisions of the European Council [...] The people who decide economic policy, of which monetary policy is no more than a means of implementation, are the politicians.'[3]

There are still suggestions that the ECB derives its authority almost by divine right without political legitimacy and trust of the people. This is not the case, the same way governments cannot abdicate their role in macroeconomic policy or uncouple fiscal policy from monetary policy. Most politicians in Europe are currently trying to repeat the

---

[3] See remarks in televised referendum debate *Aujourd'hui l'Europe*, TF1 on 3rd September 1992, immediately commented upon, mainly in Germany, by the press in article such as Lothar Ruehl's *'Paris und die Daemonen'*, *Die Welt*, 4th September 1992, Eric le Boucher's comments in *'Bonn l'exploitation de la "peur de l'Allemagne" dans la campagne irrete beaucoup'* reported in *Le Monde*, 4th September 1992 and by the *Wall Street Journal*, Brussels in 'With Friends Like These...' on 5th September 1992.

economic success of the US which enjoyed significant economic growth over recent years, apparently without endangering price stability. Many see Alan Greenspan's interest rate activism and growth as part of the Federal Reserve Bank's policy objectives as the prime success factors for sound expansionary fiscal policy, not only delivering stable prices but also creating growth and employment. Omniscient observers have started to question the golden age of the US economy in recent times and with it the retrenchment of fiscal policy. Looser fiscal policy might be a tempting option for many EU member states to deal with problems such as government debt and high unemployment. For the ECB, lax fiscal policies call for a counterbalancing tightening of monetary policy, and vice versa. Attempts on both sides to achieve credibility, legitimacy and recognition at the expense of the other may well become a pyretic undertaking. Central bankers will never be able to compete with the modern telegenic politician neither will they have the luxury to be saturnine individuals, withdrawn from public view and immune from public opinion.

In an increasing number of EU member states, including Germany, the notion of central bank autonomy has, or has at least acquired since the Single European Act and the Maastricht Treaty, political and even trade union support. Sole responsibility for the challenging areas of macroeconomic policy – including taxation, employment and what is more important unemployment as well as public spending – will remain with member states acting both collectively and individually. Demonisation of the ECB merely diverts attention from the real issue of the collective economic policies that we wish our governments to pursue together in a future EMU to tackle major problems such as worrisome levels of unemployment in most member states, both structural and regional, environmental problems

which know no borders and the need to become and remain competitive in global markets.

The ECB will be judged just like the German Bundesbank and the Federal Reserve Bank on its ability and to what degree it can reach compromises even though it enjoys considerable independence. What the ECB will not have is the Federal Reserve Bank's eighty years of experience of balancing independence (as the Executive and Congress do not exercise their full powers of intervention) and political accountability without prejudicing the policies of the government of the day. This 'earned' or 'acquired' independence appears to be the result of clear objectives for the Federal Reserve Bank coupled with a clear system of accountability as demonstrated by the appointment of the Chairman and the regular reports of the Federal Reserve Bank's activities to Congress. Alan Blinder, former Vice-Chairman of the US Federal Reserve expressed it as follows: 'In a democratic society, the central bank's freedom to act implies an obligation to explain itself to the public. Accountability legitimises independence within a democratic political structure.'[4]

The most direct way to achieve accountability would be the publication of the individual voting records of Council members and Art. 10.4 of the Statute of the ESCB permits the Governing Council of the ECB to decide whether to make the outcome of its deliberations public. The central argument remains whether publication of such voting records places accountability ahead of independence and whether accountability could endanger the ECB's independence. ECB Executive Board member Otmar Issing raises the principal concern when he stated, 'Making individual members' voting behaviour public could

---

[4] See article by Robert Chote entitled 'Bank on transparency' in *The Financial Times*, 2nd March 1998.

encourage undesirable scrutiny of members' voting pattern. This, in turn, would encourage external pressures on the [Governing/General] Council members arising from local interests. Independence, granted by the Treaty, would be at risk.'[5] Although any form of pressure by national authorities and other interested parties on 'their' nationals sitting on the Executive Board, the General or Governing Council of the ECB would be against the spirit and the letter of the EC Treaty, sceptics doubt whether full accountability can ever be achieved in practice, given the sheer number of people present at the Council meetings of the ECB.[6]

Given this relatively extensive availability of 'insider information' to national central banks and hence to national governments, why should institutions charged with the supervision of the ECB such as the EP be excluded from receiving such sensitive information? If such information were to be made available to an increasing number of interested parties, why not make it available to the public at large as 'Smoke-filled rooms and confidentiality are more likely to allow the ECB mandate and independence to be perverted by national political pressures than openness and the occasional short-term embarrassment that this entails.'[7]

The wording and the spirit of the EC Treaty has clearly tipped the balance between independence and accountability in favour of the former, in the full knowledge that complete secrecy can never be achieved in practice and that breaches of confidentiality have more forms than the Councils of the ECB have members. Recent revelations[8] in

---

[5] See letter by Prof. Buiter entitled 'Independence of ECB likely to be perverted if council voting is secret' published in *The Financial Times*, 24th September 1998.

[6] Ibid.

[7] Ibid and 'Secret voting would put the ECB independence at risk' in *The Financial Times*, 24th September 1998.

[8] *The Sunday Times*, 20th September 1998.

the UK have shown that there is even a role for the Secret Service when it comes to important matters such as the single currency. When taking independence and accountability into perspective, one must not forget that the drafters of the Maastricht Treaty have valiantly tried to keep politics out of the ECB. The ECB will be responsible for monetary policy across the entire Euro-zone and was thereby granted the 'luxury' of not having to place too much emphasis on local interests pushed by national governments or interest groups.

The idea that governors of national central banks will not act independently and only implement from time to time instructions from their respective national governments has been rejected on the grounds that peer pressure and the desire to reach a consensus at the political level within the ECB's Governing Council and General Council will be the central mechanism with which 'philosophical convergence'[9] will take place, i.e. acceptance and therefore avoidance that one member state could harm the others. This necessitates sufficient convergence of policy considerations and preferences such as price over output stability, fiscal prudence over boom and bust cycles. In order to safeguard the ECB's independence both in thought and action, Wim Duisenberg clearly set out his views: 'We would want to avoid people being able to influence or meddle through the back door with the independence of the decision making power of individual members of the board.'[10]

---

[9] See O. Sievert in '*Zur Europäischen Währungsunion – das Eigentliche und der Unrate auf dem Wege dahin*', presentation at Hamburger Sparkasse, 13th August 1997.

[10] Wim Duisenberg quoted in 'ECB poised to spread its wings', *The Financial Times*, 24th May 1998.

The high degree of independence of the ECB is already the result of a series of political compromises borne out of:

1. each member state wanting to be represented on the board of Governing/General Council of the ECB,
2. representation to be either equal for all member states, or
3. representation to be related to a member state's population or its GDP or other economic measure.

Only elaborate schemes would cater for all these considerations but they would at the same time curtail the effectiveness of the executive committee. Independence for the ECB was thus limited to price stability with only a limited number of external controls. The principal advantage of price stability is not the ongoing need to adjust almost on a permanent basis economic life for the effects of inflation (not to mention the art of predicting it) but for the certainty of knowing that the figures agreed in a contract will remain the same as close as possible to those when the contract is fulfilled. This effects almost all parts of economic life from borrowing money to buying a house, to taking out a life insurance policy or a long-term pension fund.

A French proposal[11] seeking a right for the President of the European Council or even the European Commission to postpone decisions made by the ECB for a period of up to fourteen days, which would have mirrored a similar right granted under Art. 13(2) of the Bundesbank Act 1957 to the

---

[11] See 'Managing Maastricht: EMU issues and how they were settled' by A. Italianer in Gretschmann K. (ed.), *Economic and Monetary Union: Implications for National Policy-Makers*, Dordrecht, 1993, p.51 and 'The Project of a European Central Bank' by J.-V. Louis in Stuyck (ed.), *Financial and Monetary Integration in the European Economic community: Legal, Institutional and Economic Aspects*, Boston, 1993, p.23.

German government, was not approved by the member states thus keeping the ECB free from any political interference.

2. Price Stability

EMU and the ESCB will take monetary policy out of the hands of national institutions and give it to one central institution, the ECB in Frankfurt, but with national central banks helping both to decide it and to carry it out. There must be a single European monetary policy, otherwise there can be no single European currency as the failed Latin Monetary Union taught us well over a hundred years ago.

The ECB, like the Deutsche Bundesbank, is based on the assumption that central banks that are independent are more successful in controlling inflation than those that are not. This sounds persuasive, but is it really true? There is a lot of evidence[12] to the effect that the political independence of central banks is of importance and a key determinant to keeping inflation low. The more recent evidence comes from a paper by S. Eijffinger and E. Schaling of Tilburg University showing that central banks that are politically

---

[12] See studies by Bade and Parkin (1985), Demopoulos, Katsimbris, and Miller (1987), and A. Alesina and L. Summers in 'Central Bank Independence and Macroeconomic Performance: Some Comparative Evidence', in *Journal of Money, Credit and Banking*, 25th May 1988; M.J.M. Neumann's 'Central Bank Independence as a Prerequisite of Price Stability', in EC Commission's *The Economics of EMU*, European Economy, Special Edition 1 (1991) and more recently in the discussion paper by S. Eijffinger and E. Schaling of Tilburg University entitled 'Central Bank Independence: Theory and Evidence' and published by Centre for Economic Research as Discussion Paper 9325 in April 1993, showing that central banks that are politically independent tend to produce less inflation than central banks that have to take order from the government.

independent tend to produce less inflation than central banks that have to take orders from the government.

If the central bank's objective is price stability, can it achieve this more effectively if it is independent of the government or if it is closely integrated with the ministry, finance or economics? An independent central bank is supposed to be less subject than its government to short-term political pressures, yet if it is independent and unelected, it may pursue unpopular policies but not be able to carry them through, particularly if the government is opposed. EMU would founder even sooner if it would be subject to political winds and tides, especially if monetary policy would be affected by changes caused by on average two or three parliamentary elections in a given year throughout the EC.

Where price stability has been achieved, central bank independence and monetary (and not monetarist) policy in general have been only two of a number of contributory factors. The Deutsche Bundesbank's success as an independent central bank in keeping inflation low has been helped in Germany by responsible trade union behaviour. Lack of central bank independence however did not prevent Japan from achieving even greater price stability than Germany after the 1970s. Notable Eurosceptics such as Bill Cash, Conservative MP endorse that: 'the Bundesbank's record on monetary control is not better and no worse than that of many traditional dependent central banks […] and that Germany's solid record on low inflation and of a strong and stable currency is a function […] of the strengths of its political economy, of its tradition of high skills, technical perfection, long-term corporate financing through universal banks, consensual industrial relations and above all of its

trading structures, exporting high-value goods and importing lower added-value goods.'[13]

The case against central bank independence is that the separation of key policies such as monetary and fiscal (tax and public expenditure) policy and their allocation to different and possibly conflicting agencies can lead to higher costs than otherwise in lowering inflation.[14] For example, Germany may have had higher budget deficits, higher interest rates and lower economic growth in the aftermath of reunification because the Federal Government's responsibility for fiscal policy was separated from the Deutsche Bundesbank's responsibility for monetary policy. If the German Government would have had to take the blame for high interest rates, it might have raised taxes sooner to reduce the Federal deficit quicker.

This argument can be met by showing that where the government and the central bank agree on policy objectives, welfare losses can be reduced because inflation expectations are lower than otherwise, and the unemployment cost of lowering actual inflation is therefore less. In such a case it may not matter too much whether the central bank is independent of the ministry of finance or subordinate to it, if the policy outcome is the same. Conversely, if the central bank and the finance ministry are at loggerheads, independence may not help the credibility of the central bank's inflation performance if the welfare sacrifice for policy demands goes beyond the bounds of what is acceptable to voters.

What can be expected from former high-inflation countries with a naturally higher rate of unemployment is much stronger pressure on the ECB than on the Deutsche

---

[13] Ian Milne in *Maastricht: The Case Against Economic & Monetary Union*, Nelson & Pollard, June 1993, p.12.

[14] Prof. James Meade is a leading exponent of these doubts.

Bundesbank today to be soft on inflation. That is why it is so important that the statutes of the ECB explicitly declare that the only macroeconomic objective of the European monetary policy is to maintain price stability. At the same time the ECB must be institutionally independent of the political authorities (including the European Commission and the EP). Political independence is crucial to ensure that budget deficits of the national and European governments will not be financed by printing money.

Many central banks have focused almost exclusively over recent years on price stability and conducted their policies accordingly. Monetary policy – whether expressed in terms of interest rates, exchange rates or the growth in money aggregate measurements – have all been used to achieve the high level goal of low and stable inflation. Even politicians have started to praise central bankers for pursuing such a worthy objective since they believe inflation to be costly, even a sign of weakness. Gordon Brown has now accepted that delegating monetary policy to an independent central bank with a clear mandate for price stability or low inflation can enhance the credibility of monetary authorities and governments.

Many economists now agree that there is a close link between the credibility of a central bank's monetary policy and its anti-inflationary reputation. Central bank credibility appears to be at the greatest when monetary policy is solely geared towards price stability and delegated irrevocably to a politically independent central bank. Under such an environment, the central bank would not be responsible for output or employment and enjoy full independence from government.

In a study[15] dating back to 1989, but updated and slightly modified by the author, central bank independence was measured by the political and economic autonomy of national central banks. Political autonomy related to the ability of a national central bank to conduct monetary policy without governmental influence whilst economic autonomy focused on the central bank's ability to use monetary policy instruments without restrictions.

Points A to H relate to the political autonomy of a central bank; points I to O take into account the central bank's economic autonomy from government (points I to L relate to advances to governments for monetary financing of budget deficits). The index of political and economic autonomy is the unweighted result of the sum of '*'s in each row divided by 16, i.e. the maximum number of points achievable for each category considered. The highest possible figure of 1.000 shows complete political and economic independence of the central bank. Japan has lower levels of inflation despite poor marks for central bank independence mainly due to the strong commitment by the government to price stability demonstrating that high central bank independence is not an absolute necessity for price stability.

---

[15] *Monetary Policies, Credibility and International Coordination* by V. Grilli, A. Mascianaro and G. Tabellini, 1991.

CENTRAL BANK INDEPENDENCE INDEX

	I	II¹	A	B	C	D	E	F	G	H	I	J	K	L	M	N	O²	/16
Austria	3.9	2.6						*		*							**	0.5625
Belgium	4.5	2.1										*			*	*	**	0.4375
France	6.3	2.0		*		*								*	*	*	**	0.4375
Germany	2.8	2.5		*	*	*	*	*	*	*			*	*	*		**	0.8750
Ireland	7.0	2.3		*			*	*			*	*	*					0.4375
Italy	10.6	4.1	*	*	*	*					*		*					0.3125
Portugal	17.4	5.4				*							*	*		*	*	0.1875
Spain	9.4	4.2			*	*						*		*				0.3125
Finland	7.1	1.9	*		*	*	*				*	*		*	*		**	0.6250
Netherlands	2.0	2.5		*		*	*	*		*		*	*	*	*	*		**	0.6250
Luxembourg	5.2	2.5																³
Sweden	7.7	3.2	*	*					*	*			*	*	*	*	*	0.5625
Greece	18.4	10.9			*				*									0.2500
Denmark	5.8	2.1					*	*				*			*	*	**	0.5000
UK	6.2	3.0		*		*		*			*	*		*		*	*	0.5000
ECB/EU11	6.5	2.6	*	*	*	*	*	*	*	*	*	*	*	*	*	*	**	1.0000
EU15	6.7	3.0				*	*	*	*	*	*	*	*	*	*	*		0.5000
US	4.5	2.8			*	*	*	*	*	*	*	*	*	*	*	*	*	0.7500
Japan	1.9	1.1							*	*			*				*	0.3750

NOTES
1.   I.   Average inflation 1981 – 1990 in %
     II.   Average inflation 1991 – 1998 in %

2.   A.   Governor not appointed by government
     B.   Governor appointed for term > five years
     C.   Entire board of central bank not appointed by government
     D.   Entire board appointed for term > five years
     E.   No mandatory participation of government representative in board of central bank
     F.   No governmental approval of monetary policy formulation
     G.   Statutory requirement for central bank to purse monetary stability
     H.   Legal provisions to strengthen central bank's position in conflict with government
     I.   No automatic direct credit facilities
     J.   Market interest rates for direct credit facilities
     K.   Temporary direct credit facilities
     L.   Limited amount of direct credit facilities
     M.   Central bank does not participate in primary market for public debt
     N   Discount rate set by central bank
     O.   Banking supervision not entrusted to central bank or shared with other authority

3. Luxembourg did not until recently with the Institute Monetaire Luxembourgeois have a central bank.

It is now generally accepted amongst most economists in Europe that the pursuit of price stability should be the final and absolute target of monetary policy as an important precondition for real growth and employment but without it being an end in itself. Ever since Milton Friedman and followers of the 'Chicago School' have shown since the 1970s that it is not possible to control the final target of price stability in a direct way and without considerable lead/lag effects, successful central bank policy has concentrated on the 'levers' and 'transmission belts' of

Central Bank Independence

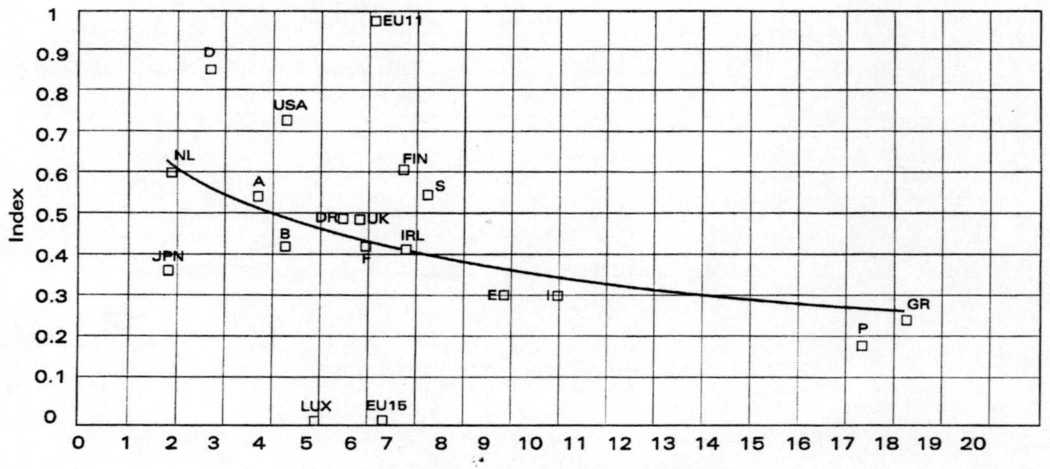

Index vs *Average inflation rate 1991-1999 in %*

Central Bank Independence

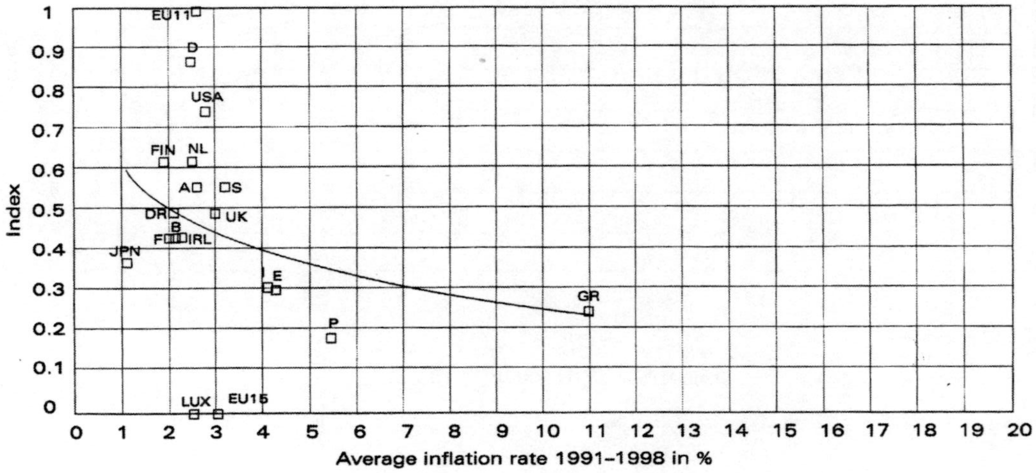

central bank operating control (e.g. the monetary base, interest rates, etc.) and so-called intermediate targets.

At the start of the transmission process there are a number of variables which are solely determined by the ECB. At the very end, the final variables of the economic process can be found such as GDP and most importantly price levels, the holy grail of central bank monetary policy. What makes the final target of monetary policy – price stability – and its achievement rather difficult is the fact that the final economic variables can only be steered indirectly with central bank instruments such as repo rate, lombard rate and the minimum reserve system.

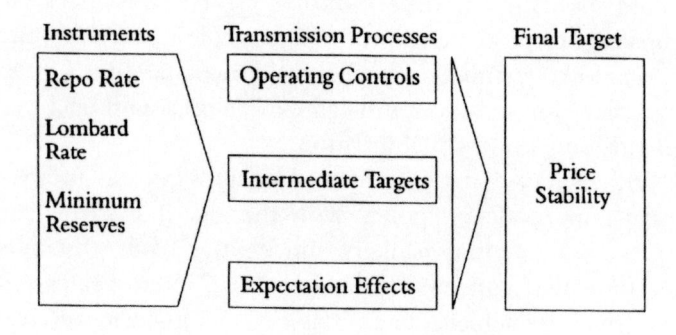

Instruments	Transmission Processes	Final Target
Repo Rate	Operating Controls	
Lombard Rate	Intermediate Targets	Price Stability
Minimum Reserves		
	Expectation Effects	

Intermediate targets are now accepted central bank indicators for the effectiveness of operating controls even as possible leading indicators for inflation rate development. Some central banks such as the Bank of England also use

the exchange rate or at least its trade weighted average as an intermediate target as a compass for their monetary policy.

When the ECB announced that it wanted its monetary policy to be forward looking, it did it for good reasons because the complex relationships usually studied by sociologists in relation to people's expectations have found their way into economics. In terms of the transmission processes of monetary policy, these expectations have become almost as important as operating controls (for example money market rates) or intermediate targets (for example external exchange rates). Almost all agreements relating to future financial commitments or receipts include expectations as to their future value. The lower the expected loss of future values due to inflation, the lower the risk to future price rises. 'Credible' central bank policy should be able, ignoring unforeseen circumstances, to achieve as close an equilibrium as possible between future expectations of inflation and actual price stability. Under any other circumstances inflated expectations will lead to a self-fulfilling build-up of inflation.

With a very complex transmission process and indirect steering of monetary policy with the aid of intermediate targets, most central bankers and central bank observers tend to heavily concentrate on short-term interest rates as a key driver to achieve price stability. Short-term interest rates therefore tend to be the central dial of a central bank's navigation system complemented by exchange rate and money base indicators. The implications of such an inflation targeting navigation system are as follows:

Interest Rate Decisions	Targeting of Money Base 'Monetary Targeting'	Targeting of Exchange Rates 'Exchange Rate Targeting'
Raise	if growth above target rate	if currency depreciates
Reduce	if growth below target rate	if currency appreciates

Chart 1: Main Channels of the Monetary Policy Transmission Process

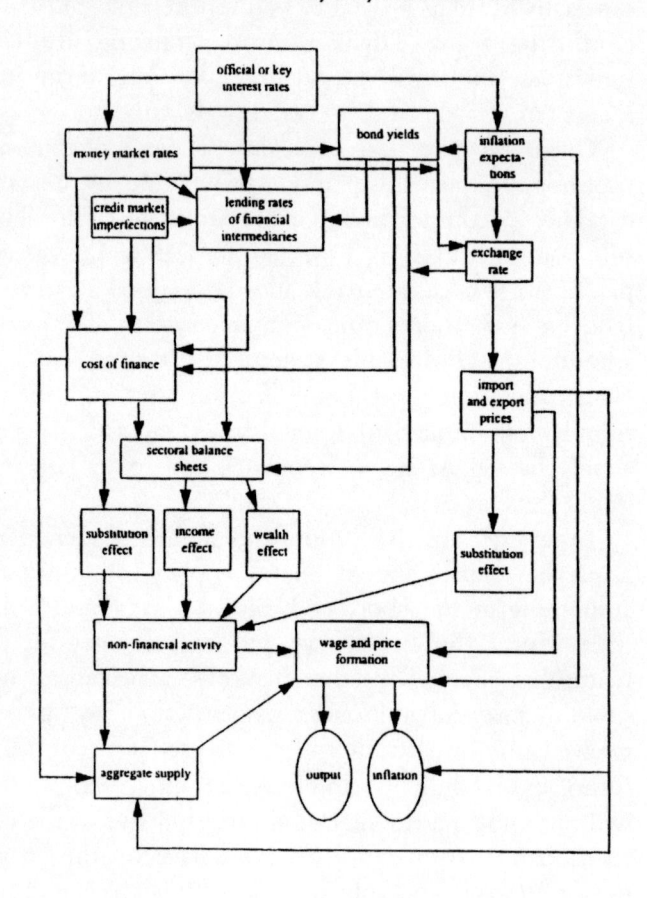

Source: De Nederlandsche Bank NV, 1997

Experiences of European central banks and the developments within the EMS during the 1980s have given this form of inflation targeting more and more credibility, especially as it has proved to be more reliable and with less conflicting signals than measures ranging from wage indicators, industrial production and long-term interest rates to money statistics and credit growth.

Given the overall complexity of the monetary policy transmission mechanism and to provide the greatest deal of certainty to counter undue expectations of future levels of inflation, the ECB is expected to follow the successful practice of the Bundesbank and the Federal Reserve Bank by using as their operating controls a system of 'interest rate smoothing'. Under this system, the central bank keeps changes in short term money market rates on a month by month basis limited to a small band, say ±0.25% p.a. and avoids having to signal frequent changes in key interest rates.

Experiences by the Bundesbank and the Federal Reserve Bank have also shown that a policy of interest rate smoothing at the short end allows a very good indirect control over the yield curve, i.e. interest rates for longer maturities, based on the market's expectation of the monthly rates corridor over a longer period, say up to six or twelve months. By attempting to achieve control over future expectations of interest rate movements although without knowing the precise timing and size of the effects[1] such change to operating controls have on the economy, the ECB would be able to achieve effective control over short-term money fluctuations, generate more accurate

---

[1] Referred to as the 'Brainard uncertainty' discovered by the American economist Bill Brainard. See 'Uncertainty and the Effectiveness of Monetary Policy', American Economic Review, Vol.57, 1967, pp.411–425.

longer term forecasts and avoid having to provide frequent sometimes possibly conflicting signals to the markets.

It is now generally acknowledged that the pursuit of price stability should be seen as a medium to long-term goal for a central bank and its monetary policy. This time horizon is necessary due to the existence of considerable and constantly changing and varying time lags[2] between the central bank using its monetary policy instruments and effects showing on the target variable and the 'time inconsistency'.[3] What makes the ECB fundamentally different from the US Federal Reserve Bank and what is the biggest criticism from most centre-left governments now in power in most EU member states is that the EC Treaty does not include employment growth as one of the key objectives to be pursued by the ECB. Justification for making employment growth a more broader and general principle for the ECB's monetary policy strategy can be found in more recent economic theory[4] which has started to confirm that monetary policy-makers who pursue price stability as well as employment growth could over the medium to long term end up with higher inflation, i.e. no price stability and no better outcome on stimulating employment than monetary policy that is solely focused on the pursuit of price stability.

Given the inherent uncertainty in the transmission process and the limitations on the cognitive capacity of the multitude of market participants or in economist jargon

---

[2] 'What central bankers could learn from academics and vice versa' by A. Blinder, *Journal of Economic Perspectives* 11, 1997.

[3] 'Rules rather than discretion: the inconsistency of optimal plans' by F. Kydland and E. Prescott, *Journal of Political Economy*, 85, 1977 and 'What is New-Keynesian economics?' by R.J. Gordon, *Journal of Economic Literature*, 27, 1990.

[4] 'Monetary policy in a game-theoretic framework' by J.J. Sijben, *Jahrbücher für Nationalökonomie und Statistik*, 210, 1992.

known as 'economic agents', the monetary transmission process should not only be seen as underpinning monetary policy (i.e. the methods used for the analysis of information) but also as a tool of monetary policy strategy (i.e. making judgements and decisions based on the information analysed). With all the uncertainties surrounding the workings of the transmission processes across the new single currency area, different structural, behavioural and institutional factors which exist throughout the EU already create an enormous challenge for the ECB to execute monetary policy for an area covering over 290 million consumers and to conduct a successful monetary policy strategy for an economic powerhouse generating a gross domestic product of over US$6,800 billion with the sole aim of achieving price stability.

The bridge from navigating behind closed doors and secret meetings at the ECB to lasting credibility and transparency essentially comes from the publication of regular inflation reports. This eliminates the need for the underlying model and navigation system to be made public the same way commercial enterprises do. Although the ECB would have the chance to cut corners, even cheat, with its regular inflation reports, the ECB will have to compete against many and the best of private, public and academic institutions which enhances the overall transparency of central bank monetary policy.

The transfer of monetary policy responsibilities from national central banks to the ECB will be very far reaching and probably without historic precedent, if one ignores the considerable preparatory work and extensive research undertaken by the EMI since 1994. Furthermore, our knowledge of the monetary policy transmission belts is still limited and based on theories which yet have to withstand the test of time or the effects of economic crisis. Although there has been extensive academic interest and research

over the last ten years relating to the still emerging topic of monetary transmission processes, most studies relating to the Euro and the ECB were based on comparisons with the US and the Federal Reserve Bank. Most research also used raw merged data for the Euro-zone with monetary policy mainly executed under the stewardship of the Bundesbank. Early results of these complex economic research undertakings have not yet clarified whether differing monetary transmission processes in Europe and the US might also lead to diverging monetary policy paths.[5] Significant differences in the structure and disintermediation of the US and European banking and capital markets will make it very difficult to predict the ECB's effects on monetary policy. At the same time, intensified competition and cross-border consolidation of the financial markets within the Euro-zone will also mean that the responsiveness and effectiveness of the monetary policy instruments and the transmission process itself must change over time.

The development of policy drivers for statistical fine-tuning and forecasting effects coming from changing technical and qualitative product developments, shifting consumer patterns to new channels of distribution and the impact of new selling mediums such as television and global internet shopping, will keep future generations of economists and statisticians occupied for some time yet.

It is no surprise that most economists and the ECB now agree that an inflation rate of less than 2% per annum is deemed as acceptable for delivering and maintaining price stability. Differences of opinion arise whether independent central bank monetary policy, prudent fiscal policies pursued by governments or simply lower expectations for future wage increases to compensate for predicted price

---

[5] See *'Design Probleme einer einheitlichen Geldpolitik in Europa'* by M. Borchert in *List Forum für Wirtschafts- und Sozialpolitik* 24, 1998

rises can claim credit for almost stable prices since the early 1990s in most leading industrial nations. It must be an equilibrium of effective operating controls, transparent intermediate targets and low inflation expectations which gives a central bank the required credibility to pursue and maintain lasting price stability and to deal with economic shocks such as severe fluctuations in major commodities, stock market crashes and natural disasters.

These theories largely work within a stable economic environment. What politicians and economists are worried about is conservative independent central bankers counter-acting governmental policy in extreme situations such as a severe collapse in stock market prices or oil price shocks. Under these situations, governments will be forced to accept recessionary consequences or be tempted to override the central bank but both alternatives imply certain if not considerable costs: either lower GDP, lower fiscal revenues etc. or higher inflationary expectations. In my opinion, short-term recessionary impacts can be counteracted with limited governmental actions but inflationary expectations are based on long-term credibility, credibility that is easily and quickly destroyed and can only be regained over a considerable period of time.

Whilst numerous studies[6] have been conducted over recent years to measure the effectiveness of central bank independence in quantitative terms no study will ever claim to have a complete list of objective and subjective criteria. Subjective criteria such as rules concerning the use of collateral, procedures for allocating profits and losses and the active participation in exchange rate policies may have

---

[6] For an extensive quantitative analysis of measuring central bank independence see study undertaken by Cukierman entitled *Central Bank Strategy, Credibility and Independence: Theory and Evidence*, Cambridge, Mass., MIT University Press, 1992.

an impact on the room for manoeuvre available to a central bank. Historical experience and customary developments can have as much if not more influence than formal law in defining the boundaries of central bank action, independence and accountability. Quite often, central bank independence tended to establish itself through a sequence of specific events, most entailing conflicts with other organs of government. The ways these conflicts are ultimately resolved seem to mark the evolutionary boundaries of central bank independence and define the limits of a central bank's future scope for action.

The problems which the ECB will ultimately have to resolve centre on the inevitable conflict and ability to reach compromises in the pursuit of maintaining 'price stability, balanced growth, converging standards of living, high employment, and external equilibrium.[7] Central bank independence under political stewardship is equal to a politically dependent central bank. Despite the rhetoric of safeguarding long-term interests and planning considerations, myopic politicians of all political persuasions always have and will always be tempted to win the next election by all means at their disposal. The most frequently used tools are short-term output stimulation or consumer demand manipulation which lead to boom and bust cycles and a related policy of 'unhedged' inflation. The downside of this policy is generally the fact that the sum of short-term gains is less than the sum of long-term losses, ignoring any opportunity gains.

The independence of the ECB enshrined in the Treaty of Rome and subject to a consent amongst all fifteen member states as well as the fact that all members of the ECB Executive Board will in future be appointed for a

---

[7] 'Report on Economic and Monetary Union in the European Community', para 16.

period of eight years should guarantee the safeguarding of uniform long-term policy interests over the risks of unhedged inflation across the Euro-zone and beyond. At the same time, the management of the application of policy instruments for the ECB's toolkit and the various transmission processes for monetary policy to achieve lasting price stability should become over time uncontroversial and largely clinical in their execution, best left to experienced administrators and market professionals.

Conflict or potential conflict with other government bodies looks like an intrinsic central bank activity even in the case in which the central bank has the primary objective of price stability and enjoys large degrees of operational autonomy. The row between the German government and the Bundesbank over the revaluation of the considerable gold reserves of the Bundesbank are a classic example. The way such conflicts are resolved usually defines the limits of independence of a central bank. Such independence is at the same time linked to accountability, i.e. the way the central bank justifies its action against the background of the objective assigned to it.

The most direct spillover of EMU into fiscal policy is the loss of so-called 'seigniorage' income. Seigniorage is the issuance of money by the government, usually involving the national central bank providing the government with non-interest-bearing loans. For some member states, this seigniorage represented at times an important source of revenue possibly as high as 2.5% of GDP. During the period 1980–1995,[8] seigniorage enjoyed by the German government amounted to 0.44% of GDP compared with

---

[8] See IMF staff paper no. 97/130 by P. Masson, M. Svastano and S. Sharma entitled 'The Scope for Inflation Targeting in Developing Countries', 1997 and 'Can Inflation Targeting Be a Framework for Monetary Policy in Developing Countries?' by the same authors in *Finance & Development*, March 1998.

0.37% of GDP in the US over the same period. Developing countries such as China and Brazil enjoyed during the period 1992–1995 seigniorage as high as 7.75% and 7.46% of GDP respectively. Economists refer to seigniorage as 'inflation tax' as it inflates the money supply and causes inflation on holders of notes and coins of the national currency. For example, China had to deal with an inflation rate during the period 1992–1995 of 16.1% whilst Brazil experienced during the same period an average annual inflation rate in excess of 1,300% p.a. No seigniorage will be permitted by the ECB as Art. 104(1) of the EC Treaty and Art. 21.1 of the Statute of the ECB prohibit 'any […] type of credit facility with the ECB or with the central banks of the member states […] in favour of Community institutions or bodies, central governments, regional, local or other public authorities, […] and the purchase directly from them by the ECB or national central banks of debt instruments.'

Even with long-term interest rates having converged ahead of the start of EMU, the most important consideration for the ECB's future monetary policy will be different lead and lag structures in the transmission from policy rates set by the ECB to lending rates set by market participants. At the same time, monetary impulses sent by the ECB will have different effects on the economy across Europe both in terms of timing and intensity. Empirical research[9] has shown that there are many factors which could explain why there are differences in the direct and indirect responsiveness of market lending rates to changes in central bank policy rates. However, in general terms the success of providing monetary policy impulses to market

---

[9] See IMF staff paper No. 41 by C. Cottarelli and A. Kourelis entitled 'Financial Structure, Bank Lending Rates, and the Transmission Mechanism of Monetary Policy', 1994 pp.587–599.

lending rates is highest if the banking system is exposed to full competition and is privately owned, when capital transfers and the foreign exchange rate regime are free of any restrictions, there is an unrestricted relationship between the banking system and the corporate sector, the non-existence of credit access constraints, and when random fluctuations in the money market rates are contained.

What makes any research relating to monetary policy and in relation to the future policy of the ECB very difficult to undertake and even more to evaluate in a meaningful manner and even with quantitative research such as the vector autoregressive systems (VAR) methodology[10] showing encouraging results in identifying cross-country differences in the real impact of monetary policy, is that many EU member states have *de facto* subordinated their national monetary policies by linking their national currencies over different periods of time to and to different degrees to an anchor currency such as the Deutschmark. The different financial structures across EU member states and the influences of the EMS and ERM have affected the course of monetary policy itself. These differences in the financial structure across Europe are likely to persist for some time after EMU and will only disappear as a result of increased competition within the Euro-zone, across Europe, and even on a global basis.

At the same time, it is increasingly acknowledged by experts[11] that central bank models tend to reflect differences

---

[10] See 'The Transmission of Monetary Policy in the European Countries' by F. Barran, V. Coudert and B. Mojon, CEPI I, Document de travail n. 96–03, 1996.

[11] See 'Central Bank Macroeconomic Models and the Monetary Policy Transmission Mechanism' in *Financial Structure and the Monetary Policy Transmission Mechanism* by F. Smets in BIS C.B. 394, 1995, pages 225–266.

in financial structures across countries, generally include short-term and long-term interest rates and often identify long-term interest rates as the driving force for investment decisions. With the increasing complexity of the financial systems, the effect of monetary policy transmission mechanisms across local markets, and the differences in the real impact of monetary policy across member states, even the most comprehensively structured central bank model will not be able to yield conclusive results.

In the recent past doubts have arisen about whether traditional techniques for measuring and predicting the rate of inflation are accurate and reliable enough. Ongoing shifts within the economy over the last thirty to forty years from manufacturing to the service sector, steady increases in product quality, ever shorter product life cycles and the impact of price reductions in sectors such as computers and telecommunications equipment despite quality improvements and the introduction of more and more sophisticated products, have created ever larger distortions in the official price indices possibly as high as one percentage point.[12] Distortions of such a magnitude could mean that with current low levels of inflation within the Euro-zone, eleven member states could be currently wavering between inflation and deflation. In the light of such problems, it must be right to question whether the ECB has sufficient insight into inflationary developments and whether as a result, the ECB will be capable of conducting adequate monetary policies especially during times of low inflation when statistical distortions can be substantial. Given these inherent uncertainties in measuring inflation correctly, the Governing Council of the ECB was wise to consider price

---

[12] See results of Boskin Commission in the US and 'Problems of Inflation Measurement in Germany' by Johannes Hoffmann, Deutsche Bundesbank Discussion Paper, March 1998

stability as a rise in the recently harmonised and measured inflation of less than 2% and to use a broad set of indicators as homing beacons for the ECB to steer its monetary policy course.

The ECB will not be able to have meaningful year-on-year comparisons of harmonised monthly data for the targeted money supply aggregates well after the start of EMU. At the same time, figures available to date will require further adjustments for seasonal effects and any potential one-off transition effects. Difficulties relating to the collection of measurements and statistical information within the Euro-zone should have been overcome by the start of Stage Three on 1st January 1999. Given these early uncertainties and teething problems, the ECB is wise to use, at least at the beginning, a broad set of economic and financial indicators to detect any possible risks to price stability.

3. Market Credibility

How effective will the policy instruments of interest rates and exchange rate intervention be and how frequently would national central bank as local policy guardians and the ECB need to make use of them? Since the ECB as an independent institution and the ESCB as a policy executor will have no history and reputation to rely upon, their credibility will have to depend, at least in the beginning, on strict rules thus allowing much reduced room for discretion for national monetary authorities.[13]

---

[13] Prof. Issing, former Board Member of the German Bundesbank publicly outlined that the ECB should publish its aims and targets on a regular basis, produce and use its own statistical information on which it can reliably base its decisions, participate in the market only occasionally (perhaps no more than once a week) to show calmness and that the ECB stands above the markets and is not driven by them as well as make good

Arguably the credibility of the ECB will also depend on the past record of participating countries with their stability minded economic and fiscal policies, hence the adoption of strict convergence criteria. For many countries, EMU will imply a double transfer of power: from the national to the European level (itself already the subject of endless debate not only in Westminster) and from politicians to technocrats (the Brussels hate figures carefully groomed by Eurosceptics), thus following the precedent set by the Bundesbank. In truth this power shift acquired an additional dimension largely due to the current democratic deficit within the European political system and the related question of legitimacy referred to later. Furthermore calls for more transparency tend to come from member states where the monetary authorities have or had little credibility (usually evidenced by high bond yields) and the publication of inflation targets are presented as a poor alternative to a solid track record. Australia and New Zealand are classic examples of countries having experimented with various mechanisms for accountability but where high bond yields (and currency volatility) signalled a lack of central bank credibility over the longer term.

Could accountability go too far and explicit inflation targeting become a problem for the ECB because of its explicitness? The Bundesbank's discretionary power and its political independence are not restricted by its broad legal mandate even if interpreted in terms of achieving price stability and on the bank's leadership role in the ERM. In theory, price stability could therefore mean anything it suited the Bundesbank to have it mean. The Bundesbank

---

use of the strong credibility of the Bundesbank in order to achieve a strong and credible track record from an early start. Remarks made by Prof. Issing on 28th October 1997 during a presentation to a EMU conference organised by DG BANK and Euromoney in Frankfurt entitled *'Europa auf dem Weg in die Waehrungsunion'*.

has given indications on a number of occasions that it considers price stability to mean measured inflation in the range of 1.5–2 %.[14]

The Statutes of the ECB or the proposals by the EMI do not give a specific definition of the concept of price stability. The ECB is therefore not only allowed independence concerning the choice and use of its future monetary policy instruments but also with respect to its goals within the framework in which price stability is the overriding objective. In his introductory statement for the presentation of the 1997 EMI Annual Report to the EP, Wim Duisenberg highlighted that 'there was a need for a clear definition of the objective of price stability and for specific targets against which the performance of the ESCB could be assessed.'[15] When the ECB finally announced in October 1998 its definition of what constitutes price stability within the Euro-zone, the ECB confirmed that 'Price stability shall be defined as a year-on-year increase in the Harmonised Index of Consumer Prices (HICP) for the Euro area of below 2% and that the task of maintaining price stability was a medium term objective.'[16] Wim Duisenberg also confirmed that 'a situation of deflation, i.e. substantial and ongoing decline in the consumer price level is not consistent with price stability.'[17]

Should the ECB publish minutes of its regular meetings? Should it even reveal how individual members of the Governing Council and the General Council voted on

---

[14] 1997 Annual Report of Deutsche Bundesbank.

[15] Introductory statement delivered by the President of the ECB for the presentation of the EMI Annual Report to the EP, 15th July 1998.

[16] As announced by the President of the ECB during a press conference on 13th October 1998.

[17] 'The role of monetary policy in economic policy', speech delivered on 3rd December 1998 to the Economic and Social Committee of the European Communities.

particular decisions? Institutions which enjoy the benefit of long track records may not need a high degree of official transparency as information on policy changes often reach the public through official and unofficial channels. Frequent speeches and other public communiqués by members of the ECB's Executive Board prior to and after 1st January 1999 may allow the development of a system of communication and signals which will allow seasoned observers to understand the actions and longer-term strategies of the ECB. To keep the public informed of the final preparations prior to 1st January 1999 and latest developments thereafter, the President of the ECB has agreed to hold a monthly press conference after the first meeting of each month of the Governing Council of the ECB which will also incorporate the quarterly meetings of the General Council of the ECB.[18]

Most of the economic independence of the ECB will only emerge fully over time and some unresolved aspects such as the allocation of profits and losses have wide margins of manoeuvre to enable the ECB to preserve its financial independence.

The credibility of the ECB will also depend on the irreversible character of the monetary reform which EMU will bring. If the political process leading up to the start of Stage Three on 1st January 1999 and the full introduction of the Euro in early 2002 shows any cracks or discords, this will risk the ECB's general principles of efficiency, market orientation, simplicity, transparency and continuity being destroyed very quickly and with it the ability of the ECB to achieve needless to say maintain price stability. Probably as everything else in life, irreversibility has its price – the price of breaching the contract of EMU. Speculators will argue if

---

[18] As announced by the President of the ECB during a press conference on 11th September 1998.

the profits are potentially higher than the costs of breaching the contract, market participants will already sense that the process is indeed reversible. Therefore it will be vital for the EU and national authorities to promote a smooth transition to the ultimate replacement of national currencies with the Euro and to give rise to risk premiums and breakage costs well in excess of potential profits.

The simple fact that the ECB's physical presence is in Germany and that the former Chief Economist of the Deutsche Bundesbank now holds the same key position within the Executive Board of the ECB must give it some of the Deutsche Bundesbank's credibility in financial markets and may reconcile hostile public opinion in Germany to the loss of the Deutschmark as a tried and trusted currency. Some commentators suggest however that the German Bundesbank was rarely challenged by politicians from all sides of the political spectrum not because of its constitution but because it was seen by Mr Average on the street to do an excellent job experienced by Germans when they went on holiday abroad and received highly favourable amounts of foreign currency for their Deutschmarks. Early experiences of EMU suggest that the ECB will remain independent as long as it delivers good economic performance out of sound monetary policy visible to the public at large. Failure to do so will mean political accountability and ultimately loss of control and independence.

Recent econometric models[19] attempted to measure central bank credibility, transparency and optimal monetary

---

[19] See 'A Theory of Ambiguity, Credibility, and Inflation under Discretion and Asymmetric Information' by Alex Cukierman and Allan H. Meltzer, *Econometrics* 54, 1992; 'Transparency and Credibility: Monetary Policy with Unobservable Goals' by Jon Faust and Lars E.O. Svensson, Sveriges Riksbank Working Paper Series No. 50, December 1997 and 'Policy Rules for Inflation Targeting' by Glenn D. Rudebusch

policy in an inflation environment of less than 5%. These models were also used to explore whether and how transparency could improve central bank performance and whether increased transparency is both in the interest of the central bank and the society at large. Some notable cross references and early applications of the model in the 'real world' could be achieved by analysing the monetary policy and monetary policy strategy of the Federal Reserve Bank in the US over the last three years. Doubts however, remain whether any such results can be used for like-for-like comparisons with the future and untested monetary policy of the ECB, in particular as the ECB will not be accountable for growth and employment.

The results of the transparency and credibility models can be summarised as follows:

1. Increased central bank transparency is not only of interest to academics and financial institutions but it is also generally socially beneficial.
2. Due to the linearity of the monetary policy rule, both low and high-credibility central banks react in the same way to supply shocks and shocks to the employment target.
3. Increased central bank transparency make the reputation of the central bank more sensitive and directly responsive to its actions, increases the costs for its deviating from the announced inflation policy and consequently deterring the central bank from attempting to fulfil its idiosyncratic (if any) employment target.
4. Society decides on the level of transparency in monetary policy, delegating it in practice to the central bank itself, provided the overall monetary policy does not upset too

---

and Lars E.O. Svensson, Sveriges Riksbank Working Paper Series No. 49, February 1998.

much the equilibrium between inflation and employment.[20]
5. A central bank's desire for a strong and credible reputation creates a powerful incentive to behave close to the 'socially optimal policy'.[21]
6. Extreme transparency could completely divorce the central bank's reputation from its actions, depriving it of any important constraint on its behaviour.
7. If society could readily and directly observe the idiosyncratic goals of the central bank, it might not tolerate such goals and instead find ways to enforce its own goals on the central bank.

Ideally the measured performance of any central bank should be the subject of the central bank's ultimate customers. This can only be society at large which benefits or not over time from price stability. The ECB's independence and accountability can at this stage only be measured by legal texts since there is not yet any practical experience to draw from. The system of accountability to the society at large or based on public opinion presupposes the existence of parliamentary representation with cross-border voting structures and at the level of the Euro-constituency this is far from present.

The only viable form of a lasting monetary union is one where a common currency has displaced the national currencies, and where one ECB independently conducts monetary policy in the union. A system where national currencies maintain their domestic legal tender and whose exchange rates is 'irrevocably fixed' will suffer sooner rather than later from a credibility problem. Therefore any

---

[20] See 'Crucial issues Concerning Central Bank Independence' by Bennett T. McCallum, *Journal of Monetary Economics* 39, 1997.
[21] Ibid.

transition period from irrevocably fixed exchange rates must be for the shortest possible period only and even then they are likely to be tested by the 'market'.

Although the only system likely to survive in the long run requires a common currency managed by a common independent central bank, this system is not without its problems. The inflationary discipline of the system will depend on what this common central bank actually does within its monetary policy stewardship, on its reputation and most importantly on its international even global market credibility. Despite the fact that on paper the ECB will be as tough on inflation and committed to price stability as the Bundesbank and with the EMI as forerunner for the 'real thing' having tried within its many limitations to build a credibility platform for the ESCB and the ECB from its location in Frankfurt, doubts will exist for quite some time about the inflationary discipline that this institution can impose throughout Europe. These doubts are together with the strict adherence to the Stability and Growth Pact the two most important hurdles on the road towards a lasting EMU.

4. Conduct and Effectiveness of Monetary Policy

The Maastricht Treaty and the Statutes of the ECB clearly explain the primary objectives of the ESCB and the general asymmetry to European Currency Union. Art. 105 of the EC Treaty and Art. 2 of the Statute of the ECB clearly set out that:

> The primary objective of the ESCB shall be to maintain price stability.

This is affirmed in Art. 3a(2) of the EC Treaty and was even legally underlined by the German Federal Constitu-

tional Court.[22] In practice, the ECB is likely to adopt intermediate targets to guide its policy and will agree internally on a specific time horizon of say one to three years. It would be damaging as well as unnecessary for the ECB to nail its colours to specific short-dated targets that proved to be an unreliable guide to inflation as the huge uncertainties at the start of Stage Three must point to caution.

Nevertheless, the ECB will also have a wider duty to support the 'general economic policies in the Community'[23] but 'without prejudice to the objective of price stability.[24]

Art. 107 of the EC Treaty and Art. 7 of the Statute of the ECB underlines that:

> When exercising the powers and carrying out the tasks and duties conferred upon them by this Treaty and the Statute of the ESCB, neither the ECB nor a national central bank, nor any member of their decision making bodies shall seek or take instructions from Community institutions or bodies, from any Government of a member state or from any other body.

which must be read together with Art. 104(1) of the EC Treaty and Art. 21.1 of the Statute of the ECB which expressly prohibit:

> Overdraft facilities or any other type of credit facility with the ECB or with the central banks of the member states [...] in favour of Community institutions or bodies, central governments, regional,

---

[22] See Brunner v. European Union Treaty [1994] 1CMLR 57.
[23] Art. 2 of the EC Treaty.
[24] Art. 105(1) of the EC Treaty and Art. 2 Statute of ESCB.

local or other public authorities, [...] and the purchase directly from them by the ECB or national central banks of debt instruments.

These seem to confirm that the drafters of the statutes of the ECB have understood the basic disparity in the incentives of countries to join the EMU. As a result, they have taken pains and made valiant efforts to ensure that the ECB, at least on paper, will be an institution akin to the German Bundesbank. It might even be said that the language used by the drafters of the statutes of the ECB is tougher on inflation and political independence than the statutes of the Bundesbank.

The question that arises here is whether the explicit recognition in the statutes of the ECB of operational autonomy, political independence and above all price stability[25] as the primary objectives of monetary policy are sufficient (they are certainly necessary) to guarantee that the ECB can manage an inflation proof single currency. One can express doubts about this, in particular for two reasons.

First of all the fact the EC Treaty has introduced a strict 'no monetary financing rule'[26] which will go some way to help the monetary policy independence of the ECB but it will not necessarily constrain fiscal deficits, since the ECB may have to purchase government debt instruments on the

---

[25] Critics such as Prof. Goodhart argue that the lack of a precise definition for price stability in the EC Treaty or any other text provides the European Central Bank with 'flexibility at the cost of relaxing accountability' and that a system constructed by, with and for central bankers would only serve to give them an easy life. Cited by Ian Milne in *Maastricht: The Case Against Economic & Monetary Union*, Nelson & Pollard, June 1993, p.25.

[26] Art. 104(1) of the EC Treaty and Art. 21.1 of the Statute of the ECB.

secondary market to prevent interest rates from rising.[27] The Maastricht treaty however does not mention the ECB as a 'lender of last resort' which might become very important in a very liquid Euro market in order to avoid severe market disruptions or even failures. The best example for such last resort lender activity was the huge cash injection and lending activity by the US Federal Reserve Bank during and immediately after the 1987 stock market crash. In theory a country could go bankrupt after EMU, just as Orange County in the US did, but it remains unclear how the ECB would respond if a country did ever threaten to default, not least because this could threaten the credibility of the whole system.

At the same time the market might be distorted by speculation or other inefficiencies, allowing, despite national debt premiums for individual member states and disciplinary proceedings by the ECB against individual member states, national debt burdens to rise so fast and to such an extent that there would be a real danger of a financial crisis which even the ECB with its considerable reserves would not be able to contain without relaxing policy and jeopardising price stability.[28]

---

[27] Rising fiscal deficits will, without raising interest rates, cause the Euro to depreciate in the event of excessive deficit. Rising interest rates will correspondingly cause the Euro to appreciate. This point was highlighted by Paul Kenen in his discussion paper entitled 'Hazards on the Road to the Third Stage of Economic and Monetary Union' for the Forum of US-EC Legal-Economic Affairs Session on Issues of Governance in the European Community in September 1995.

[28] See discussion paper by Paul Kenen entitled 'Hazards on the Road to the Third Stage of Economic and Monetary Union' for the Forum of US-EC Legal-Economic Affairs Session on Issues of Governance in the European Community in September 1995, p.93. To combat the risk of excessive deficits of member sates, the Delors Committee proposed a combined fiscal deficit (as a percentage of GDP) which would be set and

Secondly, the human beings sitting on the Executive Board of the ECB who are going to make and dictate monetary policy are subject to social and cultural influence brought into the job with their general upbringing and national identity and ideology. Some individuals come from countries where resentment towards inflation and more importantly its causes and symptoms is not as intense as it is in Germany. They may therefore argue and act differently from the individuals sitting on the board of the German Bundesbank, even if the statutes of the ECB have been designed in the image of the Bundesbank statutes. In addition, differences in the natural and historic rate of unemployment may make them more prone than the German Bundesbank to be soft on inflation.

Advocates[29] for the wait and see policy before joining the Euro expect that the Euro is likely to soften after a strong start and given the political impetus necessary to propel European Monetary Union into flight and the anxiety of the new ECB to establish tough credentials, the 'Eurobaby' will emerge fighting. But its strength might evaporate the instant that a heterogeneous Executive Board of the ECB, faced with unreliable data, hesitates to tighten monetary policy, and/or if disputes surface between governments of member states over exchange rate policy. Any disagreement over the Euro's value and the workings of the Stability and Growth Pact first agreed at the Dublin summit of December 1996 and fine-tuned at the Amsterdam summit of October 1997, however resolved, would

---

periodically reviewed by the General Council of the European Central Bank but this proposal was not accepted in the Maastricht Treaty.

[29] Advocates for a wait and see policy now firmly include the current Labour administration, the distinguished monetarist William Buiter of Cambridge University and Member of the Bank of England Monetary Policy Committee as well as Alison Cottrell, Senior International Economist at Paine Webber International.

cause a bad reflection on policy credibility and hence directly or indirectly undermine the currency.

Some economists[30] argue that changes in monetary policy (like raising or lowering interest rates) which Britain would give up as part of monetary union, do not actually affect long-term wealth creation in any case and that monetary policy can only make an impact during transitional periods, hence it is not the stuff of which the wealth of nations is made. Nevertheless, the EMI is of the opinion that following its close monitoring of fiscal and monetary developments over the last three years that '[t]here is a link between sustainable fiscal adjustment and an improvement of growth perspectives over the medium term.'[31] At the same time, the EMI clearly spelt out that things are not going to change overnight and that the ESCB will not be able to move mountains even with its operational independence as it 'will face a complex transmission process from policy actions to price developments which will be characterised by several interlinked transmission channels with long variable legs'[32] especially as the decisions of the ECB will also have to withstand the guiding principles of effectiveness (which also includes credibility and consistency), accountability and transparency.

The EMI has defined a set of monetary policy instruments for use by the ESCB mainly through use (if possible sporadic but clearly visible[33]) in open market operations.

---

[30] William Buiter, Professor of International Macroeconomics at Cambridge University has undertaken extensive research on the subject of governments' ability to influence fiscal and monetary developments.

[31] EMI 1996 Annual Report, p.5.

[32] Report by EMI entitled 'The Single Monetary Policy in Stage Three – Specification of the operational framework', p.6.

[33] Prof. Issing, former Board Member of the German Bundesbank stated in public that the ECB should participate in the market only occasionally, perhaps no more than once a week, to show calmness and that the ECB

These policy instruments, in order for the ECB to achieve the EC Treaty obligation of maintaining price stability, were defined as one of the key tasks by the EMI and crucially having taken into account 'guiding principles such as effectiveness, accountability, transparency, medium-term orientation, continuity, consistency with the ESCB's independence and considering the environment likely to prevail in the Euro area.'[34] They include:

1. Main refinancing operations (i.e. regular liquidity-providing reserve transactions with a duration not exceeding two weeks).
2. Longer-term refinancing operations (i.e. liquidity-providing reserve transactions up to three months duration intended to cater for a limited part of the ESCB's overall refinancing volume).
3. Fine-tuning operations depending on liquidity in market and principally for steering interest rates.
4. Structural operations intended to affect the structural liquidity position of the banking system vis-à-vis the ESCB.

In addition, the ESCB as a central clearing house will have facilities to provide or absorb overnight liquidity together with the complex but effective minimum reserve

---

stands above the markets and is not driven by them. Remark made by Prof. Issing on 28th October 1997 during a presentation to a EMU conference organised by DG BANK and Euromoney in Frankfurt entitled *'Europa auf dem Weg in die Waehrungsunion'*.

[34] EMI report entitled 'The Single Monetary Policy in Stage Three – Specification of the operational framework', p.11.

system copied from the German Bundesbank for stabilising money market interest rates.[35]

Regarding the conduct of monetary policy by the ECB, there are two technical issues which still require a lasting solution:

1. Should the ECB aim at an inflation target (like the Bank of England) or a money-supply target (like the Deutsche Bundesbank)?
2. Since the Maastricht treaty gives the ECB control over monetary policy and ECOFIN responsibility for external exchange rate policy, what arrangements will enable the ECB and ECOFIN/EURO X to co-ordinate these two crucial areas of policy?

The ECB announced after the meeting of its Governing Council on 13th October 1998, the main features of its future monetary policy strategy which will be based on:

1. A quantitative definition of what constitutes price stability.
2. The use of a reference range for domestic monetary aggregates.
3. The use of various other indicators.

However, the focus of monetary policy strategy will be geared towards the ESCB's primary objective of price stability as enshrined in the EC Treaty. In relation to a meaningful quantitative definition of what precisely constitutes price stability but also as a public guide for expectations concerning future price developments, the

---

[35] See proposal by EMI for a draft EU Council Regulation concerning minimum reserves as published in report entitled 'The Single Monetary Policy in Stage Three – Specification of the operational framework', p.63.

ECB defined price stability in terms of 'Price stability shall be defined as a year-on-year increase in the Harmonised Index of Consumer Prices (HICP) for the Euro area of below 2%.' [36] With the HICP already having served well and reliably as a key parameter for the assessment of a member states' compliance with the inflation limit set under the EMU convergence criteria, the ECB considers this indicator as the most appropriate measure for defining and assessing price stability across the Euro-zone. Accepting variations during different stages of economic cycles, the ECB considers price stability to be a medium-term objective. For this reason, the ECB also intends not to publish its forecasts of year-on-year inflation.

Money aggregates and with it monetary targeting will be given by the ECB a prominent role despite various definitions of broad money which have shown during the run up to EMU similar and stable rates of growth of between 3% and 5% per annum. Targeting broad money represents a continuation of one of the key monetary policy indicators used by the Bundesbank even with the ECB only setting a reference value rather than a clear target figure. Nevertheless, the Governing Council of the ECB again intends to provide the results of its analysis of broad money developments on a regular basis to the public.[37] It also intends to again explain the impact of its analysis of monetary policy decisions. In addition to monetary and inflation targets, the ECB plans to take a large number of other economic and financial variables into consideration in order to achieve a 360 degree assessment for its ongoing monetary policy, the evaluation of future price developments and the possible risks to price stability.

---

[36] Announced at ECB Press Conference on 13th October 1998.
[37] Likely to be on a quarterly basis following the regular meetings of the Governing Council.

Although the ECB intends to keep an eye on short-term volatility and events affecting the global financial markets, its monetary policy will generally have a medium-term orientation both in terms of using and interpreting forecasting models and their actual outcome. Appreciating its role as public servant but also to foster market credibility, the Governing Council of the ECB not only intends to publish detailed assessments of the monetary, economic and financial situation in the Euro-zone but also provide the public at the same time with reasoning for their specific policy decisions. In order to show consistency and some level of transparency, the ECB has agreed that statistics relating to money and banking will also be made available to the public once a formal harmonised system of reporting has been completed under the stewardship of the ECB. Although no details were provided as to the regularity of such assessments, it is generally expected that such reports will be available on a quarterly basis in line with the regular meeting schedule of the Governing Council of the ECB.

Critics argue that whilst the ECB was right to opt for a flexible strategy and to use a broad set of indicators to achieve both a high level and a detailed overview for future risks to price stability, the transparency and with it the ECB's willingness to accept more scrutiny still leave much to be desired. Of particular concern to sceptics are the ECB's unwillingness to issue details how it will operate, its refusal to release forecasts on which the ECB's secret decisions are based and for which it could be held accountable and the already stated policy that no minutes of ECB meeting will be available for a considerable period of time. The mere publication of reference values rather than clear targets and the discretionary use of an unspecified mix of economic and financial indicators, represent in the eyes of many doubters a clear lack of transparency and a substantial deficit in accountability.

The use of a wide variety of monetary instruments, discretionary interpretation rather than rule based monetary targeting and unpublished forecasts of inflation as well as the use of an unspecified mix of other economic and financial indicators will mean that the ECB will not be a reincarnated Bundesbank but will conduct its operations more like the US Federal Reserve Bank.

Following the lead of the German Bundesbank but also with the Banque de France and the Bank of Italy having made favourable experiences with a minimum reserve system, as it allows a relatively simple fine-tuning of monetary policy and aids the gathering of reliable statistical information, the ECB decided[38] in October 1998 that banks operating within the Euro-zone should be required to hold 2% of their deposits[39] as involuntary reserves with the ECB. With minimum reserves to be held as a monthly average, the minimum reserve system will act as an effective buffer in the money markets where unforeseen fluctuations in the demand for short-dated liquid funds can be catered for without the need for any major intervention of the ECB in the markets.

Whilst minimum reserve requirements are intended to ensure financial stability and can not be easily bypassed, they have also been criticised as an 'outdated monetary tool'[40] and for disadvantaging banks within the Euro-zone against banks operating from countries outside the single currency or other EU member states not participating in the single currency such as the UK where there is no

---

[38] Minimum reserve system is made available to ECB under Art 19.1 Statute of ESCB. See Recommendation of the ECB for a Council regulation concerning the application of minimum reserves by the ECB contained in European commission Euro Papers No. 25, July 1998.

[39] Each bank has a free deposit pool of 100,000 Euros.

[40] Rolf Breuer, Chairman of Deutsche Bank AG in 'ECB cracks its whip', *The Financial Times,* 10th July 1998.

requirement to maintain such deposits with national central banks. To counteract criticism such as that minimum reserves represent another form of taxation on the intermediation of credit by banks, the ECB decided to pay interest at the prevailing repo-rate (securities repurchase rate) – the ECB's key short-term interest rate. Most observers were surprised that the ECB had adopted interest levels so close to market rates thereby ensuring the most generous system of compensation. Even if one could argue that minimum reserves have largely been replaced by the far more flexible repo market for absorbing liquidity, paying interest at rates close to general market levels will alleviate the desire or attempts to avoid it, like any other form of taxation. At the same time, they no longer discriminate vis-à-vis financial centres where a reduced or even no requirement exists to maintain minimum reserves such as Luxembourg or London. There will still be a 0% minimum reserve on securities repurchase operations, the regular monthly money market tenders through which the ECB but mainly national central banks within the Euro-zone will inject liquidity into the Euro financial markets. A minimum reserve requirement of 0% will also apply to debt securities and deposits with a maturity of over two years. In order to be able to enforce compliance, Art. 7 of the draft Council regulation concerning the application of minimum reserves by the ECB coming into force on 1st January 1999 will allow the ECB to impose severe sanctions on institutions failing to hold all or part of their required minimum reserves.

In the true spirit of a European tradition of compromise, the ECB will most likely operate a monetary policy which involves both monetary and inflation targets. Although the ECB is by all accounts inclined to use monetary targeting as its key policy instrument instead of inflation targeting, the actual collection and aggregation of reliable monetary

statistics is extremely complicated and cumbersome. The production of a single set of European monetary statistics, essentially around M3, has turned out to be a large pool of quicksand for ECB officials. For example, Italy does not publish M3 data and the French M3 figures have been affected by so many changes that they are nowadays essentially meaningless.

Following the production and publication of the first set of monetary aggregates for the Euro-zone on a consolidated basis, which showed M3[41] growing at an average rate of 4.5% p.a., the Governing Council of the ECB approved a growth rate for M3 of between 3.5% and 5.5% as 'broadly compatible with continued price stability in the Euro area'.[42] The ECB intends to revise the reference value on an annual basis although it made it clear that it does not wish to lock itself into a monetary target for its monetary policy strategy. Although the Governing Council of the ECB agreed at its meeting on 1st December 1998 a 4.5% reference value for annualised growth in the broad money supply figure of M3 and the President of the ECB provided at the press conference on the same day a full and detailed explanation of how the Governing Council came to this decision, the co-ordinated cut in interest rates by all national central banks participating in the single monetary policy from 1st January 1999 on 3rd December 1998 did not meet universal approval. Some economists argued that with M3 growing within the target corridor of 3.5% to

---

[41] M3 will consist of Euro currency in circulation plus overnight deposits, deposits with an agreed maturity of up to two years, deposits redeemable at notice up to three months, repos, debt securities with a maturity of up to two years, unit/shares of money market funds and money market paper (net) of monetary financial institutions resident in the Euro area and, in the case of deposits, the liabilities of some institutions that are part of central government (such as post offices and treasuries).

[42] ECB press release, 14th December 1998.

5.5%, there was no need to cut interest rates. Even more stinging has been criticism describing the publication of quantitative reference values for monetary growth as 'monetary masquerade'[43] under which the ECB spells out the assumptions made for prices, real GDP growth and velocity, only to ignore them forty-eight hours later through a co-ordinated interest rate cut by eleven national central banks. Early indications of the ECB making full use of its discretionary powers and broad set of indicators suggest that the ECB will follow the time honoured tradition of the Bundesbank of second-guessing the market for major policy decisions.

Even if a Herculean task would start to generate reasonably accurate and reliable data,[44] more fundamental changes caused by EMU could undermine the interpretation of historic relationships between money supply and inflation, both for inflation and monetary targeting. The biggest danger for the economists at the ECB will be an over-reliance on either set of economic forecasting models even to the extent that the combination of two poor policy indicators does not create in aggregate a good one.

Some economists[45] have even proposed incentive schemes for the key ECB policy-makers so that it would make it more likely that they pursue non-inflationary policies. One such imaginative scheme consists of paying the members of the Executive Board of the ECB a fixed

---

[43] '"Monetary masquerade"' cuts across the rules.' *The Financial Times*, 8th December 1998.

[44] See draft Council regulation concerning the collection of statistical information by the ECB as reported in European Commission Euro Papers No. 25, July 1998.

[45] Prof. M.J.M. Neumann's 'Central Bank Independence as a Prerequisite of Price Stability', in EC Commission's 'The Economics of EMU', European Economy, Special Edition 1, 1991, and Roland Vaubel, 1989.

nominal salary[46] but to reduce their salary by a considerable percentage margin for every point of inflation. These schemes may help in the short term, but they are unlikely to eliminate completely the risk that the ECB will not be as inflation-conscious as the Bundesbank is today. One could indeed argue that if central bank independence comes without proper accountability, central bankers may feel inclined to pursue their own policies and often in an opportunistic manner, thereby putting themselves above the society's policy objectives such as price stability, full employment and growth. But these shortcomings could be overcome[47] without too much bureaucratic implications through the establishment of clear objectives including personal incentives. The clear target of price stability as enshrined in the EC Treaty significantly limits the ability of the ECB to behave in an opportunistic manner and provides an overriding principle and credible authority.

More radical solutions for the possible conflict between monetary and fiscal policy could for example be the development of a quasi-European federal budget structure under which governments of member states would transfer a sizeable portion of national taxation and public expenditure into a central EU budget or to give ECOFIN or another Community body a central fiscal authority with the right to influence national fiscal balances or even set deficit ceilings. Such transfers of power would clearly impose

---

[46] Following pressure from Euro MPs, the President of the ECB admitted that he earns around £160,000 p.a., a figure which has been set at 40% above the highest earning EU official for reference purposes. As reported in *The Daily Telegraph*, 16th July 1998. The terms for salaries of ECB officials are contained in the amended EC Regulation No. 260/68.

[47] See central bank law of New Zealand as discussed in 'Central bank independence in New Zealand: analytical, empirical and institutional aspects', G.E. Wood, 1994, paper presented at the Paoli Baffi Conference on Central Bank Independence and Accountability, Milan, March 1994.

further limits on the prerogatives of national governments and would be under the current political climate impossible to achieve. Further political union on the other hand should not be contemplated without a transfer of fiscal authority to the EP.

European developments of fiscal harmonisation or mere fiscal co-ordination are a political minefield which even the experienced central bankers have carefully avoided. With unanimity rule in the EU on taxation matters still firmly intact, tax policy is one of the last bastions of national sovereignty. The problem has not been an unwillingness to start with a joint approach, for example with the agreement by EC finance ministers on a voluntary code of business taxation, but how far to go. EMU entails economic and monetary union, but still many governments believe that different tax policies are immune from the effects of economic union. But these different tax regimes are inviting unfair methods or policies to gain competitive advantages and thus undermine national sovereignty instead of fostering it. Member states should use greater fiscal co-ordination and even harmonisation within the European Union to safeguard sovereignty, otherwise efficient global money markets and tax havens from Switzerland to the Bahamas will expose EMU to predatory tax competition on a global scale.

Although Eurosceptics continue to argue that a single monetary policy cannot be applied effectively to eleven independent member states, economic and monetary experience since World War Two nevertheless has shown that stable money is an essential precondition for both poor and richer countries alike in order to achieve sustainable long term levels of growth. Recent studies[48] have also

---

[48] See 'Comparing the Monetary Transmission Mechanism in France, Germany and the United Kingdom: Some Issues and Results' by E.

shown that differences in the monetary transmission process, i.e. the economic impact of interest rate changes is much smaller throughout EU member states, as was previously thought, providing the platform for a lasting convergence of financial structures both inside the Eurozone and the EU as a whole.

The fact that not all EU member states will be joining the single currency at the start of Stage Three on 1st January 1999 will not stop the increasingly widespread use of the Euro in all EU member states, as well as in Central and Eastern European countries which will start to use the Euro as a replacement for the Deutschmark for domestic and international transactions and reserve holdings. This might complicate the developing monetary policy of the ECB should it heavily rely on money aggregates as transmission tools and as an intermediate target. Some commentators[49] however, argue that a general policy of openness and reconcilable targets for variables such as money supply will lead to a strong credibility for the ECB and thus avoid any possible undercurrents for its monetary policy.

5. Limits on Operational Independence

As outlined above, the ECB is not free to enter into agreements concerning monetary or foreign exchange regime matters between the Community and non-Community States or international organisations for example the World Bank or the International Monetary Fund. Before concluding any formal arrangements for the Euro vis-à-vis

---

Britton and J. Whiteley, *Bank of England Quarterly Bulletin*, May 1997, pp.152–162.

[49] See comments by Ramana Ramaswamy in 'Monetary Frameworks: Is There a Preferred Option for the European Central Bank?' in Research Department, International Monetary Fund, January 1997.

non-Community currencies, the Council of Ministers must consult with the ECB to 'ensure that the Community expresses a single position.'[50] The Council of Ministers has however confirmed that the ECOFIN Council, helped by the ECOFIN Committee, the European Commission and the ECB within their respective fields of competence, will monitor and assess the situation and suggests that prior to Stage Three, the Council of Ministers provide the ECB within agreed margins the ability of intervention on a discretionary basis.

Should the Council of Ministers, when acting unanimously, force its will on the ECB however much the ECB might protest? Highly unlikely, as this would not represent a consensus position between the Council of Ministers and the ECB, a point which in my opinion the ECJ would highlight when called upon to adjudicate on the exercise of the powers granted to the Community institutions.

The separateness of monetary policy from exchange rate policy and the limits imposed on the ECB concerning the conduct of exchange rate policy could lead to possible conflicts, in particular if ECOFIN should adopt an external exchange rate policy in Stage Three which turns out to be inconsistent with the ECB's prime objective of price stability, i.e. imported inflation forcing the ECB to take action in order not to jeopardise its objective. Although the Maastricht Treaty has given ECOFIN a strong mandate for overall exchange rate policies, the fact that the EC Treaty also requires unanimous decisions for formal international exchange rate agreements provides the ECB with a relatively strong position as it has to provide ECOFIN with its recommendations on exchange rate systems and on any parity adjustments. Experiences with the Federal Reserve

---

[50] Art. 109(3) of the EC Treaty. See Council of Ministers, annexes to the conclusions of the Presidency (4/108), Bulletin EU 6–1996.

Bank in the US have shown that a consistent ECB monetary policy would help little with respect to long-term exchange rate stability or exchange rate predictability.

Although the ECB will be in charge of the day-to-day management of the Euro's exchange rate and over the large majority of foreign exchange reserves of member states participation in the single currency, ECOFIN will still have the right to enter into international agreements involving the new single currency or 'formulate general orientations for exchange rate policies'[51] in relation to non-Community currencies. Most commentators suggest that this was a compromise granted to member states that regarded exchange rate policy as their prerogative and that they will not have to entirely abandon this right when participating in EMU. Only experience will tell whether the fears of some critics[52] will materialise and the division of responsibility for monetary policy and exchange rate policy prove to be impracticable or even potentially damaging.

Any attempts by the ECB to build a solid foundation for a medium to long-term Euro-zone exchange rate policy will be directly linked to its monetary policy (measured by price stability, interest volatility and long term economic growth) and the management of foreign currency reserves both by the ECB and by national central banks. At the same time, central bank credibility based on sound monetary policy will also be linked to fiscal policies by not only Euro-zone member states but by all EU member states.

Early signals that the ECB might clash with politicians over the formulation of future exchange rate policies have

---

[51] Art. 109(2) of the EC Treaty.

[52] See comments by D. Begg in 'Alternative Exchange-rate Regimes: the Role of the Exchange Rate and the Implications for Wage-Price Adjustment' in *The Economies of EMU* published by the European Commission in European Economy, Special Edition 1, 1991.

emerged from the German government when its Finance Minister Oskar Lafontaine tabled ideas that the Euro should float within target zones against the yen and the US dollar in order to foster European growth and with it to fight unemployment. The German proposal quickly found favour with the Socialist government in Paris which stated that both governments have a responsibility to pursue a strategy of growth and job creation to bring down mass unemployment. The speed and size of capital movements on an almost global scale has made it almost impossible for any central bank to control exchange rates through any regulatory regime. General exchange rate accords also act like conductors for possible effects on price stability across different currency blocks rendering monetary policies and their transmission processes almost worthless. It remains to be seen whether these new policy ideas remain political rhetoric or whether they will be turned into practice within ECOFIN where the two major countries driving EU policy-making and at the heart of the single currency project and the majority of other EU member states are now managed by left-of-centre governments.

Despite possible conflicts between the exchange rate policy adopted by ECOFIN and the day-to-day running of the same by the ECB and the ECB's monetary policies in fulfilment of its prime task of maintaining price stability, the separation of monetary policy from other policies, in particular foreign exchange policy, should in practice be achievable for a number of reasons:

1. Member states' participation in the single currency will have a strong vested interest to see EMU succeed.
2. Member states are unlikely to enter into agreements which are in direct conflict with the interests of EMU and which challenge the authority of the ECB.

3. The EC Treaty provides strong protection of the interests of the ECB and the ESCB with a need to consult the ECB 'in an endeavour to reach a consensus consistent with the objective of price stability'.[53]
4. Initiatives by the Council will require recommendation from the Commission or the ECB and unanimity.[54]
5. Although ECOFIN may formulate 'general orientations' for exchange rate policies, mainly vis-à-vis larger currencies such as the US dollar and the Japanese yen, they 'shall be without prejudice to the primary objective of the ESCB to maintain price stability.'[55]
6. Policies pursued by the G3, G7 and G20 nation currencies over recent years have excluded any formal agreements in favour of fully floating exchange rates.

As long as not all member states participate in the single currency after the start of Stage Three, arrangements under the new ERM II will continue for the foreseeable future, provided they do not prejudice the ECB's prime objective of price stability and hence do not oblige the ECB to adjust its policies or intervene without limit to support currencies of non-participating member states.

6. National Central Banks

Although Art. 107 of the EC Treaty and Art. 7 of the Statute of the ECB clearly spell out that:

> neither the ECB nor a national central bank, nor any member of their decision making bodies shall seek or take instructions from Community institutions or

---

[53] Art. 109(1) of the EC Treaty.
[54] Ibid.
[55] Art. 109(2) of the EC Treaty.

bodies, from any Government of a Member State or from any other body.

it is unclear how far national central bank governors will be accountable in their own jurisdiction in Stage Three. The statute of the ESCB does not bar them from appearing before their own respective parliaments or more likely parliamentary committees, but the strong prohibition on taking instructions as outlined above suggests that they could not be required to attend (unlike the position now in the United Kingdom). All in all it might seem unlikely that governors would refuse their parliaments' requests for hearings, but they could and should object to discussing policy details on grounds of confidentiality. Under Art. 10.4 Statute of ESCB governors of national central banks as members of the Governing Council of the ECB are nevertheless bound to keep their deliberations confidential unless and until the Governing Council decides to make them public.

Following approval by the EMI Council in 1996 of the accounting principles to be followed by national central banks and for the overall reporting of the ESCB, the ECB is still in the process of fine-tuning the necessary and uniform techniques to allow national central banks to adapt their local accounting procedures and systems to correctly and consistently apply the accounting principles for the financial reporting of the ESCB as a whole. National central banks will also have a vested interest in separating income achieved from purely domestic operations from income arising from the performance of the ESCB's monetary policy function.[56] Furthermore, agreement will have to be reached with national central banks of those member states not participating in the first phase.

---

[56] Art. 32.2 and 32.3 Statute of ESCB.

7. Supervision of the ECB

The principal bodies of the ECB will be its Executive Board and the Governing Council but they will both be limited to the relevant persons from member states without derogation. However there is a third body, the General Council, which is established under Art. 45 of the Statute of the ESCB (without prejudice to Art. 106(3) of the EC Treaty) and its function is set out in Art. 47 of the Statute of the ESCB. When no member state has a derogation, the General Council will become otiose and its largely contributory functions may become blurred as interests are no longer forthcoming from countries wishing to join the Euro but cannot rely on their right of derogation to be represented within some of the workings of the ESCB.

Was it a wise move to leave the conduct of monetary policy to an independent ECB and will the balance of power between the very independently run and centrally organised ECB and the Council of Minister which leaves the responsibility to the member states to conduct their respective national economic policies, not be unbalanced?

The independence of the ECB will not isolate it from having to interact with economic policy makers as it will almost be unthinkable that the ECB could in any way conduct a proper monetary policy without taking into account the ongoing economic situation in the EC and the direction of national even regional economic policies. The sustainability of the right balance of power between the ECB, the ECOFIN council and the European Commission will depend on the quality and maturity of this dialogue. It will have to take place at four different levels:

1. At the level of the General Council of the ECB.

2. At the level of the Governing Council of the ECB, (at least for as long as some member states have decided not to participate in the single currency).
3. At the level of the ECOFIN council (which will also enforce the commitments of the Stability Pact).
4. At the level of the Economic and Financial Committee.

8. ECOFIN/EURO X

At the final stage of EMU, the Monetary Committee, consisting of two members from each member state and the European Commission, will be replaced by ECOFIN[57] when it will be joined by representatives from the ECB.[58] Its principal role will be to link the member states participating in the single currency, the European Commission and the ECB and to act as the only real joint discussion forum for policy matters of the ECB. The Council of Ministers as representative of the Members and on a proposal from the European Commission, but after consulting the ECB and the Committee itself, have yet to lay down detailed provisions for the composition, functioning and role of this important forum.[59] Early guidance can be had from the Council decision on 21st December 1998[60] on the composition of ECOFIN and its formal statutes[61] (see Appendix V) agreed by the Council of Ministers on 31st December 1998.

In principle it will continue the work of its predecessor on a wider scale, including the review of the monetary and

---

[57] See proposal for EU Council Decision 98/C125/11 on the detailed provisions concerning the composition of the Economic and Financial Committee, European Commission, Euro Papers 25, July 1998.

[58] Art. 109c(2) of the EC Treaty.

[59] Art. 109c(3)(4) of the EC Treaty.

[60] OJ 1998 L358.

[61] OJ 1999 L5.

financial situation and the general payment systems of the member states that have obtained opt-out or wait-and-see stances toward the EMU system. It will report its findings to the European Commission and the Council of Ministers. But does it act as a policeman for the ECB without any real power? What is its proper role? The division of responsibilities between the ECB and ECOFIN appears to be still unclear. With the ECB having been committed to the objective of maintaining price stability, the ESCB is also committed to the 'support of [the] general economic policy set at the Community level by the competent bodies'.[62] This will leave in my opinion ample room for acrimonious debate between national finance ministers and the ECB both within ECOFIN and on a national level.

The debate will largely home in on the question of whether the general economic policy of the European Community was consistent with price stability and hence to be supported by the ECB. Furthermore, I feel that there are danger signals from recent ECOFIN Council Meetings which called for the external exchange rate to be determined by ECOFIN. If fiscal policy is left to be determined by national governments and the external European exchange rate to be determined by ECOFIN (essentially finance ministers acting for political reasons), then monetary policy is formally pinned down or even cornered to such an extent that the ECB's independence will be gravely weakened.

With regards to policy co-ordination between the ECB and ECOFIN it appears that ECOFIN currently lacks political clout and for this reason ECOFIN, whose ministers are accountable to their national parliaments, should be strengthened to make it a more balanced political counterweight to the ECB. Alternatively, an even more

---

[62] Art. 105 of the EC Treaty and Art. 2 Statute of ESCB.

powerful EU Financial Council could be established, consisting of heads of government and finance ministers, to address the imbalance between the ECB and policy-makers and to ensure a constructive trade-off between fiscal and monetary policy, to combine low inflation with reasonable growth.

ECOFIN will be a macroeconomic policy forum comprising of the finance ministers of all fifteen member states of the EU and could be regarded as an 'Economic European Government'. For as long as some member states are not participating in the single currency, the so-called Euro X could become the more powerful body clearly upstaging ECOFIN. EU politicians however have realised the political damage which could occur from conflict between Euro X and ECOFIN.[63]

The provisions of Art. 109 of the EC Treaty provide ECOFIN with a broad policy input when it comes to the exchange rate policy of the Euro. The Maastricht Treaty however does not give ECOFIN an explicit authority over exchange rate policy which would have an in-built conflict with the ECB. Most monetarists now agree that exchange rate policy cannot be set independently of monetary policy and that interventions in the foreign exchange market are generally ineffective if they are not accompanied by changes in monetary policy. The main reason for this is the experience gathered by many central banks that foreign exchange interventions by open market operations do not affect the money supply and hence have no lasting effect and are the fastest way to depleting a central bank's foreign currency reserves. In order to avoid any foreign exchange policy clashing with the monetary policy pursued by the ECB which could lead to significant speculation in the foreign

---

[63] See 'Austria say Euro X will not exclude UK' in *The Financial Times*, 11th May 1998.

exchange markets and to the detriment of the Euro, Art. 109(2) of the EC Treaty clearly provides for any exchange rate policy set by ECOFIN that 'The general orientations shall be without prejudice to the primary objective of the ECB to maintain price stability.' Even if the ECB takes or is forced to take into account any exchange rate considerations put forward by ECOFIN, Art. 3a of the EC Treaty unambiguously states that the objective of price stability ranks ahead of exchange rate policy.

There will essentially be a two-tier ECOFIN, tier one including representatives from all member states without derogation and tier two including representative from all member states of the EU. Whilst Art. 109c(2) of the EC Treaty sets out the tasks of ECOFIN, Art. 109c(4) of the EC Treaty also gives the Committee additional tasks in relation to member states with a derogation. Press reports[64] and ECOFIN meetings since the Birmingham summit in May 1998 suggest that ECOFIN will remain the crucial body for economic policy-making and that a way had been found of informing those countries remaining outside the single currency of issues which the Euro member states had agreed. The likely solution appears to be some sort of observer status but one must be fearful that any compromise will not withstand the test of time. Many practical aspects and political implications for the Euro X still remain undefined but countries such as France and Germany have shown their determination that it will play a central role in defining the key policies and common interests of the Euro-zone. Its leverage on short-term European monetary policy and vis-à-vis international institutions such as G7 or even the IMF should not be underestimated. Affected will

---

[64] See 'Britain wins Euro safeguard' in *The Guardian*, 19th November 1997 and 'UK rebuffed on 'Euro-club' entry' in *The Financial Times*, 2nd December 1997.

be those member states not participating in the single currency for the time being as they will not be allowed to vote on sanctions against member states breaching the provisions of the Stability and Growth Pact and on the external exchange rate policy for the Euro. Symbolic evidence of the Euro X's power was displayed in early June 1998 when Gordon Brown, Chancellor of the Exchequer, was not allowed to participate in the meeting of the eleven member states initially joining the single currency even though he had officially opened the meeting at the Luxembourg chateau of Senningen as part of the United Kingdom's presidency of the European Union at the time. Only clever logistical arrangements and behind the scenes manoeuvres similar to opera house scenery changes avoided embarrassing press attention. This still did not save Mr Brown from being described by a European diplomat as a 'gatecrasher'[65] and criticism at home that Britain had been seriously embarrassed.

The last level will be the most important one as ECOFIN will have the task assigned to it for keeping under ongoing review the financial and economic situations of member states and of reporting it back on a regular basis to the Council of Ministers and to the European Commission. Against this background, ECOFIN will play a key role in the preparation of broad economic guidelines and limits for economic convergence. The members of the European Commission and the ECB on the Economic and Financial Committee should provide the necessary and most suitable platform for regular dialogue between the different factors of macroeconomic co-ordination. The constitution and the workings of this vital committee must strike the right balance between the notions of European economic

---

[65] See 'Opt-out Britain "gatecrashes" euro club part' in *The Times*, 5th June 1998.

governance (yet fully democratic and capable of engaging member states in a direct manner) and the principle of subsidiarity according to which national competence is the rule and the Community competence the exception. The question however remains whether ECOFIN will ever be able to deliver fiscal policy co-ordination without being dominated by national political interests and agendas. The broad vision for Europe has always and will always be provided by the European heads of state meeting at least twice a year.

Probably the most powerful but through its sheer size never to be highly effective body will be the new Economic and Financial Committee[66] which will comprise of officials from national treasuries, central bankers and two members of the European Commission. Transparency would be highly welcome at this level as this new body replaces the secretive Monetary Committee[67] which prepared ECOFIN meetings. With economic management in the Euro-zone becoming increasingly dependent on the co-ordination and preparation of forums such as the Euro X and the ECOFIN meeting of EU Finance Ministers, the Economic and Finance Committee will still allow central bankers a powerful say in the political counterweight to the ECB.

As far back as 1990, the European Commission started to explore whether EMU will lead to greater international policy co-ordination between the Euro-bloc and other major countries representing currency blocs such as the United States and Japan. In its publication 'One Market, One Money',[68] the European Commission came to the

---

[66] Art. 109c(2) of the EC Treaty.

[67] Art. 109c(1) of the EC Treaty.

[68] 'One Market, One Money: An Evaluation of the Potential Benefits and Costs of Forming an Economic and Monetary Union' in *European Economy*, No. 44, European Commission, October 1990.

conclusion that there are incentives for various currency blocs to co-ordinate monetary policy as spillovers from either side would have to be taken seriously. Other and more recent commentators are less convinced as it will take Europe some time to become a single currency bloc.[69] Factors which will hinder European representation and which are necessary to produce beneficial results include the current evanescence of responsibilities with monetary policy being the responsibility of the ECB, exchange rate responsibility being shared by the ECB with ECOFIN and fiscal responsibility still the clear responsibility of member states. Further hindrances will come from structural uncertainties relating to future European monetary policy, relative immunity of EU economies from exchange rate fluctuations and a general lack of genuine openness of most European economies.

Political interference in the activities of the ECB is likely to come from ECOFIN and Euro X deals struck for political reasons with little regard for fiscal and monetary policy. A recent example must be a deal engineered by the French government and approved by ECOFIN at their meeting in July 1998 under Art. 109(3) of the EC Treaty which essentially commits Europe to bail out former French colonies through existing exchange rate links with the French franc being continued unchanged with the Euro as from 1st January 1999. With the formal approval of ECOFIN, such an exchange rate agreement is legally binding upon the ECB. It can be expected that France will not be happy with the general wording of Art. 109(3) of the EC Treaty which states that the Council 'shall decide on

---

[69] See *Economic Cooperation in an Uncertain World* by Atish R. Ghosh and Paul R. Masson, Basil Blackwell, Oxford, 1994 and C. Randall Henning's 'Europe's Monetary Union and the United States' in *Foreign Policy* No. 102, Spring 1996.

the arrangements for the negotiation and for the conclusion for such agreements' and that the French government will seek formal ratification of the exchange rate agreement under the terms of Art. 109(1) of the EC Treaty which would commit the ECB to support the exchange rate of former French colonies having been turned into French monetary dependencies. One could argue that the size of the former French colonies in relation to the Euro makes this only a token gesture but it establishes two important precedents. First, member states could use the provisions of Art. 109 of the EC Treaty to pass on fiscal problems such as having to support ailing monetary dependencies from budgets of member states to the ECB by forcing it to support exchange rates or by asking the ECB to tolerate the printing of Euros by a member state, whether the ECB likes it or not. The second consideration would be even more serious as it clearly entails the use of the Euro for political purposes. If the Euro can be used as a shield to support the economies of far-off dependencies,[70] who and what stops the Euro from being used as a sword? It would be intolerable for the ECB to sit down with institutions such as the Federal Reserve Bank to discuss greater monetary policy co-ordination at the same time as ECOFIN and its political masters threaten to conduct a trade war with the US government.

An additional area where the ECB could sooner or later start to clash with the political interests of ECOFIN is in the field of exchange controls. Art. 73 of the EC Treaty allows individual member states to impose exchange control mechanisms (even in secrecy or urgently if proven necessary) should 'movements of capital lead to disturbances in the functioning of the capital market in any

---

[70] See also Art. 227(2) of the EC Treaty as amended by the Treaty of Amsterdam.

member state',[71] i.e. if their balance of payment position was under severe pressure or threatened to come under pressure. This provision however, was incompatible with the free movement of capital and the general development of a single currency and abolished under the terms of [72]the Maastricht Treaty effective from 1st January 1994, the start of Stage Two.

In order to safeguard the overall interests of EMU and the single currency, being well aware of the powers of speculators such as international hedge funds, the Maastricht Treaty introduced a new Art. 73 into the EC Treaty which provides ECOFIN (voting by a qualified majority) with the right to impose exchange control regimes between all EU member states (not just member states participating in the single currency) and third-party countries (essentially the rest of the world), if large movements of capital to and from third countries, usually triggered by severe economic shocks or massive speculative attacks, would 'cause, or threaten to cause, serious difficulties for the operation of economic and monetary union.' Whilst Art. 73(f) of the EC Treaty limits the time span for such 'safeguard measures […] in exceptional circumstances' to a maximum period of six months, there are no provisions contained in the EC Treaty which would prohibit ECOFIN to impose such controls time and time again. Whilst ECB technocrats are likely to ponder over the possibility and clear definition of what constitutes serious difficulties for the operation of EMU, the politicians within ECOFIN will be far more tempted to use the provisions made available under Art. 73(f) of the EC Treaty if they serve European interests and ask questions about their legality later.

---

[71] Art. 73 of the EC Treaty.
[72] Art. G(15) of the Maastricht Treaty.

In may be tempting for EU Finance Ministers to use Art. 73(f) of the EC Treaty in order to clamp down on tax havens such as the Channel Islands or the Isle of Man, especially since they are trying to establish a common withholding tax system. The problem is that Art. 73(f) of the EC Treaty could be used to avoid capital shifts within the EU for example from the current favourite Luxembourg to Austria with its numbered savings accounts or the United Kingdom with its lower tax levels, but it could not be used to stop funds being transferred to the Channel Islands which are not part of EU. Even if the United Kingdom sought to protect its special constitutional relationship with the Channel Islands, more likely however to safeguard the interests of the City of London, the qualified majority in ECOFIN under Art. 73(f) of the EC Treaty provides the government in Westminster with no right of veto to block exchange control measures being designed and erected within the EU to block large movements of capital out of the EU and to the Channel Islands. Nevertheless, when taken into perspective, tax havens around the world have been around for a long time and are here to stay. As long as private enterprise and the banking community at large, ignoring the criminal fraternity, have a vested interest in such facilities, monetary and fiscal policy makers will be directly exposed to the global competitive forces for funding from private and institutional investors. The ECB will learn to deal with these forces just like the Federal Reserve Bank in the US has learnt to deal with tax havens such as the Cayman Islands, Bermuda, etc.

9. Role of The European Parliament

The EC Treaty contains a system of compulsory consultation under which the EP has to be consulted with the EP's greatest weapon under the consultation procedure

being delay. At Maastricht new areas of consultation were added to the EC Treaty that affect the EMI and the ECB:

1. Under Art. 108a(3) of the EC Treaty, the EP must be consulted for the limits and conditions under which the ECB will be able to impose fines or periodic penalty payments for failure to comply with ECB regulations and decisions.
2. Under Art. 109f(7) of EC Treaty, the EP must be consulted for conferring upon the EMI any tasks during the second stage of economic and monetary union for the preparation of the third stage not expressly given in the EC Treaty.
3. Under the assent procedure introduced by the Single European Act, the EP must approve[73] in a single reading any proposal of the Council for amendments to the protocol of the ESCB[74] and/or to entrusting the ECB with new tasks.[75]

The assent procedure is a cruder form of co-decision as there is no scope for the EP to put forward amendments to the measure in question. This compares with the consultation procedure for important institutional matters such as the appointment of the President and members of the Board of the ECB.

On the non-legislative front, Art. 109f(1) of the EC Treaty stipulates that the EP is to be consulted in the second stage of EMU on the appointment of the President of the EMI and Art. 109a(2) of the EC Treaty states that it is to be consulted in the third and final stage of EMU on

---

[73] The EP has to approve the proposed measures by a simple majority of those voting.
[74] Art. 105(5) of the EC Treaty.
[75] Art. 105(6) of the EC Treaty.

the appointment of the President, Vice-President and other members of the Executive Board of the ECB. Given the significant powers that will be enjoyed by the Executive Board of the ECB, these appointments are of great importance.

Although the EP's role is only consultative, it is potentially crucial. As for other appointments where the EP is consulted, when it comes to a public vote in an elected parliament on an individual it would be surprising if that individual wished to take office should the EP reject his or her candidacy. If he or she wished to proceed, it is equally unlikely that the member states would retain the necessary unanimity to proceed with the appointment. It is therefore likely that the required consultation of the EP will amount, in practice, to a vote of confirmation in which the EP enjoys a virtual right of veto. In exercising this right, the EP will organise public confirmation hearings at which candidates are invited to defend their suitability for office. In November 1993, when Mr Lamfalussy as Council nominee for President of the EMI, appeared before the Economic Committee he had replied in writing beforehand to a series of specific questions and answered detailed oral questions for three hours at a public meeting. Subsequently, the EP gave its approval for his nomination and later appointment.

As already outlined above, the ECB must produce an annual report on its activities and on the monetary policy of both the previous and current year to the EP, the Council, European Council and the Commission. The President of the ECB must present this report to the Council and the EP, and the latter can hold a debate on it.[76] The presentation to the EP or any of its relevant committees will be verbal and in person following the US-style hearings of the

---

[76] Art. 109b(3) and EP's Rules of Procedure (1994) Rule 39.

Federal Reserve Bank Chairman under the Humphrey-Hawkins procedure.[77] In addition, the EP can invite the President and other members of the Executive Board to be heard by one of its committees with competence in this area.[78]

Scrutiny within EP committees takes a number of forms including reports on implementation of particular policies and regular questioning of Commissioners, their civil servants and other executives such as the President of the EMI, the Director of the EIB and heads of various Community auxiliary organs. These procedures have already begun well with the President of the EMI as forerunner of the ECB.

However, the independence of the ECB is such that it can and should choose if necessary to ignore the views of the EP and its President and members of the Executive Board can refuse to answer particular questions. This right of refusal is even more potent considering that the tasks and objectives of the ECB and hence the Ten Commandments for all its members and servants can only be changed by amending the EC Treaty itself or its protocols – a far from easy or quick process.[79] Members of the key Monetary

---

[77] See 'The Project of a European Central Bank' by J.-V. Louis in Stuÿck (ed.), *Financial and Monetary Integration in the European Economic Community: Legal, Institutional and Economic Aspects*, Boston, 1993, p.24.

[78] Art. 109b(3) of the EC Treaty and EP's Rules of Procedure (1994) Rule 39 which requires the President of the ECB, and in the second stage of EMU, the President of the EMI, to appear before the relevant committee twice a year and makes it possible for the President and other Executive board members to be invited to make statements and answer questions at other meetings of the committee.

[79] See comments by David Dunnett in *Legal and Institutional Issues affecting Monetary Union*, p.144 who laments that 'The extent of the delegated power given to the ECB is all the more remarkable in that it is virtually irreversible. To reverse the transfer of power would require an amendment of the Treaty, to be ratified with the consent of the

Policy Committee of the EP have gone one step further in their attempts to extract answers from the ECB. It has called for the EP to play a role in supervising the ECB including its interest rate policies. The Monetary Policy Committee pointed to the role of Congress as a possible role model for the oversight and supervision of the US Federal Reserve Bank. Even if this US role model might fall on fertile ground and resemble a reasonable balance between independence and accountability, such direct parliamentary oversight would clearly represent a major shift in text and spirit of the complete independence of the ECB as set out in the EC Treaty. The Monetary Policy Committee may well become a future battle ground for conflicting European interests, especially from France and Germany, where disagreements about the control of monetary policy are still suppressed for political motives within national authorities in order to minimise political and public disapproval of EMU. Eurosceptics still fear that the complete independence of the ECB and the goals of monetary policy with price stability at its heart will become sources of serious conflicts between member states inside and outside the Euro-zone, especially if the conflict is measured in terms of inflation versus employment.

In order to enhance the credibility of the new single currency and EMU as a whole, the EP proposed a freely circulating 100 Euro gold coin. This did not meet with approval from the EU finance ministers. As a compromise solution, the EU finance ministers approved at their meeting in November 1998 the issue of collector coins, provided such issues are approved by the ECB. No collec-

---

legislature of all member states.' Ian Milne describes the independence of the European Central Bank as a 'democratic deficit of immense proportions.' (See *Maastricht: The Case Against Economic & Monetary Union*, p.21).

tor coins in Euro should be issued before January 2002, when national currencies are going to be physically replaced by Euro notes and coins. Although collector coins will be legal tender they will only be so in the country of issue. This means that there will be a single currency but some currency will not be valid throughout the eleven Euro-zone member states. Even if collector coins are not meant for entry into general circulation, the fact that they will be denominated in Euro and issued with the express approval of the ECB should not restrict their legality within the Euro-zone.

10. Other EC Institutions

The Maastricht treaty did not create any new institution for the conduct of fiscal policies which will remain a national responsibility, nor was there any mention of fiscal federalism that might lead to the creation of a much bigger EU budget. The treaty did however make provisions for the strengthening of existing mechanisms of multilateral surveillance, while also attempting to define in some detail what constitutes 'economically correct' behaviour.

Without outright interference in the independence of the ECB, the President of the Council of Ministers and a member of the Commission may participate in ECB meetings but under no circumstances are they allowed to vote.[80] This right of attendance undoubtedly goes a very long way towards accountability thus restoring the balance of power between European institutions into an improved state of equilibrium. Furthermore, the Council may formally submit a motion for deliberation at the Governing Council of the ECB.[81] This instrument of a motion could

---

[80] Art. 109b(1) of the EC Treaty.
[81] Ibid.

also be construed to amount to a full question and answer session where the ECB can be held under carefully worded motions to account for its plans and activities.

Almost as a matter of reciprocity and further outlined below, the President of the ECB will be invited to attend and participate in Council meetings when discussing matters relating to the objectives and tasks of the ECB.[82] Although the European Commission has been unusually silent on the powers to be enjoyed by the ECB and its leading role in the conduct of monetary policy, past experience indicates that a future power struggle between the European Commission and the ECB should not be ruled out.

11. Guardian of the Banking System and Lender of Last Resort

Neither the EC Treaty nor Article 2 of the Statute of the ESCB mentions any specific objective for the ECB to sustain the health and effective functioning of the banking and financial systems. There is also no reference to the possible role of the ECB as 'lender of last resort' to be found anywhere in the Statute of the ESCB or the EC Treaty. Wider interpretation of Article 2 together with Article 3 of the Statute of the ESCB is not necessarily to be ruled out. One of the tasks for the ESCB in Art. 105(5) of the EC Treaty and Article 3 of its Statute is 'to ensure the smooth operation of payment systems'. A justification why central banks have acted as lenders of last resort has often been the fact that bank failures could endanger such a smooth operation.

The Statutes of the ESCB also state the task of having 'to participate as necessary in the formulation co-ordination

---

[82] Art. 109b(2) of the EC Treaty.

and execution of policies relating to prudential supervision and the stability of the financial system'[83], but it is silent on the question of who is to decide what is necessary. Although this specific advisory function for the ECB in the field of Community legislation applies to all EU member states, the Banking Advisory Committee of the European Commission is preparing new proposals for directives in the sphere of banking legislation. There is clearly a conflict between the operation of the ECB acting as lenders of last resort, the fact that under Art. 105(6) of the EC Treaty the right of initiative lies with the European Commission and the obligation of the ECB concerning the maintenance of price stability. It opens the possibility of the ECB draining liquidity in support of its monetary policy objectives but at the same time as a central bank injects it into the market to ward off financial panic.

The Eurosceptic Brian Connolly points out when commenting on the ECB's possible role of lender of last resort that in the United Kingdom and the United States the central bank function in the Anglo-Saxon banking system is to ensure the stability of the financial system, i.e. it is intended to provide a 'public good'[84] enabling private markets to operate more safely and effectively. But where was the Bank of England when Barings Bank collapsed and did the US Federal Reserve Bank step in to stop the collapse of the US Savings & Loans Industry during the late 1980s?

The comparison of central banks in the United Kingdom and the United States with its counterparts in Europe does not really hold. In Continental Europe, central banks have a much greater political role and function

---

[83] Art. 25(1) Statute of ESCB.
[84] See Bernard Connolly, *The Rotten Heart of Europe*, London, Faber & Faber, 1995, p.248.

differing considerably from one country to another. For example in France the central bank has traditionally been an agent or facilitator of government policy but no clear mechanism makes it fully accountable to the electorate. In Germany, the framework governing the Bundesbank is subject to interacting qualifications that are explained in the statute of the Bundesbank placing price stability ahead of accountable political choice and reducing the authority of central government in a federal political system. The Maastricht Treaty and the Statute of the ESCB merely try to reconcile in the area of central bank philosophy the seemingly irreconcilable, but in practice there can be little doubt that with its strong track record the Continental bank lending-driven system will hold sway.

As guardian of a banking system with strong bank lending activity the ECB will be at the centre, not a peripheral facilitator for private markets such as in the highly liquid US paper market. Whether the power that comes with it will be exercised by the ECB stepping into the shoes of German monetary domination or by strict dogmatic central banking policy adherence to override electoral preference, if need be, is still the subject of controversy and conflict. The ECB will be a very different animal from the central banks with which Anglo-Saxon financial markets have had a symbiotic relationship. Prudential supervision will after the commencement of Stage Three of EMU remain within the competence of national authorities according to the principle of 'home country control'. Such control will however be based on the harmonisation of the main national legislative provisions and cross-border co-operation among supervisors under the stewardship of the ECB. To achieve a common understanding on relevant supervisory policy issues, the ECB will set up specific committees composed of representatives of national central banks and national supervisory

authorities from all fifteen EU member states even though Art. 105(5) of the EC Treaty will apply strictly only to those member states participating in the single currency. The Banking Supervisory Sub-Committee of the EMI has already started with this process and a similar committee within the ECB is expected to continue.

The broad framework for financial surveillance and supervision within the EU to ensure financial stability under EMU is gradually evolving, both in terms of the supervisory role the ECB, national central banks and national supervisory authorities and the development of pan-European money and capital markets which a single currency is expected to bring.

In addition to the general state of the European financial sector already being challenged by exposure to Asian countries, Russia and other emerging markets, the ECB is also concerned with the safeguarding of the European financial markets and its participants from systematic risk, i.e. the settlement of international settlement transactions through a network of local and central clearing and payments systems. For this reason the ECB agreed that under specific conditions credit institutions from the four member states not participating in the single currency will be allowed to access TARGET, the ECB's settlement system for clearing EU-wide payment instructions based on a network of many real-time gross settlement (RTGS) national payment systems.

The implementation of EU-wide RTGS systems to settle cross-border payments will undoubtedly help to reduce the risk of losses due to settlement failures but a number of considerations still leave the European financial sector and hence the ECB at its centre wide open to systematic risk:

1. Large value transactions within TARGET use a financial safeguard device called 'intraday credit' which requires financial institutions to lodge and maintain collateral in order to obtain such intraday credit.
2. Although techniques such as 'pooling' and 'earmarking' collateral lodged for the purpose of obtaining intraday credit may help to offset some of the costs of maintaining eligible security with the ESCB, the TARGET price structure for providing payment settlements services appears to be more expensive than established systems.
3. Alternative Euro payment settlement services offered by organisations such as ECS (Euro Clearing Systems privately owned by the European Bankers' Association), EAF (Euro Access Frankfurt 2) or Euro-SWIFT which settle their payments at regular intervals (usually at the end of each working day) have not only announced price structures much lower than those of the ECB, they also do not operate any intraday credit systems and therefore do not require any costly collateral to be placed with them.

The most sensible compromise between the undoubted need to safeguard the European financial markets from systemic risk and the different cost structures would be a compulsory requirement for all high value payments to be settled through TARGET on a real time basis but with a cost structure equal to that of other established service providers such as those mentioned above. Having secured the bulk of high value payments within the EU all settled on a real time basis through TARGET would go some way to reduce the substantial risk of one European bank failure generating a domino effect throughout the Euro-zone. The potentially vast risks and the unexpected speed associated with a financial institution failing in Europe became

painfully clear to regulators when the US hedge fund LTCM (Long-Term Capital Management) had to be bailed out for US$3,500 million. Failure to safe LTCM would have resulted according to an official from the Federal Reserve Bank of New York in 'the potential paralysis of the global financial system'.[85]

Even with TARGET in place, the expected restructuring of the European banking system in an environment where many parts of Europe are simply 'overbanked' but downsizing or even closure of whole banks are almost impossible to achieve, will not bring the expected reduction in systemic risk. Against the background of difficult market conditions in Asia, Russia and throughout the Emerging Markets, cross-border unsecured interbank lending and higher credit risk in local markets to achieve increased yields are expected to grow considerably in Europe even without EMU.

Whilst the ECB will have no direct input in the inevitable restructuring of the European banking sector, the introduction of the Euro will bring even more centralised systems of market surveillance and crisis management. Even if the ECB has been given the mandate to focus almost exclusively on monetary policy and only a limited, peripheral role in banking supervision and no responsibility for providing liquidity support to individual financial institutions, the spirit of the EC Treaty places the ECB at the heart of any European banking crisis. It is yet unclear how a bank crisis in Europe would be handled under the current institutional and relatively vague legal framework of the EC Treaty and the Statute of the ESCB.

Effective crisis management for a possible bank failure in Europe will focus hard on supervisory and regulating responsibilities shared between the ECB and national

---

[85] See 'Rescue' in *The Sunday Times*, 27th September 1998.

authorities and effective mechanisms in order to secure that a particular financial institution can meet all its payments obligations sent through TARGET or any alternative payment settlement systems operated within the Euro-zone. With the ESCB and ECB mirroring in many respects the operations of the German Bundesbank, it is expected that the ECB's main emphasis will be on supervision and prevention as well as behind the scenes brokering of national authorities. The EU however does not have any form of Community-wide deposit insurance and must therefore rely on local schemes to protect the interests of depositors and to ensure that financial institutions are able to settle its payment instructions.

The current institutional framework provides no clear picture as to the first and second line responses to a bank failure within the Euro-zone or with any other EU member state, and the arrangements already agreed between the ECB and national central banks and supervisory authorities concerning the sharing of information appear to be wholly inadequate for a sudden crisis situation. The speed and magnitude of past banking collapses have shown that speed is indeed the most critical factor when handling a financial and systemic crisis, combined with a clear sense of leadership. In the event of a bank failure in Europe, the authorities, politicians and the public at large will look very quickly for a solution to the crisis and who has been responsible for it. The current decentralised approach creates a massive lack of transparency and a vacuum for effective and efficient crisis management. The ambiguity of the EC Treaty and related provisions also reduce any clear accountability on the part of the ECB to a mere moral hazard. The expected pan-European integration and development of European banking groups will sooner rather than later outgrow the capabilities of even the largest national central banks to provide adequate liquidity support

for the market and the ECB will despite its unclear mandate be forced to assume a leading role in European financial crisis management and supervision of financial institutions.

With the ECB expected to assume the mantle of Euro area banking supervision supervisor, where central banking and banking supervision will be conducted strictly at arm's length, the handling of major banking problems with their impact on payment system integrity and central/clearing bank liquidity will create a proximity to monetary stability where the ECB will have to be closely involved in any crises management. Experiences over the last twenty years from the problems afflicting the US savings and loans industry, the banking crises in Scandinavia as well as the banking problems in Japan, other parts of the Far East and in a number of emerging market countries have shown that there are essentially three solutions to handling possible bank failures:

1. Central banks acting as lenders-of-last-resort.
2. Provision of private money.
3. Provision of taxpayers' money.

The separation of central banking from banking supervision, different standards of banking supervision throughout the EU and the consolidation of the banking market as a result of or facilitated by EMU places significant pressures on the ECB to act as lender-of-last-resort. The provisions of the EC Treaty nor the Statutes of the ESCB provide any clear guidance or mechanism how the ECB would act in emergency situations. In addition, the resources available to the ECB raise serious doubts whether the ECB will have sufficient management capacity to successfully handle a bank crises under the current institutional framework. However, with the remit of the ECB

acting as lender-of-last-resort narrowed down to providing emergency funding to financial institutions which are solvent but illiquid and unable to raise central bank funding due to the lack of sufficient or eligible collateral, the likelihood of the ECB having to act as lender-of-last-resort must be considered as remote in the modern banking industry.

With the large majority of bank crises caused by the fact that financial institutions have become insolvent (mainly caused by poor lending policies and asset quality), crises management will usually consist of public or private funds bailing out ailing institutions. Although public authorities have assisted in the provision of market solutions to potential crises, such as the involvement of the Federal Reserve Bank of New York in the rescue of the LTCM hedge fund, the handling of solvency crises within the EU does not fall within the mandate of the ECB nor of national central banks, although the latter will continue to be consulted by national supervision authorities.

The baptism of fire will come for the ECB with possible recurrence of a major stock market crash, a major banking crisis, high price rises for commodity products such as oil or the occurrence of major events such as the outbreak of war or natural disaster. In its 1997 Annual Report, the EMI acknowledges that EMU is expected to increase competition, aid the phenomenon of banking disintermediation and strengthen the need to restructure the EU banking system by means of reduction in excess capacity. The EMI expects a three-layer EU banking system to emerge in which (i) the first layer would be composed of a large number of small, locally based institutions, (ii) the second layer would comprise EU regional players, and (iii) the third layer would consist of very large EU-wide banks which consider themselves to be global players. The challenge for the ECB in its supervisory capacity will be to

monitor the activities of national supervisory authorities in their task to detect the weaker credit institutions and to ensure that they take steps to adapt to the increasing pressure. The ECB has already explored in this respect the use of macroeconomic data in the supervision process in order to explore links between macroeconomic developments and the fragility in the banking systems both as a whole and at the local level.[86]

In the wake of the financial crisis in the Far East and most emerging markets, it has become clear that those countries must improve their standards of transparency and banking supervision. Even banking supervision in the highly industrialised world has been found to be lacking in particular in relation to the secretive hedge funds. The ECB must play a leading role, even become a role model and standard bearer, for modern, efficient, pro-active and innovative banking supervision as the combination of globalised, fast-moving capital markets and fragile emerging market economies can inflict serious damage on the financial systems not only in Europe but on a global scale. Revelations that the Bank of Italy had invested US$250 million in the controversial US hedge fund LTCM Long-Term Capital Management only highlights possible conflicts of interest between European regulators and high risk players able to destabilise local even global financial markets.[87]

Perhaps the ultimate policy conflict for the ECB will be attempts by the global political and financial community to deal with a global threat to the confidence in the institutions of the world's financial system and the fear of recession now having reached all parts of the global

---

[86] See EMI, Annual Report 1997, May 1998, p.78.
[87] 'Bank of Italy put $250m into LTCM', *The Financial Times,* 2nd October 1998.

economy. Under normal circumstances, central bankers would respond to a foreign exchange crisis with tighter monetary policy, but the most appropriate remedy for a banking crisis is looser monetary policy. With both factors likely to exist at the start of EMU, the ECB is pushed in a natural dilemma to which there is not easy remedy.

Current economic wisdom suggests that sound monetary policy can only be pursued in tandem with prudent fiscal policy. Prudent fiscal policy will ultimately reach into the pockets of the private sector either through higher taxes or more indirect means of ensuring that the private sector shares the burden of resolving crises. The taxpayer may however be reluctant to foot the bill especially with the faith in the international financial system badly dented. Although the IMF has borne the brunt of the criticism for the handling of the crises with its intellectual foundations and inflexible bureaucracy repeatedly questioned, it may be the only safety net for risky uncoordinated and untried attempts to haul the global financial system out of its depressive state. International institutions such as the IMF, the World Bank or the BIS may have to be provided with sufficient financial resources to act as the global lender of last resort.[88] It is doubtful whether the ECB could remain outside such a global safety net where ultimately political considerations will come into conflict with the ECB's independence. It is also unclear how the ECB can achieve a lasting balance between credibility, supporting European growth, achieving and maintaining price stability and its responsibilities to the world economy.

---

[88] The US still owes the IMF US$17,900 million in overdue contributions (US$3,400 million for the IMF's credit facilities and US$14,500 million to raise the IMF's core capital. As reported in 'Clinton has clout to end US isolation by funding the Fund', *The Times*, 8th October 1998.

Chapter V
Comparison with German Bundesbank

At its heart, the ECB is closely modelled on the German Bundesbank where the state banks of the German Lander form part of the Bundesbank. Its physical presence in Frankfurt is also expected to give it some of the Bundesbank's credibility in financial markets and may reconcile growing hostile German public opinion to the loss of the Deutschmark as a tried and trusted currency.

	Deutsche Bundesbank (prior to EMU and ESCB)	European Central Bank
Primary (ultimate) monetary objective	Defence of the value of the currency	Maintaining price stability
Secondary monetary objective	General support for the government's economic policy as long as it does not prejudice primary objective	Support for general economic policies in the Community as long as it does not prejudice primary objective
Specification of targets	Target rate/zone for money growth which implies certain inflation target	No obligatory targets other than achievement of primary objective
Independence	Completely independent from government instructions; it may consult government but is not forced to agree with it	Independent from government/other EC institution instructions
Can decisions be overridden	Temporary veto for maximum of two weeks	Only via amendment of EC Treaty (with limited exceptions)
Changes	Through change in legislation (Bundesbank Act)	Most provisions can only be changed through an amendment of the EC Treaty
Appointment of officials	'Zentralbankrat' appointed by mixture Executive Board appointed by mixture of federal and Laender governments	Executive board appointed by member states without derogation and subject to EP approval
Legal personality	Yes, enshrined under Bundesbank Act	Yes under Protocol attached to Maastricht Treaty

The ECB follows the model of the Bundesbank.

There are however, a few crucial differences. There will be no adequate political counterpart to the ECB at the European level, and this absence will give the ECB a degree of real power and non-accountability not experienced by any other central bank in a national system. In addition, the popular attachment to price stability may not be as strong in other European countries as it is in Germany, mainly for historical reasons. This means that popular attitudes towards trade-offs may also be different.

Difficult (i.e. unpopular) decisions will need to be taken, decisions that imply a trade-off between price stability on the one hand and growth and employment on the other, even if many economists claim that a trade-off can only exist in the short term. It will take some time before the ECB will be able to draw on a reservoir of legitimacy that is currently available to its national counterparts. The independence of the ECB is essentially compromised through the Council formulating general orientations for exchange rate policy in relation to non-Community currencies in the absence of an exchange rate system and the Council being responsible for decisions about formal agreements on an exchange rate system. The conclusion to draw is that a truly independent ECB will find it very difficult to function without a more developed European political system.

The Bundesbank, generally acknowledged to be one of the most independent central banks in the western world, albeit in its special area of competence, is subject to reform of its powers and objectives by the German parliament which could change them by amending the Bundesbank Act. A similar situation exists in the United States, where in addition the Federal Reserve Board must promote plural goals between which it must strike a balance acceptable to the administration and Congress.

The ECB will mirror the Bundesbank both as far as its primary goal is concerned – the pursuit of price stability – as well as its organisational structure. The ESCB will be a federal system with a large network of local central banks.[1] Hence the ECB is the nerve centre of an extensive network, officially named the European System of Central Banks. Through the traditional system of local central banks, the ECB will be able to tap into a formal and informal relationship with the commercial banking sector throughout the European Union. Effective monetary control practised by the German Bundesbank has also shown that in addition to the public setting of interest rates or passive reserve/deposit requirements, it also requires a certain amount of 'arm-twisting' by passing messages to commercial banks.

Some experts have argued that the German model, which preserves discretion entirely for the central bank, may be more suitable to economies where there is a history of hyperinflation which 'has entered the public psyche' and where the wish to constrain the powers of central government has played a large role in recent political history.[2] Others have argued that with 'one country [being] able to impose an alien and underperforming model on the eleven

---

[1] Jean Claude Trichet, Governor of the Banque of France in speech entitled 'Economic and Monetary Union as seen by the Banque de France' on 5th June 1998 at the Intermoney XXV Jornadas de Mercado Monetario 1974–1998, Madrid.

[2] See contribution of M. Guitian in paper entitled 'Central Bank Independence: Issues and Diversity of Models' prepared for a workshop on 'Independence and Accountability: The Role and Structure of the South African Reserve Bank' in Pretoria in January 1995. Ian Milnes argues that hyperinflation alone is not just associated with economic mismanagement (for example in Brazil) but with other psychological factors such as military conflicts of the size and destruction of two world wars.

others is a reflection not of common sense or rigorous analysis but of German power.'[3]

However much the ECB will look like the German Bundesbank and however much it were dominated by Germany, it would not of course be the Bundesbank. Whilst the German Bundesbank conducts in a very direct way money market operations through which it injects liquidity into the markets and fine-tunes interest rates, the ECB is not expected to so in such a direct fashion.

The ECB will not automatically enjoy the same market credibility nor political legitimacy (absence of the second being enough on its own to ensure the absence of the first) as the Bundesbank has done for the last forty years. Even if the ECB does resemble in key parts the Bundesbank, Germany is certainly not Europe. It can be assumed with reasonable certainty that the ECB will try to mimic the Bundesbank in the way it interacts with financial markets and that it will attempt to draw from and build on the credibility of the Bundesbank. The ECB will ultimately not be able to behave in the same ways as the Bundesbank, as the culture, structure and behaviour of the European financial markets do not provide a mirror image of the present German system of conservative universal banks. The London financial community which is largely self-regulated, increasingly securitised, disintermediated, internationally orientated and innovative is a good example for the diversity of the European financial markets.

Central banks such as the German Bundesbank and the Federal Reserve Bank have demonstrated with their track record that politically independent and credible central banks are in a position to achieve good results with their monetary policy even without explicit inflation targets and in particular their public announcements as practised by

---

[3] *Maastricht: The Case Against Economic & Monetary Union*, p.13.

central banks such as the Bank of England, the Reserve Bank of New Zealand or the EMU central banks of Spain and Sweden. Without an established track record and to accelerate credibility and accountability, the ECB should perhaps make additional investments in transparency. Inflation targeting as the central driver for monetary transmissions processes leading to price stability and policy transparency seems to be the most appropriate toolkit for the ECB rather than monetary targeting as practised not without its problems by the Bundesbank.

Critics and political alarmists have suggested that the inclusion of soft currencies such as the lire, the peseta and the escudo will imply a softer stance for monetary policy, with higher inflation and essentially a weaker Euro. Nevertheless, the ECB is likely to build on the experience and track of the German Bundesbank and may emulate monetary policy in its early years like the Federal Reserve Bank did under Paul Volcker in the 1980s. This will, if necessary, boil down to offsetting lax and undisciplined fiscal policies with higher interest rates. The experiences of the US dollar in the 1980s have shown that this must lead to the Euro becoming overvalued and volatile. But overvaluation, high interest rates and exchange rate volatility would only rub salt into European wounds of unemployment and lacking competitiveness.

Just like the Federal Reserve Bank under Paul Volcker, the German Bundesbank and probably all other central banks around the world, the ECB will from time to time come under severe criticism from participating member states and even the public at large. Some of this criticism will even be justified as the ECB is bound to make technical errors when setting Euro interest rates, in particular because the ECB will have to overcome during the first couple of years considerable technical difficulties when

trying to establish reliable figures for monetary measurement tools across the Euro-zone.

Chapter VI
Judicial Review

The ECB legislation will be subject to the usual procedures for judicial review in the EC Treaty under Article 173. The ECJ has to ensure the conformity of the EMU system with the provisions of the Treaty as a whole. Whilst the ECJ will not concern itself with the technicalities of EMU it has to exercise judicial control over its implementation. Thus it may be called upon to adjudicate on the exercise of the powers granted to the Community institutions, the conduct of the member states in the performance of their duties and the constitutional issues arising from the creation of the new institutions. It may also have to adjudicate on any potential conflict when the Community conducts external relations in support and relating to EMU, or if there is any conflict what each institution might see as their own prerogative.[1]

Most importantly it will have jurisdiction for any disputes between the ECB and the national central bank, in particular if the national central fail or appear not to fulfil their obligations under the EC Treaty and the statute of the ESCB.[2]

More specifically the CFI will have in accordance with Art. 168 of the EC Treaty jurisdiction[3] in any dispute between the ECB and its servants[4] in matters concerning

---

[1] Art. 173 of the EC Treaty.
[2] Art. 180d of the EC Treaty and Art. 35.6 Statute of ESCB.
[3] Declaration No. 33 annexed to EC Treaty OJ C191.
[4] Art. 36.2 Statute of ESCB.

their employment. In this role, the CFI treats the ECB just like any other EC institution.

The acts or omissions of the ECB will be and are subject to review or interpretation by the ECJ just like the acts or omissions of all other EC institutions. Conversely, the ECB will be able, within its fields of competence, to institute proceedings in accordance with Articles 173 to 178 and 184 of the EC Treaty. The ECJ shall also have jurisdiction to hear cases pursuant to any arbitration clause contained in a contract concluded by or on behalf of the ECB[5] irrespective of whether the contract in question is governed by public or private law.

Since the ECB is subject to non-contractual liability in accordance with Art. 215 of the EC Treaty, cases in that category too would be heard by the ECJ.

The duties of the national central banks under the EMU and the statute of the ESCB will be enforceable by the ECB in a manner analogous to the enforcement actions of the Commission under Art. 169 of the EC Treaty. Accordingly, if the ECB considers that a national central bank has failed to fulfil an obligation under the statute of the ESCB it shall deliver a reasoned opinion to the national central bank with a given time limit in which they can reply and/or comply and, in the event of non-compliance, may bring the matter before the ECJ.[6] A decision of the ECB to bring an action before the ECJ must however be taken by the Governing Council of the ECB.

Decisions for the compulsory retirement of the President and of the Members of the Executive Board of the ECB are within the exclusive jurisdiction of the ECJ.[7]

---

[5] Art. 35.4 Statute of ESCB.
[6] Art. 35.6 Statute of ESCB.
[7] Art. 11.4 Statute of ESCB and Art. 9.7 Statute of EMI.

In line with normal commercial litigation, disputes between the ECB and its creditors or any other person fall within the jurisdiction of the competent national courts unless jurisdiction in such cases has been specifically conferred upon the ECJ.[8] When not performing functions and entering into liabilities that are regarded as being part of the functions of the ESCB, national central banks are liable according to their respective national laws.[9] The ECJ will have jurisdiction to give judgement to any arbitration clause contained in a contract by or on behalf of the ECB, whether that contract is governed by public or private law.[10]

Time is going to be of the essence in order to allow the ECB and the national central banks under the ESCB to react fast to market developments, often within hours, which could otherwise seriously undermine or even destroy the system. How is this going to be ensured? The current judicial process involving the ECJ is far too slow and ineffective. For this reason, the ECB would have to intervene in the market directly instead of the national central bank(s) failing or theoretically even refusing to perform their functions. Alternatively, the ECJ could be granted the capability of passing emergency measures and instruments such as injunctions or orders for specific performance as interim solutions similar to those already in existence under English law.

---

[8] Art. 35.2 Statute of ESCB and Art 19.2 Statute of EMI.
[9] Art. 35.3 Statute of ESCB.
[10] Art. 35.4 Statute of ESCB.

Chapter VII
Stability and Growth Pact

The ever increasing need for co-ordination of budgetary policies between all member states of the EU for a common budgetary policy stance at European level with a view to ensuring a desired policy mix for the EU as a whole will be imperative to resist inflationary pressures and to win favourable consideration for economic situations of individual member states (in particular during economically unfavourable periods) in order for the ECB not having to tighten its monetary policy. Unlike the Federal Reserve Bank in the US, the ECB does not have a dual mandate for price stability and employment which means that it cannot rely on labour mobility and flexibility together with competition to hold inflationary pressures at bay.

The budgetary and monetary disciplines now enshrined in the Stability and Growth Pact, agreed in principle by the December 1996 Dublin European Council, are not only a question of budgetary prudence but also the way to re-establish the possibility of implementing contracyclical budgetary policy provided national budgets are flexible enough (i.e. based on sound public finances) to face up to adverse cyclical economic developments. Member states can rely on the flexibility of the goods and the job markets to preserve the growth potential of their respective economies instead of being able to use devaluation in order to accelerate the adjustment of national economies.

The idea for a budgetary and monetary stability pact stems largely from a proposal by the German government

in order to ensure that budgetary disciplines are adhered to on an enduring basis within stinging penalties for non-compliance. The Stability and Growth Pact was also a second attempt by the French government to create a 'European economic government' as a political counter-weight to the new ECB after not having succeeded with this idea during the negotiations leading up to the Maastricht Treaty. Other EU member states however twice declined to support French proposals considering existing bodies such as ECOFIN and Euro X able enough to handle issues. The ECOFIN Council finally submitted its suggestions for the main elements of a Stability and Growth Pact[1] and agreed in principle to a European Council resolution.

In March 1997 however the European Commission presented amended proposals for Council regulations on the strengthening of the surveillance and co-ordination of budgetary policies[2] and for speeding up and clarifying the implementation of the excessive deficit procedure[3] and both were accepted by the June 1997 Amsterdam Summit together with the Resolution on Growth and Employment.[4]

The ECOFIN Report to the December 1996 Dublin European Council in essence provides under a separate legislative proposal for the continuance of the convergence criteria beyond Stage Three on a rolling basis including those member states which have not adopted the single currency. The budgetary disciplines required for the stability and convergence programmes for the Euro area will be carried outward into the European Union as a

---

[1] Presidency Conclusion (SN401/96 ANNEX), Annex I.

[2] COM (97) 116 final. The regulation entered into force on 1st July 1998 by which time the first wave of member states participating in Stage Three had been identified.

[3] COM (97) 117 final. For the positive opinion of the draft regulation see OJ C211, 12th July 1997.

[4] Presidency Conclusion (D/97/2), Annex I.

whole. Primary supervisory role thereto is assigned to the European Commission. However, updated programmes are to be examined by the Economic and Financial Committee on the basis of European Commission assessments.

Here again lies potential conflict with ECOFIN examining the stability and convergence programmes as well as the avoidance of excessive government deficits for the EU as a whole. ECOFIN would have to assess member states with the strict price stability discipline of the ECB separately from member states not (yet) part of the single currency. Is this really possible especially if monetary sanctions were to apply? At the same time is it fair for the 1997 Amsterdam European Council to agree that the proceeds of sanctions should only be distributed to those member states participating in the Euro?

Critics have argued that the strict no bail-out rule contained in Art. 104b of the EC Treaty and the prohibition of the ECB to grant credit to government bodies essentially to finance fiscal deficits makes the Stability and Growth Pact and with it the strict adherence to fiscal criteria and fiscal sustainability a needless set of rules. Their reasoning is based on the argument that a fully independent central bank and its statutory task of maintaining price stability will no longer allow member states to use inflation as an easy option to eliminate government debt and that the no bail-out rules in Art. 104b of the EC Treaty isolates fiscal policies from other Euro-zone member states. In order to achieve and maintain price stability, the ECB must establish and prove its credibility. Permitting member states to pursue non-conformist fiscal policies would be the first nail in the ECB's credibility coffin. A lax approach by the ECB to sound fiscal policies would sooner rather than later be followed by a test whether the ECB would in practice implement its no bail-out obligations as per Art. 104 of the EC Treaty.

Even with the Stability and Growth Pact in place, there are still no grounds for assuming that disciplined fiscal policy will be automatically observed by all EU member states inside or outside EMU. The provisions of Art. 104b of the EC Treaty and its strict application of the no bail-out rule must lead to different risk premiums becoming payable for the government debt of Euro-zone member states depending on their fiscal discipline. Experiences to that effect can be gleaned from the US where the creditworthiness of different states is reflected in their rating from specialist credit rating agencies and with it directly the rate at which they can borrow funds in the money markets. The aim to achieve the highest possible credit rating is not driven by central bank monetary policy but in many cases strict rules for states to enact a balanced budget and a prohibition to carry forward any budget deficits into the next fiscal year.

Without such strict budgetary discipline in the Stability and Growth Pact, the potential spillover of loose fiscal policies within the Euro-zone places greater political pressure on the strict adherence to the no bail-out rule contained in Art. 104b of the EC Treaty. The credibility of the no bail-out rule is however already undermined by the provisions of Art. 103a(2) of the EC Treaty which allow the granting of financial assistance by the EC to a member state if 'a member state is in difficulties or is seriously threatened with severe difficulties caused by exceptional circumstances beyond its control.' Although the Council must act unanimously[5] before granting such financial assistance, the EC Treaty does not contain any reference what might be considered 'exceptional circumstances'. Benefit has been granted for severe difficulties caused by natural disasters,

---

[5] Art. 103a(2) of the EC Treaty.

where the Council can approve financial assistance by a qualified majority.[6]

The ECB is expected to be vigilant when it comes to the fiscal policies of all EU member states participating in the single currency. Should fiscal prudence of a member state cause a crisis, the ECB will have to make difficult decisions. Should it remind member states of the strict no bail-out provisions contained in the EC Treaty or turn a blind eye to member state solidarity and avoid a possible international banking and finance crisis, especially if the problems are caused by a large sovereign borrower? In the short term, the ECB will have no choice but to increase interest rates and use its discussions within ECOFIN to create peer pressure within the EU and to call on the mechanisms of sanctions and fines to bring member states back into line.

In support for the Stability and Growth Pact but also to answer questions of the future relationship between member states participating in the Euro area and non-participating member states which were already raised in the December 1995 Madrid European Council.[7] The ECOFIN Council made it clear in its progress report to the June 1996 Florence European Council[8] that a new exchange rate mechanism could encourage convergence among the member states not participating in the single currency and assist them in their efforts to eventually join the Euro area. The Dublin European Council endorsed the subsequent conclusions of the ECOFIN Council and the EMI and invited the ECOFIN Council to prepare a draft resolution setting out the fundamental elements of the revised

---

[6] Ibid.

[7] Presidency Conclusions (SN400/95) Part a. and paper published by European Commission entitled 'Exchange Rate Relations between Participating and Non-Participating Countries in Stage Three of EMU' (CSE(95) 2108).

[8] Document 7940/96 of 4th June 1996.

Exchange Rate Mechanism (ERM II) and the EMI to prepare a draft for an inter-central bank agreement for submission to the ECB and national central banks of member states outside the Euro area.[9] The June 1997 Amsterdam European Council[10] in adopting the ECOFIN Report decided that there should be a new ERM from Stage Three of EMU.

This new ERM II is vital for the success of EMU for a number of reasons:

1. It is necessary to safeguard the statutory requirement for the ECB to maintain price stability and new exchange rate orientated measures should force national central banks in non-Euro member states also to pursue the primary object of price stability.
2. Providing the Euro with the necessary stability will further foster the Euro's role as an anchor currency both in terms of monetary and exchange rate policy.
3. There will remain a sufficient degree of flexibility between the Euro and currencies of non-participating member states fostering strategies for economic convergence.

This is provided that any adjustment in central rates can be made in a speedy manner in order to avoid significant misalignments as seen towards the end of the ERM I and that equal treatment of all member states in the fulfilment of the convergence criteria, including the exchange rate stability criterion, is maintained prior to any member state joining the single currency.

To provide the ECB with the necessary tools and controls over exchange rate developments between the

---

[9] Presidency Conclusions (SN401/96 (Annex) II.1).
[10] Resolution of the European Council (97/C236/03).

Euro and non-Euro currencies, the EMI proposed and the European Council accepted that central rates and fluctuation bands should be set by mutual agreement between the ECB, the Ministers of the Euro area member states and their respective counterparts from non-Euro member states. Following a common procedure involving the European Commission and after consulting ECOFIN provided that ERM II can function without prejudice to the primary objective of the ECB to maintain price stability.

With ECOFIN representing participating and non-participating member states in the single currency, it will together with the European Commission be the most suitable body to review the functioning of ERM II and the underlying monetary and financial situation of member states. However, it will be up to the General Council of the ECB to administer the intervention and financing mechanisms as already provided for in Art. 44 of the Statute of the ESCB. As a follow-up to the agreement on a new exchange rate system at the Amsterdam summit in June 1997, the General Council of the ECB endorsed at its meeting on 11th September 1998 an agreement signed between the President of the ECB and the governors of the four national central banks not participating in the single currency on 1st January 1999. The agreement which will have a normal fluctuation margin of 15% either side of a central rate against the Euro will lay down the operating procedures for the new ERM II. However, the Danes already indicated that they would adhere to a tighter trading range of ±2.25% once the agreement became operational on 1st January 1999.

The central rates under the new ERM II for the Danish krone and the Greek drachma to the Euro were set at the same time the irrevocable conversion rates of the eleven EMU member states against the Euro were agreed. The Euro central rate for the Danish krone was fixed at 7.46038

krone (with a fluctuation margin of ±2.25%) whilst the Euro central rate for the Greek currency was set at 353.109 drachma (with a fluctuation rate of ±15%). Although the Euro equated to £0.7058 sterling or 9.5183 Swedish krone on the conversion weekend, the United Kingdom and Sweden are not formally part of the new ERM II.

The new exchange rate mechanism and its membership will be an important condition precedent for future Eurozone member states. Whilst the conventions and procedures of the new exchange rate mechanism will be very similar to those of the existing ERM, there will be one key difference: the signature of the national central bank governors of the four member states not participating in the single currency to the new Central Bank Agreement governing ERM II confirm in principle their acceptance of the operating procedures of the new ERM II, but it does not imply actual participation thus the ECB and the central banks of the member states participating[11] from the non-Euro area will be able to suspend their otherwise automatic unlimited interventions at the margins 'if this were to conflict with their primary objective of maintaining price stability.'[12]

The new ERM II must only be seen as a short-term adjustment mechanism in order to support a member state's willingness to defend the central rate as part of its progress towards convergence and joining of the single currency. Interventions in the foreign exchange markets in order to stabilise exchange rates at either end of the permitted band must be seen as secondary measures as

---

[11] At this stage only Greece and Denmark have indicated that they will participate. The United Kingdom and Sweden have stated that they will not be joining the new ERM II as reported in 'ECB offer link to non-Euro countries' in *The Financial Times* dated 12th September 1998.

[12] As reported during ECB press conference on 11th September 1998.

convergence requires stability-orientated monetary and fiscal policies. The same will also apply to any decision for the possible suspension of compulsory intervention. Improvements within the ERM II compared to the previous EMS include the right of all central banks participating in ERM II to initiate a confidential procedure to reconsider adjustments to the central rates if shifts in economic fundamentals such as purchase power parities warrant it. By transferring this right of action to the ECB and the national central banks this should help to largely neutralise political considerations out of any central rate adjustments and speed up adjustment procedures. With the General Council of the ECB being charged with monitoring the functioning of the new ERM, greater stability between the Euro and EC currencies of member states not yet having joined the single currency should develop as an important yardstick to see how quickly and how successful member states and in future other countries wishing to join the single market and the single currency will be able to adapt their economic, fiscal and monetary policies, thus achieving necessary convergence for joining the Euro at a future date.

The Stability and Growth Pact signed at the Amsterdam summit in June 1997 and coming into force on 1st January 1999 was designed to ensure post-EMU discipline for public finance through an ongoing commitment by each member state to 'avoid excessive government deficits.'[13] When an excessive deficit occurs, the terms of the Stability and Growth Pact set out several steps involving an increasing amount of pressure to be applied on member states through recommendations and notices that they have to take effective measures to correct the excessive deficit. In technical and legal terms the extensive provisions contained

---

[13] Art. 104c of the EC Treaty.

in Art. 104c of the EC Treaty are guided by four key definitions relating to exceptional and temporary circumstances, time limits as well as the application and level of fines.

By claiming exceptional or temporary circumstances, a member state may have the opportunity to escape the sanctions provided by the Stability and Growth Pact even if its deficit exceeds 3% of GDP[14] provided that the deficit[15] is the result of an unusual event beyond its control or in the case of a 'severe economic downturn'. The case for a 'severe economic downturn' has been defined as a fall in real GDP of 2% over a period of four calendar quarters'.[16] A fall of 0.75% to 2% of real GDP over a period of four quarters might be outside the normal range of situations and be regarded as 'exceptional'[17] if there is evidence to support that, for example the abruptness of the downturn or an accumulated loss of output relative to past trends. In addition to the fluctuating balances, the Stability and Growth Pact also stresses that governments of member states must aim to run budget balances or surpluses over the course of an economic cycle.[18]

The Stability and Growth Pact imposes a time limit of 1st March of each year by which member states must submit their final figures relating to 'actual government deficit' and 'government debt'. These figures will be

---

[14] Art. 1 of Protocol No. 5 on the Excessive Deficit Procedure as attached to the EC Treaty.

[15] Art. 2 of Protocol No. 5 on the Excessive Deficit Procedure as attached to the EC Treaty.

[16] Art. 2(2) Council Regulation (EC) No. 1467/97 on excessive deficit procedure, OJ L209.

[17] Art. 2(3) Council Regulation (EC) No. 1467/97 on excessive deficit procedure, OJ L209.

[18] Art. 1 of Protocol No. 5 on the Excessive Deficit Procedure as attached to the EC Treaty.

analysed under the terms of Art. 104c of the EC Treaty by the European Commission to consider whether a member state has not complied with the terms of the excessive deficit procedure. The EU then has three months to make recommendations and to notify member states that they have an excessive deficit.[19] A member state has four months from the date of notification to announce remedial action, which should aim to correct the deficit in the year after it was recorded.[20] In most cases, member states must first attempt to identify the nature of the underlying economic disturbance causing the excessive deficit including its own fiscal policies. If a member state fails to take such action in the four-month period, then the European Council will be able to impose sanctions on the member state involved. The terms and procedures of the Stability and Growth Pact do not distinguish between different types of recession or whether the excessive deficit is home-made or not. The aim is to counteract political pressures with inappropriate policy responses (so-called quick fixes) and restrict the leeway for recessions which would require the use of budgetary stabilisation policies. Hence governments will be forced to 'save for a rainy day' once in EMU, in order to have the necessary room for manoeuvre for budgetary policies during periods of recession.

Sanctions will be initially in the form of non-interest bearing deposits to be lodged with the European Commission.[21] If the deficit persists this deposit becomes a fine after

---

[19] Art. 3(3) Council Regulation (EC) No. 1467/97 on excessive deficit procedure, OJ L209.
[20] Art. 3(4) Council Regulation (EC) No. 1467/97 on excessive deficit procedure, OJ L209.
[21] Art. 11 and 12 Council Regulation (EC) No. 1467/97 on excessive deficit procedure, OJ L209.

two years.[22] If the deficit is successfully corrected, the deposit is returned to the government of the member state. The level of fines[23] payable by a member state has been set at 0.2% of GDP plus 0.1% of GDP for every one percentage point that the deficit exceeds 3% of GDP. The maximum fine is 0.5% of GDP, equivalent to a maximum deficit of 6% of GDP. Interest earned on the deposits lodged with the European Commission and any fines payable under the excessive deficits procedure will be treated as revenue referred to in Art. 201 of the EC Treaty and will be distributed among participating member states without an excessive deficit.[24]

No one denies that the Stability and Growth Pact was a German inspired and, with the benefit of limited hindsight, important feature for ongoing convergence and the macro-economic framework operating within the Euro-zone and indirectly across the EU as a whole. Many sceptics however believe that the mechanics of the fines process against transgressors running excessive deficits of more than 3% of GDP are essentially unworkable. Whether the fines process will ever have to be fully utilised will also depend on whether the European institutional framework can no longer utilise the combination of peer pressure and economic policy co-ordination which has worked so well since Maastricht and the scrutiny of the ECB. The biggest threat to the Euro-zone and the survival of the Stability and Growth Pact will come when economies within Europe have started to converge, and hence the slowdown of economic growth will pose a problem for all governments

---

[22] Art. 13 Council Regulation (EC) No. 1467/97 on excessive deficit procedure, OJ L209.
[23] Art. 12 Council Regulation (EC) No. 1467/97 on excessive deficit procedure, OJ L209.
[24] Art. 16 Council Regulation (EC) No. 1467/97 on excessive deficit procedure, OJ L209.

within the EU. At the same time, governments will start to look for fiscal shortcuts and quick fixes for long term problems. Willem Buiter, Member of the Bank of England's Monetary Policy Committee, even remarked that '[t]here are signs of PMF syndrome or Post-Maastricht-Fatigue in a number of countries.'[25]

Warnings by the President of the ECB that governments within the Euro-zone must aim to achieve balanced budget positions, in particular those member states with high levels of government debt, started to draw the first front lines between fiscal and monetary policy objectives. Wim Duisenberg's 'yellow card' to Finance Ministers was quickly criticised from the sidelines, when French government officials attacked the reasons for the ECB's tough lines. The ECB's reference to preliminary monetary data for the Euro-zone drew the rebuttal 'They just pulled this figure [forecast for structural deficits] out of a hat. They could have chosen any other figure.'[26]

Signals from the new German government and centre-left governments in most EU member states suggest that the ECB will be at the receiving end of political pressure right at the start of EMU, especially if the ECB is prepared to run a tight monetary policy thereby making it harder for Euro-zone member states to generate growth and with it prospects for employment. Greater government spending has raised calls for the temporary[27] relaxation of the Stability and Growth Pact's rigour.

---

[25] 'The UK and Emu' by Willem Buiter, EmuNet, 8th July 1998.
[26] As reported in *The Financial Times* on 11th July 1998 in 'ECB squares up to Finance Ministers'.
[27] Called for by Heiner Flassbeck, Chief Deputy to Oskar Lafontaine, German Minister of Finance, as reported in 'Germany opens door to demise of EMU budget pact' by Henry Engler in Reuters, 10th November 1998.

Of particular concern to the ECB are proposals by Mario Monti, the EU's internal market commissioner, to apply the 'golden rule' economic interpretation to the Growth and Stability Pact. Mr Monti's proposals suggest a different treatment for spending and capital investment, permitting member states to incur structural deficits for capital investments without attracting automatic fines.

Whether Champagne Socialism or Communist-led coalitions, the current political climate in the EU 'has raised the spectre of a Red Euro.'[28] Of particular concern to the guardians of the new single currency are calls from the governments in Bonn and Paris to influence the monetary policy of the ECB and by calling for controls on capital markets. How much this political vocabulary will lead to actual changes in the EMU's constitutional set-up will largely depend on the economic governance practised by Euro X and ECOFIN, the effectiveness of the Stability and Growth Pact and the unanimity within the Council of Ministers. Predictions that the Stability and Growth Pact will eventually be dismantled are clearly unwarranted at this stage.

---

[28] As reported in *The Times* on 14th October 1998 in 'Bankers scared of Red euro'.

Chapter VIII
Legitimacy

The question of legitimacy in the EU should also be considered when looking at the role and functions of the ECB especially in the light of the public debate, even outright opposition, surrounding the Maastricht Treaty.[1] The question of legitimacy within the EU arises if 'the power of the Community institutions to act is seriously challenged and their purpose questioned, if their very existence is opposed by a significant proportion of the public.'[2] At the same time, it is often linked to transparency and accountability from the democratic systems of the EU member states up to the various European institutions, including the ECB.

Essentially all member states of the EU are both market economies and democracies. But having these two common denominators does not mean that we can merge them like a simple mathematical equation and concentrate only on the numerator. Creating a single European market is different from creating a single European democracy and this problem lies at the heart of the fact that political union has made comparatively so little progress when compared with economic union. This has been magnified by the fact that the European Union is a highly complex and still evolving entity without equal in the modern world.

---

[1] Manifested in the initial negative outcome of the Danish referendum, the close result in France and the intense political debate in the UK.
[2] Grainne de Burca, *The Quest for Legitimacy in the European Union*, (1996) 1 MLR 349 at p.351.

Developments already on the horizon ranging from future enlargement to reforms to the common agricultural policy as well as ongoing questions concerning sovereignty, subsidiarity and legitimacy will add further challenges to the emerging model constructed with reference to and based on conventional political theory.

Critics commonly blame the uneasy evolution of the Community as a whole on an inherent democratic deficit within the EU institutions whilst at the same time describing them as extensions of national democratic institutions. But if one accepts that European together with local, regional and national institutions build up several layers of democratic interaction, even competition, one could argue that the EU does not suffer from a democratic deficit but enjoys a healthy yet somewhat untidy democratic surplus, at least since the 1996 inter-governmental conference.

Although there appear to be no clear and immediate answers to the question of legitimacy within the EU, despite constant calls for further reforms of the EC institutional structure, the ECB will have in response to the underlying causes for criticism concerning legitimacy, multi-level governance, a proper constitutional design and administration, a sufficient level of transparency and openness of procedures and most importantly through its primary task of maintaining price stability a singular set of values on which everyone can agree down to the individual citizen of the EU.

The development of European democratic principles and hence a lasting counterbalance to questions of legitimacy can only be the sum of unselfish behaviour between member states, equal treatment of all member states and the pursuit of common goals and objectives supported by the EU institutions as the machinery to put those principles into effect. The first visible signs can be found in the EP where political parties already have to address in far greater

detail the political agenda of the European Union and not only deal with the politics of member states.

So far we have not yet completed the machinery for such a monumental task, a task made more difficult by the fact that the plans are still being changed. Similar to the ECJ, the ECB as a non-political institution must refer the task of drawing up any possible amendments to the democratic process of the EU and should only consider proposals strictly limited to those which are relevant to its own institutional position.

Most observers now agree that EMU entails the transfer or delegation of national sovereignty to a centralised policy driver. Any doubts as to the legitimacy of this transfer or delegation of hitherto national powers could lead to a loss of authority for the ECB and the ESCB. Affected parties may openly start to question, even legally challenge the legitimacy of the ECB and with it the EU's supreme monetary institution. The European integration process over the last twenty years and the constitutional backing of the ECB within the EC Treaty should provide it with sufficient certainty as to its powers and purpose.

Instead of questions relating to the legitimacy of particular institutions, EMU will add to some extent to the uneasy evolution of the Community as a whole and the questions relating to an inherent democratic deficit within the EU institutions to which the ECB has been added since the Maastricht Treaty. Questions relating to legitimacy will have to be assessed against a number of expected developments:

1. Will EMU create political and social pressures for greater co-ordination, even centralisation of European macroeconomic policies?
2. Will these forces push Europe into a decision-making paralysis where subsidiarity will be in open conflict with

calls for greater centralisation to ensure effectiveness and efficiency?
3. Will EMU and the Euro affect relations with the rest of the world, in particular the United States and within organisations such as GATT, the IMF and the World Bank?

The clear mandate of the ECB, somewhat handicapped by a limited supervision role of the EP, will lead to a significant shift of power from member states to a central institution based in Frankfurt, at least in terms of monetary policy and related policy instruments. At the same time, the Growth and Stability Pact forces member states into fiscal corridors with what critics argue is one arm tied behind their backs when member states aim for no or only small deficits, say up to 1% of GDP. The Growth and Stability Pact still allows those with deficits up to 3% of GDP considerable freedom within national fiscal policies to deal with cyclical economic forces including mild recession. In case of severe national recession, the effects of which are likely to be felt across the EU, the Growth and Stability Pact contains safety valves and override mechanisms.

When the founding fathers of the European Union signed the Treaty of Rome they had a grand vision which had to be filled with political and economic life and institutional arrangements which accompanied expansion to the current fifteen member states. EMU represents a new development in the evolution of the EU because it is the first EU project which actively considers a two tier system. At the same time, the EU is considering expansion to perhaps as many as twenty-five member states. The question of legitimacy comes right to the forefront if the EU develops into an *à la carte* union where member states start to choose those elements of the EU which are to their liking, hence the commitment by all member states to all

agendas is no longer required. Developments since the Single European Act have shown that the benefits for member states from co-operating on a wide range of issues and from granting concessions when pursuing a single agenda are greater than from just choosing those elements of EU policies which are advantageous for a member state at the time. Nevertheless, the EU might have to fine-tune or even change some of its decision-making processes before it can seriously consider enlargement without a resulting paralysis and the further development of European democratic principles.

Most economists believe that the ultimate objective of all economic activity is consumption and that consumption increases the welfare of the individual consumers. Hence many economists since Adam Smith have been primarily concerned with demonstrating how an economic system would maximise the welfare of the community. With the objectives of maximising social welfare in a democratic society defined in the most nebulous terms and depending who is in power, there can be no substitute for informed judgement in the evaluation of benefits. If the net benefit cannot be defined in a rigorous, readily measurable and unambiguous manner, it is unlikely that any project, including the single currency, has maximised the benefits of society.

The question of legitimacy will under the current institutional framework which accompanies EMU be debated again when it comes to international co-ordination of monetary and fiscal policy. A particular painful experience for the UK will be the fact that the voting arithmetic within the Euro X will mean that decisions made by the Euro X will carry the day in ECOFIN and hence deprive the UK of its voice.

Many international institutions such as the EBRD, IMF, the World Bank, G7 and GATT will accept the Euro as an

international trading and reserve currency in partial replacement of the US dollar. These institutions will increasingly look to the representatives of the Euro when conducting and agreeing direction on monetary and fiscal policy at an international level. The growing use of the Euro when trading with the rest of the world will undoubtedly foster further awareness of Europe as a single entity but it will also lead to a demotion of some member states and their currencies. The standing of Canada and the implied inclusions in the US dollar bloc serves as an example.

European representation on an international basis has been divided in the Maastricht Treaty. Whilst European monetary policy will be determined by the ECB and hence be represented by the President of the ECB, European fiscal policy remains the prerogative of member states and will be represented internationally by a formula of common denominators of national fiscal policies expressed externally through Euro X by the eleven member states participating in EMU at the start of Stage Three on 1st January 1999. This however, clearly demotes the role of ECOFIN, a distinction which will carry little weight for international trading interests.

Chapter IX
Risk of Failure and Possible Alternatives

Although the Delors Committee, which was not an official one in the conventional sense, was more specific than Werner in many ways, it did not develop an economic rationale for EMU as its academic member Dr Thygesen admits. This was understandable given its terms of reference which requested a technical blueprint, not an academic study. Less defensible was the Report's reluctance to consider alternative routes to EMU, apart from a brief review of the parallel currency approach which despite a respectable European pedigree received rather summary dismissal.[1]

One possible compromise that has been mentioned, and adopted in New Zealand, is for the government to subcontract monetary policy to the central bank, and make it responsible for achieving precise inflation objectives albeit with some escape clauses. This has worked well in New Zealand, but it does not ensure long-term credibility because the government can change the central bank's objectives from one period to the next. Without a EU federal government, this solution is not open to the EMU in any case.

Sir Leon Brittan advocated an independent ECB of a federal nature administering a single currency as part of

---

[1] Report on Economic and Monetary Union in the European Community, Luxembourg, 1989, p.33.

monetary union and urged the British Government as far back as 1990 not to reject monetary union and 'end up in the slow lane of a two-speed European Community.'[2] At the time, the British Government was advocating a 'hard ECU', a parallel rather than single currency, and was totally opposed to the idea of handing over control of monetary policy to an independent central bank of any shape and form.[3]

Although not specifically an alternative to EMU, it had been suggested that a trial period should be conducted before full EMU becomes effective in which monetary policy would be co-ordinated on a pan-EC basis.[4] Instead of the Bundesbank (which had become the unofficial ECB anyway through its dominant position within the ERM and with central banks of other member states such as Belgium, Luxembourg, Holland and Austria shadowing the majority of its monetary policy actions) targeting the German money supply and the other ERM members simply targeting in effect their exchange rate movements against the Deutschmark, all members of the ERM would target the domestic components of their respective money supplies. The aim and overriding interest would be to achieve a commonly agreed monetary target for the ERM area as a whole in order to produce a commonly agreed target for the money supply, inflation, output and employment within the area as a whole and not for each participating member state on an individual basis. Not surprising was the opposition of the German Bundesbank to this proposition as it essentially did

---

[2] Sir Leon Brittan in *The Times*, 28th March and 18th July 1990.

[3] The 'Major plan', announced in a speech to the German Industry Forum by John Major at the time Chancellor of the Exchequer on 20th June 1990 and reported in *The Times* on 21st June 1990.

[4] Marcel Letelier (pseudonym) in 'Axes pour sortir de la crise du SME' in *De Pecunia*, Brussels, August 1993, revealing existence and details of such plan.

not like the suggestion of having to share responsibility for monetary conditions inside the recently reunited Germany and it did not believe that central banks of other member states would act irrevocably and single-mindedly according to price stability rules.[5] The plan was finally rejected by the politically astute members of the European Commission as nobody would ever believe that any member states would grant priority to Community interests over national interests.

There are still advocates (largely from those who oppose EMU altogether and those who are concerned that economic convergence is not sustainable) for postponing EMU or even abandoning Stage Three. The thrust of their argument are the dilemma of achieving the triplicate goals of strict economic convergence, the largest possible number of member states participating and the fixed start date of 1st January 1999. Although postponement is technically conceivable at any stage, both EMU and the start date of 1st January 1999 are unequivocally enshrined in the EC Treaty and cannot be undone simply by declaration. One way to enact the delay would be to change the Maastricht Treaty, but this would require unanimity, plus parliamentary ratification and referendums in some member states – a course of action that should be considered as highly unlikely. A second way to enact a delay of EMU would be to create an empty shell. Under this scenario, EMU would proceed as planned and on schedule to satisfy the formal requirements of the EC Treaty, but no member state would actually take part following a decision by the European Council that no country has strictly fulfilled all conver-

---

[5] See Bundesbank's Monthly Report for February 1992 which mentions a possible 'all for one and one for all'. The rejection of the plan was confirmed by Erik Hoffmeyer, Governor of the Danish Central Bank in a conference speech on 'Denmark and the European Union' in Luxembourg on 9th February 1994.

gence criteria. Again this course of action must be considered as highly unlikely as some member states are on course for achieving convergence criteria. In any case, the political heavyweights of Germany and France ensured that EMU will go ahead and start on schedule on 1st January 1999.

There is hardly any historical precedent as an answer to the question of whether there can be a central bank without a corresponding political authority, and most critics of EMU do not propose alternatives to the current framework as set out in the Maastricht Treaty but suggest an immediate cessation of further integration not only in terms of monetary policy but also political integration. As their most common features, such critics suggest that the wielding of a veto by a member state in the Council of Minister gives it substantial power, and within a Europe of Nations powers are to be transferred away from EU institution back to governments of member states to achieve a Europe with flexible architecture. In addition, some critics see the biggest problem to be the power of the ECJ as the most federal of all the European institutions and allege that it is the role for every judge at the ECJ to push the present structure of EC ever onward in a federal direction. Nevertheless, the ability and the right of the ECJ to independently interpret the updated preambles, articles and other constituent parts of the EC Treaty will in the long run also benefit EMU and the ESCB.

If things went wrong after Stage Three, participating member states would have available to them the ultimate possibility of leaving EMU. At the same time, it would be difficult to expel member states from EMU against their will. The reintroduction of a new local currency instead of common money would not only be costly but also hardly stop citizens of one region using the previous single currency. The political consequences of one member state

wishing to withdraw from EMU and/or even the EU would undoubtedly be extremely damaging and likely to facilitate the collapse of EMU. The provisions of the EC Treaty do not cater for a member state leaving the EU and it would have to be considered by a member state as a last resort. Nevertheless it should not be ignored together with the notion that fiscal coherence within EMU would inevitably lead to closer political union.

Whilst Euro-sceptic economists in the United Kingdom and even in the United States have made their fair share of headlines predicting that EMU will eventually collapse after a slow and painful death rather than as a result of a sudden disaster, reality suggests that a single currency will replace national currencies early in the new millennium. Even at this late stage member states could decide to withdraw from EMU but this would require time to implement and most national governments would have to seek a mandate of their electorate to do so – most likely through a referendum or a difficult to achieve two thirds majority in parliament. The reintroduction of national currencies would also require a considerable period of preparation. Once EMU has been fully established, the risk pendulum will swing firmly in favour of continuing with EMU on the grounds that it will be more predictable and hence calculable.

EMU will after the start of Stage Three on 1st January 1999 set in motion the final portion of an irrevocable and irreversible process finalised in Maastricht and under which:

1. Currencies of participating member states will cease to exist as independent national currencies and will be tied to each other with fixed rates of exchange.
2. Member states will legally no longer be allowed to bring national currencies back to life.

3. National currencies of participating member states will be Euro surrogates and only have representative form for the Euro until its physical introduction in 2002.

As already mentioned above, even though national currencies will have been irrevocably abolished, economic and/or political considerations may still entice member states to withdraw from EMU and in this process introduce a new local currency. The withdrawal from EMU and the introduction of a new local currency and its relating complexities as well as the enormity of its effects must not be underestimated and are without modern historic precedent. The break up of the former Yugoslavia and the introduction of local currencies in Croatia and Bosnia-Herzegovina offer no conclusive lessons as political uncertainty and economic life in both countries saw in practice the introduction of the Deutschmark as the unofficial currency.

A sudden break-up of EMU would entail massive risks with national currencies floating freely on an erratic basis with no ERM holding them together and driven apart by massive speculative attacks. Hence any hint of a break-up of EMU would never be an orderly process and not without serious political fallout across the EU.

The collapse of EMU can never be fully ruled out but the likely trigger will almost exclusively come from political events in times of severe economic pressures and imbalances not witnessed since the 1930s. However, experiences over the last sixty years have shown that conditions of periodic hardship and distress have not led to the break up of ever closer political and economic ties but the opposite.

A long and detailed report[6] published by the Association for the Monetary Union of Europe concluded that the higher the uncertainty about the real costs of leaving EMU, and unless overwhelming benefits can be had or at least perceived to be had from leaving EMU, the less the probability of a member state leaving EMU. The report also points out that the pursuit of price stability is a powerful incentive for member states staying within EMU, unless EMU will consistently result in higher inflation compared with the previous track record of a member state on a national basis. What makes this reasoning such a subjective matter is the Keynesian view that member states have the possibility of a trade-off between inflation and unemployment although experience since the late 1970s has shown that the higher the rate of inflation, the lower the possibility of a successful and lasting trade-off.

In addition to this trade-off between inflation and unemployment, governments in some member states have also used flexible exchange rates as a monetary policy instrument. Their real impact on active economic demand management must be questioned and weighed up against the far more tangible benefits which can be had from efficient monetary policies.

The intention of any member state seeking withdrawal from EMU will not produce a repeat of what has become known in the UK as 'Black Wednesday', when the Chancellor of the Exchequer was forced to withdraw from the ERM, but will represent a mammoth task to be undertaken against the background and with reference to international treaty obligations enshrined in the Treaty of Rome and all its related undertakings.

---

[6] 'The sustainability of monetary stability' by Stefan Collignon in *The Sustainability Report* published by the Association for the Monetary Union of Europe.

Member states can essentially choose between two forms of withdrawal from EMU – a friendly one completed after multilateral negotiations or an unfriendly unilateral exit without the explicit agreement of fellow EU and EMU member states. The decision by a member state to unilaterally withdraw from EMU would very likely be the result of a fundamental change of circumstances ('*clausula rebus sic stantibus*'). Such a severe change where a member state would have to face an unforeseeable and intolerable situation would permit under public international law the member state's severance of treaty obligations.[7] Even if the terms of the Stability and Growth Pact could create such drastic circumstances, i.e. an annual fall of GDP well in excess of 2%, all treaty mechanisms for dispute settlement and control mechanisms must previously have been exhausted.[8]

A negotiated exit from EMU and hence the EU as a whole would be preceded by complex and lengthy negotiations with the remaining member states. With reference to the activities of the ECB and the ESCB, a number of financial matters would have to be resolved:

1. Withdrawal of the Euro within the territory of the member states leaving EMU.
2. Re-introduction of a new local currency by the departing member state as replacement for the Euro.
3. Refund or sale of member state's share capital in ECB and share of foreign currency reserves deposited with the ECB.
4. Release of withdrawing member state's national central bank from ESCB.

---

[7] Art. 62 of the Vienna Convention of the Law of Treaties.
[8] Art. 219 of the EC Treaty.

The refund or sale of the share capital and foreign currency reserves deposited with the ECB will be crucial for the member state leaving EMU as those funds will be crucial for supporting any new local currency. The valuation of the original contribution to the share capital and the original share of foreign currency reserves will be very difficult to calculate as the denomination and structure of the ECB's foreign currency reserves will have changed over time in line with its monetary and reserve policy considerations. At the same time, the central bank of the member state leaving EMU will claim its share of any profits achieved but retained up to a level of 20% of net profits by the ECB under the terms of Art. 33 of the ESCB statutes.

Whilst terms are being negotiated for the exit of member states, the fiscal positions of the remaining member states and the stability of the Euro as a whole might also be seriously affected. For this reason, a sale of the share capital and foreign currency reserves with the ECB of the member state leaving EMU to the remaining member states would be far more preferable to an outright repayment or a partial retention with the ECB. This could counteract any possible crisis in market confidence in the Euro as sufficient funding would be retained by the ECB and the ESCB to provide strong support for the Euro. Should the remaining member states not be able or willing to buy out the withdrawing member states this would put the entire EMU under significant pressure and severely undermine the credibility of the ECB as it would no longer be able to effectively defend the Euro which would lead to extreme volatility in the Euro's external value vis-à-vis other major trading currencies. Given the implications for all parties involved, no difference should be made if a member state decides to withdraw prior to the completion of Stage Three in 2002 or at any time thereafter.

If the obstacles for a negotiated withdrawal from EMU seem to be daunting, the implications and hurdles for a member state unilaterally withdrawing from EMU must be monumental. The starting point for any such considerations will be difficult to find as the EC Treaty does not make any express or implied references for a member state leaving the EU either by negotiation or by an unilateral course of action. In international treaty terms, an implied[9] right of withdrawal may be argued by a member state but ever since the Maastricht Treaty references to EMU speak of its irreversibility and irrevocability. As with any contractual agreement, a breach of contract by one side, such as the member state unilaterally seeking to withdraw from EMU might give rise to a claim for damages and compensation by the other side, the remaining member states.[10] Whilst both sides would have to wait for a judgement by the ECJ, commercial and practical realities would suggest that both sides would start to protect their own interests by withholding payment or freezing assets of the member states wishing to withdraw followed swiftly by measures in the other direction.[11]

The turmoils in the financial markets of the Far East and Russia escalating into an almost global financial crises and the apparent inability of the IMF to offer early and effective remedies to those countries affected have rekindled the debate for a new international monetary order. Politicians have started to suggest that: 'We should not be afraid to think radically and fundamentally. We need to commit ourselves to build a new Bretton Woods for the next

---

[9] See Art. 56 of Vienna Convention of the Law of Treaties and cases Danisco Sugar v. Alimänna, Case C-27/96 and Opel Austria GmbH v. EC [1996] ECR-II 39.

[10] Royal Hellenic Government v. Vergottis Ltd. [1945] 78 Lloyds List Rep. 292.

[11] See USA v. France Air Services Agreement [1978] 54 ILR 304.

millennium'.[12] These ideas do not seem too far-fetched considering that the ECB will have to build as the representative of one of the three leading currency blocks in the world international co-operation into its own rule book for monetary policy. The ECB is also aware that some of the high expectations in a system of flexible exchange rates have not been met and that so-called 'currency pegs' allowed countries to achieve unrealistic exchange rates which could only be maintained for a limited period of time.

The intellectual and ideological discussions of the economist community, political and economic think tanks as well as central banks at the beginning of the twenty-first century will focus again on achieving what the IMF had defined as its main purpose: 'To promote exchange stability, to maintain orderly exchange arrangements among members, and to avoid competitive exchange depreciation.'[13] Systemic risks exposed by exchange rate instability and free movement of huge amounts of capital on a global scale have developed into real threats to price stability.

Political initiatives for a 'New Bretton Woods' are also accompanied by calls from politicians and even some economists to re-impose capital controls in order to limit the impact of speculators and to restore public confidence in the financial markets, especially in those countries most affected.[14] Any New Bretton Woods international monetary

---

[12] Tony Blair as quoted in Peter Bofinger's paper for the Conferenza Annuale dalla Facolta' di Economia, Universita' Pavia, entitled 'The Euro and the "New Bretton Woods"', 10th October 1998.

[13] Art. 1, Articles of Agreement, International Monetary Fund.

[14] 'If allowing free capital movements means that economic policy must play by the rules of the confidence game, sooner or later the world is going to decide that this game in not worth playing.', Paul Krugman in 'The Confidence Game', *The New Republic*, 5th October 1998. 'The hour-to-hour and day-to-day behavior of exchange rates is largely

order would have to accommodate a vast range of experiences and expectations gained since 1973. It would have to:

1. Provide solutions to the dilemmas between the flaws contained in both fixed and floating exchange rate regimes.
2. Provide exchange rate stability without the tensions caused by currency pegs or other forms of artificial currency links.
3. Tame the speculative elements of foreign exchange markets.
4. Provide regulators and central banks with tools to deal with asymmetric shocks supported by an efficient and timely system of transparency and accountability of the private sector, national authorities and international financial institutions.

The message from most central banks including the ECB is the rather basic view, one could call it 'central bank instinct' that monetary stability in the international markets is built on the assumption that the whole is as good as the sum of its parts, i.e. if each country keeps its own house in order the global financial markets will also enjoy the benefits of stability. However, as long as elaborate econometric studies are unable to explain the actual behaviour of flexible exchange rates based on fundamental macroeconomic variables, central bankers including the ECB will continue to consider the flaws contained in the system of flexible exchange rates as an acceptable price for their economic and political independence.

Economists accepting such a challenge have started to outline the potential framework of such a 'New Bretton

---

determined by the instincts of interbank traders', Peter Isard in *Exchange Rate Economic*, Cambridge Surveys of Economic Literature, p.23.

Woods'.[15] They do not propose the reintroduction of capital controls to stop 'abnormal' capital flows (modern technologies used by both the private and the banking sector would make it impossible in any case to control short-term capital movements) but to strengthen central banks in their ability to defend exchange rates. The framework of a 'New Bretton Woods' is based on the assumption that the establishment of the Euro creates three major currency blocks (US dollars, yen and Euro) of equal importance and with it requiring equal treatment. Other currencies would be linked to these three anchor currencies based on their 'regional proximity or trade structures'.

The framework for the three core currencies would be based on a parity grid with the central banks of each currency area agreeing a sustainable set of exchange rates with an intervention mechanism similar to the European exchange rate mechanism which would permit each currency to float freely within an agreed band either side of the parity rate. Should a currency break outside its agreed intervention point, all three central banks would be obliged to intervene in the foreign exchange markets by buying or selling foreign currency assets without a corresponding obligation to repurchase or sell these foreign currency assets later. This would provide the financial markets with substantial 'firepower' and an extended time horizon to withstand speculative pressure. Such an extensive mutual support agreement would require the central banks within those core areas to closely align their monetary policies with a central objective of maintaining price stability.

---

[15] See 'The Euro and the "New Bretton Woods"' by Peter Bofinger, paper for the Conferenza Annuale dalla Facolta' di Economia, Universita' Pavia, 10th October 1998. Prof. Bofinger of University of Würzburg comes from the same academic stable as Otmar Issing, former chief economist of the Bundesbank and now Executive Board member of the ECB.

Non-compliance, perhaps independently observed and adjudicated, by one central bank would lead to the termination of the unlimited intervention support guaranteed by the other central banks. Long-term economic development and unexpected shocks would still require one-off adjustments to the central parity rates from time to time. The costs incurred by the central bank with the appreciating currency would have to be shared under a mutual support mechanism on a pre-agreed formula (perhaps equally) by all central banks. Central to this system of core currencies would be economically and politically fully independent central banks, each committed to achieve price stability and equipped with the same armoury of monetary policy instruments.

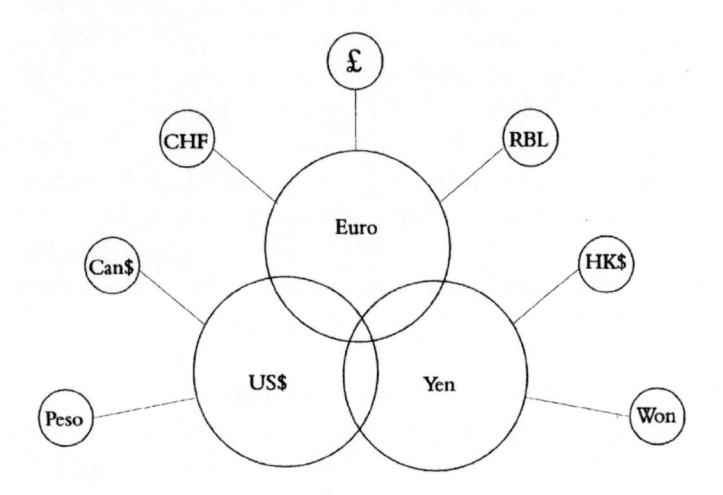

In order for currencies of satellite countries not to impose inflationary risks on the core currencies, each country would have to establish economic and monetary safeguards similar to those countries wishing to join EMU. These would include an independent central bank, prudential supervision of the financial markets and fiscal policy within the limits imposed by the Stability and Growth Pact. An actual link to a core currency would only take place after each country has satisfied certain 'alignment criteria' similar to the convergence criteria contained in the EC Treaty.

Chapter X
The Opt-out of the United Kingdom

Under a special protocol annexed to the Maastricht Treaty, the United Kingdom has negotiated the right to opt out of Stage Three of the EMU without the positive decision of the government and parliament. In any case, the United Kingdom should have notified the European Council by 1st January 1998 if it intended to move to Stage Three.

If the United Kingdom does not join Stage Three, and all indications and statements by the present government so far point towards the fact the United Kingdom will not do so until 2002 even though all economic indicators suggest that the United Kingdom would comply with all convergence criteria except EMS membership. It will retain control of the monetary and exchange rate policy[1] and will be free from the participation in the ESCB with its primary objective to maintain price stability.[2] It will not issue Euro bank notes and coins,[3] free from the regulatory framework of the ECB[4] and will therefore not be subject to EC discipline. However, having accepted Stage Two, it will still be able to benefit from Community assistance in cases of

---

[1] Art. 109 of the EC Treaty.
[2] Art. 105(1), (2), (3) and (5) of the EC Treaty.
[3] Art. 105a of the EC Treaty.
[4] Art. 108a of the EC Treaty.

difficulty[5] but in return is bound to avoid excessive public deficits.[6]

The United Kingdom is still obliged to fulfil the large majority of its treaty commitments, in particular in respect of structural funds which could become very important should the policies of the ECB foster economic divergence. In relation to monetary policy, the United Kingdom will still be subject to obligations of central bank independence[7] and may be represented in the Economic and Financial Committee.[8] This could cause a difficult but interesting dilemma. Not being able to influence the monetary policies of the ECB under its opt-out clause would not free Britain from having to pay up its not inconsiderable share to deal with problems such as high unemployment through the various systems of transfer or EC structural funds.

During its absence the weighted vote of the United Kingdom will be inapplicable when computing the qualified majority for the EMU decisions. Moreover, the United Kingdom cannot participate in the appointment of the Executive Board of the ECB, the ECB statutes will not apply to the United Kingdom and references to the Community or the member states will not include the United Kingdom. References to national central banks will not include the Bank of England. Although the Bank of England must not pay its subscription to the capital of the ECB, it will indirectly provide contributions to its operational costs on the same basis as national central banks of member states without a derogation.

EMU has often raised the question of sovereignty and opinions remain divided whether they are surrendering or

---

[5] Art. 103a(2) of the EC Treaty.

[6] Art. 104c(1) of the EC Treaty.

[7] Art. 107 of the EC Treaty.

[8] Art. 109c(2) and (4) of the EC Treaty.

'pooling' national sovereignty under the umbrella of a single currency. Strictly speaking this is not the case. Member states are delegating powers over which they enjoyed a virtual monopoly to European institutions. Just like in a marriage member states, if instructed by their electorate, could elect to withdraw from EMU, or even the EU, and after a messy divorce go their separate ways. The consequences would be bitter and severe for both parties – for the country withdrawing and for the remaining member states. The institutions of the EU would be affected just like children where symbolic links and traditional willingness to be bound together would violate hitherto existing taboos and diplomatic precedents. But unlike a divorce under national laws of a member state, the EC Treaty does not cater for the withdrawal from EMU or the EU.

The United Kingdom is free to change its mind and move at any time to Stage Three if it satisfies the four criteria of convergence and complies with the consequential obligations.

Member states not participating in Stage Three from day one are likely to suffer some penalty in the form of an increased interest rate premium but its size is hard to predict. Whether the interest rate rises during 1997 and 1998 in the UK, arguably to stop the domestic economy from overheating, will already include such a premium is difficult to predict. The present UK government's stated intentions to continue their domestic fiscal policy against the convergence criteria and with a view to participate by the year 2002 should make this possible penalty very small.

Can the UK stay out when the rest of Europe deals in Euro? When the ECB moves its interest rates up or down, would Britain not have to follow suit? The logic of Britain's trade pattern with the rest of Europe would suggest that sterling should stick closely to a particular value of the Euro, adjusting its interest rates as and when necessary. But

the British public might find it unacceptable to pay the full cost of shadowing the Euro, which would probably involve higher interest rates, when it was denied the benefits of participation such as, in crises, the support of the ECB.

Political developments over recent months suggest that the current Labour government is warming to the idea of joining EMU especially since the UK's economic and budgetary performance do not cause concern for meeting the strict convergence criteria although the EMI was not happy with sterling's volatility.[9] By continuing to sit on the fence of EMU and with the practical benefits of retaining monetary jurisdiction, often expressed as the 'right to devalue' which speaks volumes for British post-war policy and industrial performance, Britain will have the opportunity and political breathing space to gradually come to terms that further European integration with EMU at its heart will entail further surrender of national sovereignty.

Limiting the ECB's political accountability to secure its operational independence is at odds with fundamental British democratic traditions and with directions of reform proposed by the Treasury Select Committee[10] and the Roll Committee.[11] However, strengthening it would entail

---

[9] See comments by Wim Duisenberg, then President of the EMI, who told a German newspaper that he takes seriously the provision of the Maastricht Treaty that calls for a stable exchange rate for at least two years before joining the single currency. 'So far we have seen nothing but sizeable fluctuations' which would make it unrealistic for Britain to join the single currency in 1999. As reported in *The Times*, 17th October 1997.

[10] See Treasury and Civil Service Select Committee report on 'The Role of the Bank of England' First Report, Volume 1, House of Commons Sessions 1993/94, HMSO, December 1993.

[11] See report of an Independent Panel chaired by Eric Roll on 'Independence and Accountable: A New Mandate for the Bank of England' published by the Centre for Economic Policy Research, London in October 1993.

extending the powers of the other EC institutions – something that would be very difficult to sell to the British electorate. Yet it would not be logical for supporters of the Maastricht model to block further specific enhancements of the monetary powers of the EP on national sovereignty grounds, as they will be yielded away to an ECB Governing Council over which national central bank governors will be only able to exercise limited individual influence. Resistance to such additional transfers of power is naturally to be expected from those who would oppose any strengthening of ECB's accountability on the ground that it would weaken the institution's credibility, but their viewpoint assumes an absence of popular consensus on the EC Treaty's enshrined price stability objective.

The absence of a uniformly pro-European political mainstream does not make Britain the odd one out, though it does naturally limit the number of her friends and supporters. Even if Britain would suddenly warm to EMU, there are from a European perspective valid reasons why Britain should not seek rapid entry into EMU. These reasons are not based on the likely number of participants in the first phase or degree of convergence or even the start date of EMU but the current landscape of British politics which separates the political establishment into two large opposing blocks. Whilst one half proudly calls on the contents of a pre-nuptial agreement under a supposedly arranged Euro-marriage, the other half behaves like the reluctant bride who looks coyly at the ground and prays not to be asked to dance at the European wedding. A small pro-European rest neither has any political influence nor represents the public at large. The two-party system in which incoming governments can execute policy U-turns on a scale and with a speed that coalitions in other European member states can only dream about makes British membership in EMU less desirable and a risky

proposition as a lack of political commitment to EMU would be fatal, especially during the transition period to full EMU when national currencies are not yet fully replaced by the single currency.

With these inconsistencies and contradictions, not least a fundamental lack of faith by the British public in the national authorities to run monetary policy successfully, there will be no quick solutions in domestic UK politics for any matters concerning EMU.

In any case, has the United Kingdom already missed the boat? All important decisions about the single currency have already been taken. The convergence criteria, the restrictions on national tax policies under the Stability and Growth Pact, and above all the statutes of the ECB, have all been settled on an almost irrevocable basis. The only issues remaining surround personal appointments and monetary techniques to be used by the ESCB. By not participating in the 1999 start, the United Kingdom will lose its chance to lobby for a Briton to get one of the places on the powerful and all-important Executive Board of the ECB. The Presidency, Vice-Presidency and the job of Chief Economist of the ECB have already been taken by a Dutchman, a Frenchman and a German. If Britain does eventually join EMU, the Governor of the Bank of England will have a right to vote in the Governing Council of the ECB and not just in the General Council, but Britain would have to wait at least four years before it could seek the appointment of a Briton on to the Executive Board of the ECB or even eight years before it could propose a Briton as President of the ECB. Once the UK has joined the single currency, its option to join Stage Three will have lapsed and be rendered ineffective thereby providing no provision for opting out once in. The same applies to the provisions governing the participation of Denmark.

The British Government acting through HM Treasury and the Bank of England are part of Britain's unique state structure, which places the levers of power in the hands of gentlemanly capitalists, and has shown signs that it is no longer able to control the excesses of a market-based financial system. The government is no longer able to use the Bank of England as an important spokesman in the powerful and independent financial markets and as the arbiter of sound monetary policy, even with the clearing banks remaining at a prudent distance from British industry. Any role of the Bank of England as an integral part of the ESCB must be seen against the background and the experiences of the Bank of England's formal job to this day which is not to run the City of London markets but to act as the government's in-house banker. The Bank of England is an instrument of the government's financial policies, raising money so that the government of the day can pay its daily bills as well as managing the state's foreign exchange reserves and its overall currency policy.

Chapter XI
Summary

Central bankers, who are absolutely crucial for the successful implementation of the EMU project, have been closely involved from an early stage, notably through their participation in the Delors Committee and subsequently in the drafting of the ESCB statutes and within the framework of the EMI. They have also been responsible for the everyday running of the EMS. In contrast, domestic interest groups and the wider public have played hardly any role during the negotiations. EMU became a political issue only after the signing of the Maastricht Treaty, and popular reactions came as an unpleasant surprise to most politicians. EMU has since become identified with deflationary policies at times of high unemployment, and this hardly helps to make it an object of love for European citizens.

The success of the changeover to the single currency and EMU as a whole including the largely academic questions concerning legitimacy will depend on the Euro winning full and wholehearted public acceptance. The replacement of national currencies with the Euro will inevitably upset people's day-to-day habits and will for ever change the commercial activities of financial institutions and businesses. However, if the transition to full EMU is to proceed smoothly and without any major derailment, and the ECB is to gain the all-important public confidence and acceptance, the information available to the public at large will need to be clear yet comprehensive, but most importantly free of political spin doctoring.

In economic terms, EMU *de facto* already exists since May 1998 when the eleven member states participating in the Euro-zone were determined and crucially their bilateral entry rates into the single currency were fixed. The markets have also accepted these entry rates and with it the transition to EMU as an irreversible process allowing the ECB to build investors' confidence in the Euro at an early stage. In January 1999, the setting of interest rates will simply transfer from increasingly co-ordinated actions by EU central banks to a single entity setting interest rates for a single currency at a single level.

The EC is not an optimum currency area. There are no adequate adjustment mechanisms such as labour flexibility and mobility as well as budgetary transfers to act as effective substitutes for the exchange rate. There is therefore a major economic risk involved in a complete monetary union.

Perhaps the biggest challenge for the ECB will be the temptation for so many to blame the ECB for an overwhelming amount of ills – from unemployment, fiscal strains imposed by the Stability and Growth Pact to general differences in economic and monetary philosophy from the Arctic to the Mediterranean. If the European electorate were to start to blame EMU and the ECB for high unemployment, the alternatives to EMU are less than clear cut. Should the ECB indeed fail to deliver lasting price stability, its failure will be transparent and directly attributable to the benefits of leaving EMU very evident indeed. The benefits of leaving EMU will be much more uncertain and difficult to predict if the ECB generates too much price stability with low economic growth and high unemployment. One could argue that the odds are counted heavily in favour of EMU, except under the worst case scenario of persistent high levels of inflation.

The convergence criteria used in the EC Treaty have undoubtedly been worked out at the highest political level

and in consultation with the European Commission and EUROSTAT. A more interesting indicator for convergence for those member states still outside the single currency but also for measuring adherence to the fiscal prudence regime of Euro-zone member states contained in the Stability and Growth Pact is the level of 'real' interest rate (long-term interest rate less HICP inflation) as it usually gives an indication of the risk premium which the markets attach to an individual member state.

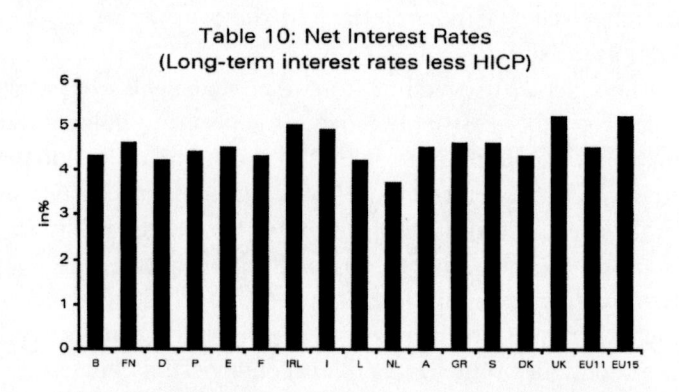

**Table 10: Net Interest Rates
(Long-term interest rates less HICP)**

As shown above, a number of 'in' and 'out' member states have not yet met the artificially-created criteria of real interest rates. This suggests that the markets place different risk premiums on different countries bringing their fiscal households in order. Although Greece, Sweden, Denmark and the United Kingdom will not participate in the single currency from 1st January 1999, the markets expect with reduced real interest rates participation of those countries in the single currency in the near future.

With the introduction of a single currency, the above measurement of real interest rates would no longer be under the control of individual governments in those member states participating in EMU but it would

predominantly become an individual market risk assessment of the fiscal policies in each participating member state.

The journey to full EMU in 2002 will be dangerously long and prone to many accidents. The credibility of the project will depend on the continuous interaction between governments, societies, and markets. Until then, the controversy between 'economists' and 'monetarists' will also play its role perhaps most crucially when agreeing the fulfilment of the convergence criteria to allow as many member states as possible to join the journey to EMU as early as possible.

The fact that several EU member states will not participate from the start, coupled with economic, political and institutional importance of EMU, means that a major new step will have been taken in the direction of a multi-tier and multi-speed Community. Although the rights and obligations of those who stay out, willingly or otherwise, still require further definition, it will be the independence of the experienced bankers of the ECB which can secure in the cool light of the day a political and social acceptability of the EMU project.

Central questions remain:

1. How much economic policy making should remain in the hands of elected representatives?
2. Can there be a central bank without a corresponding political authority?

With the decision to proceed to a complete EMU, European political leaders have decided to play with very high stakes. EMU could divide Europe, it could destabilise it politically if the new institutions do not enjoy the legitimacy that is necessary to carry their policies through,

and it could create economically depressed countries and regions.

On the other hand, if it works it will much accelerate the process of economic integration thus giving a much more concrete and stable form to the internal market, and it is also bound to create a new momentum for political integration as a necessary corollary to monetary union at a time when increasing economic internationalisation is an undeniable fact.

EMU in itself will not be the creator of an economic nor even a technical base for greater harmonisation of policies ranging from taxation, inward investment to subsidy policies, even the Common Agricultural Policy. The base case and main generator for greater market integration will come from shifts of more and more mobile production and with it employment and prosperity. Increased harmonisation of economic and social life will only be one step away from a federal European budget, European Federalist politics leading ultimately to a United States of Europe, with a name yet to be created, perhaps a Union of European Nations.

A high degree of fiscal decentralisation will be no match for the powers of the ECB in terms of monetary policy in the final stage. Risk may however also be treated as a challenge. Thus EMU could act as another powerful push on the accelerator in terms of both economic and political integration precisely in order to deal with the problems mentioned above.

The retention of fiscal sovereignty in national hands creates important risks for EMU in the form of bias towards excessively expansionary fiscal policy among governments concerned to ameliorate structural problems exposed by EMU. Safeguards in the form of sensible fiscal rules have a part to play but the rules agreed at Maastricht are likely to constrain unduly the ability of responsible

national governments to accommodate shocks and cycles in activity. The rules could be improved by giving the excessive deficit procedure an independent control mechanism under the control but existing structure of accountability of the ECB and by making the sanctions under the procedure more explicit and therefore predictable. But such modifications would have to be agreed by unanimous decision in the Council of Ministers as the body with the power to amend the EC Treaty.

In almost all member states the creation of a central bank followed political unification and in no case did the establishment of a central bank provide the lead for political unification. But can this theory hold true for the ECB? We live in an age where markets for goods and services become ever closer. Even the degree of impact on individual member states from economic shocks outside the European Union such as the recent crisis in the Far East and increased interactions and interdependencies between the economies of member states provide signals that monetary integration, i.e. common monetary denominators, have started to precede common budgetary policies.

The idea of a single currency in Europe is not new and John Stuart Mill already wrote in 1894:

> So much of barbarism, however, still remains in the transactions of most civilised nations, that almost all independent countries choose to assert their nationality by having, to their own inconvenience and that of their neighbours, a peculiar currency of their own.[1]

In response to valid questions of legitimacy and the EU's much criticised 'democratic deficit' as well as to increase grassroots interest in the European institutions as a whole,

---

[1] John Stuart Mill, *Principles of Political Economy*, New York, 1894, p.176.

it should be possible to bolster through uncontroversial modifications involving a greater long-range democratic surveillance role for the EP and ECOFIN the visible accountability of the ECB without abandoning the Maastricht commitment to maintain price stability or exposing it to short-term political pressures. A truly independent ECB however will find it very difficult to function without a more developed European political system as well as the trust and full support of the citizens of Europe.

Bibliography

ABN Amro, 'Fiscal Policy in EMU' in *European Strategy & Economics*, April 1998, vol.5, no.13

Agell, J., Calmfors, L. and Jonson, G., 'Fiscal Policy when Monetary Policy is Tied to the Mast' in *European Economic Review*, August 1996, vol. 40, no.7

Akerlof, G., Dickens, W. and Perry, G., 'The Macroeconomics of Low Inflation' in *Brookings Papers on Economic Activity*, 1996, 1, pp.1–59

Alesina, A. and Perotti R., 'The Political Economy of Budget Deficits' in *IMF Staff Papers*, 1995, 42

Alesina, A. and Perotti, R., 'Fiscal Discipline and the Budget Process', in *American Economic Review Papers and Proceedings*, 1996, 86

Alesina., A. and Summers, L., 'Central Bank Independence and Macroeconomic Performance: Some Comparative Evidence' in *Journal of Money, Credit and Banking*, 25th May 1993, vol.25.

Andersen, C., *Influencing the European Community*, Kogan Page, 1992

Arrowsmith, J., *Opting out of Stage III: Life in the lower tier of EMU*, London, National Institute of Economic and Social Research, 1995

Artis, M., *Alternative transitions to EMU* in *The Economic Journal*, 1996, vol.106, no.437

Artis, M. and Lee, S., *The Economics of the European Union. Policy and Analysis*, Oxford University Press, 1994

Artis., M. and Winkler, B., 'The Stability Pact: Safeguarding the Credibility of the European Central Bank' in *National Institute's Economic Review*, January 1998

Baibridge, T. and Teasdale, A., *The Penguin Companion to European Union*, Penguin, 1996

Ball, L., Mankiw, N. and Romer, D., *The New Keynesian Economics and the Output-inflation Trade-off*, Brookings Papers on Economic Activity 1988, 1, pp.1–65

Bank for International Settlements, *Financial Structure and the Monetary Policy Transmission Mechanism*, 1995

Bank for International Settlements, *Core Principles for Effective Banking Supervision*, September 1997

Bank for International Settlements, *International Banking and Financial Market Developments*, Monetary And Economics Department, August 1998

Barran, F., Coudert, V. and Mojon, B., 'L'union Européene est-elle une zone harmogéne pour la politique monétaire?' in *Economie Internationale*, 1996, no.65

Barran, F., Coudert, V. and Mojon, B., *The Transmission of Monetary Policy in the European Countries*, CEPII, 1996, Document de travail no.96–03

Barrell, R. (ed.), *Economic Convergence and Monetary Union, Association for the Monetary Union of Europe*, Sage Publications, 1992

Barro, R. and Grilli, V., *European Macroeconomics*, Macmillan Press, 1994

Bayoumi, T. and Eichengreen, B., *Shocking Aspects of European Monetary Integration*, Centre for Economic Policy Research, 1992, Discussion Paper 643

Bayoumi, T. and Taylor, M., *Macroeconomic Shocks, The ERM and Tri-Polarity*, Centre for Economic Policy Research, 1992, Discussion Paper 711

Begg, D., 'Alternative Exchange-rate Regimes: the Role of the Exchange Rate an the Implications for Wage-Price Adjustments' in EC Commission, *The Economics of EMU*, European Economy, Special Edition 1, 1991

Begg, D., *The Design of EMU*, IMF Staff Studies, December 1997

van den Bempt, P. and Quintyn, M. (eds.), *European Financial Integration and Monetary Co-operation*, European Policy Study Group, IFR Publishing Ltd., 1989

Berg, C., *Monetary Policy Strategies for the European Central Bank and their Implementation*, Sveriges Riksbank, July 1996, Arbetsrapport no.31

Berk, J., *Monetary Transmission: What Do We Know and How Can We Use It*, De Nederlandsche Bank, 1997, DNB-Staff Reports No.15

Berlin, G., *Interaction Between Lawmaker and the Judiciary within the EC*, Legal Issues of European Integration 1992, 17, 2.

Bernanke, B., *How Important is the Credit Channel in the Transmission of Monetary Policy? A Comment*, Carnegie-Rochester Conference Series on Public Policy 39, 1993, pp.47–52

Bernanke, B. and Blinder, S., 'The Federal Funds Rate and the Channels of Monetary Transmission' in *American Economic Review*, 1992, pp.901–921

Bernanke, B. and Gertler, M., 'Inside the Black Box: The Credit Channel of Monetary Policy Transmission' in *Journal of Economic Perspectives*, 1995, 9, pp.27–48

Bernanke, B. and Mishkin, F., *Central Bank Behaviour and the Strategy of Monetary Policy: Observations from Six Industrialized Countries*, NBER Macroeconomics Annual 1992, pp.183–238

Bernanke, B. and Mishkin, F., 'Inflation Targeting: A New Framework for Monetary Policy?' in *Journal of Economic Perspectives*, 1997, 11, pp.97–116

Bernanke, B. and Woodford, M., 'Inflation Forecasts and Monetary Policy' in *Journal of Money, Credit and Banking*, 1997, 29, pp.653–684

Berndsen, R., *The EMU Debt Criterion: An Interpretation*, De Nederlandsche Bank, 1997, DNB-Staff Reports No.18

Bini Smaghi, L., *How Can the ECB Be Credible*, European University Institute Working Paper RSC No. 96/24, May 1996

Black, R., Macklem, R. and Rose, D., *On Policy Rules for Price Stability*, Bank of Canada, Working Paper, 1997

Blinder, A., *Central Banking in Theory and Practice: The 1996 Robbins Lectures*, Cambridge, MA, MIT Press, 1997

Blinder, A., 'What Central Bankers Could Learn from Academics and Vice Versa' in *Journal of Economic Perspectives*, 1997, 11, pp.3–21

Bofinger, P., 'Is Europe an Optimum Currency Area?' in *European Monetary Integration*, London, Alfred Steinherr 1994, pp.38–56

Bofinger, P., *The Euro and the "New Bretton Woods"*, paper for the Conferenza Annuale della Facolta' di Economia, Universita' Pavia, 10th October 1998

Bofinger, P., Reischle, I. and Schaechter, A., *Geldpolitik, Ziele, Institutionen, Strategien und Instrumente*, München, Verlag Vahlen, 1996

de Bondt, G., van Els, P. and Stokman, A., *EUROMON: A Macroeconometric Multi-country Model for the EU*, De Nederlandsche Bank, 1997, DNB-Staff Reports No. 17

Borchert, M., 'Design Probleme einer Einheitlichen Geldpolitik in Europa' in *List Forum für Wirtschafts- und Sozialpolitik*, 1998, 24, pp.37–56

Bovis, C., *Business Law in the European Union*, Sweet & Maxwell, 1997

Brainard, W., 'Uncertainty and the Effectiveness of Monetary Policy' in *American Economic Review*, 1967, vol.57, pp.411–425

Britton, E. and Whiteley, J., 'Comparing the Monetary Transmission Mechanism in France, Germany and the United Kingdom: Some Issues and Results' in *Bank of England Quarterly Bulletin*, May 1997, pp.152–162

Brown, A. and Mayes, D., *Achieving Monetary Union in Europe*, Sage Publications, 1992

Brunner, A., *Bank Reserve Management, Reserve Requirements and the Implementation of Monetary Policy*, Federal Reserve Bank of New York, 1993, pp.285–330

de Burca, G., *The Quest for Legitimacy in the European Union*, (1996) 1 MLR 349

Buiter, W., Corsetti, G. and Roubini, N., 'Excessive Deficits: Sense and Nonsense in the Treaty of Maastricht' in *Economic Policy*, April 1993, 16

Buti, M., Franco, D. and Ongena, H., *Budgetary Policies during Recessions-Retrospective Application of the 'Stability and Growth Pact' to the Post-War Period*, European Commission, DGII, Economic Papers No. 121, May 1997

Buti, M. and Sapir, A., *Economic Policy in EMU*, Oxford University Press, 1998

Cameron, D., 'Economic and Monetary Union: Underlying Imperatives and Third-Stage Dilemmas' in *Journal of European Public Policy*, September 1992, 4

Cangiano, M. and Mottu, E., 'Will Fiscal Policy Be Effective Under EMU?', Fiscal Affairs Department, International Monetary Fund, December 1998

Canzoneri, M. and Grilli, V., *Establishing a Central Bank: Issues in Europe and Lessons from the US*, Cambridge University Press, 1992

Cecchetti, S., 'Policy Rules and Targets: Framing the Central Banker's Problem', in *FRBNY Economic Policy Review*, Federal Reserve Bank of New York, June 1998

Ceccini, P., *The European Challenge: 1992, the Benefits of Single Market*, 1988

Clarida, R. and Gertler, M., *How the Bundesbank Conducts Monetary Policy*, National Bureau of Economic Research Working Paper 5581, Cambridge, MA., 1996

Collignon, S., *Geldwertstabilität für Europa. Die Währungsunion auf dem Prüfstand*, Gütersloh, Verlag Bertelsmann Stiftung, 1996

Collignon, S., *European Monetary Union, Convergence and Sustainability. A Fresh Look at Optimum Currency Area Theory*, November 1997

Collignon, S., 'The Sustainability of Monetary Stability', The Sustainability Report, Association for the Monetary Union of Europe, Paris, February 1998

Commission of the European Communities, *Report to the Council and the Commission on the Realisation by Stages of Economic and Monetary Union in the Community (Werner Report)*, Supplement to Bulletin 11-1970, Luxembourg, 1970

Committee for the Study of Economic and Monetary Union (Delors Committee), *Report on Economic and Monetary Union in the European Community*, Luxembourg, 1989

Connolly, B., *The Rotten Heart of Europe*, Faber and Faber, 1995

Cooper, R., 'Yes to European Monetary Unification, but No to the Maastricht Treaty' in Steinherr, A. (ed.), *Thirty Years of European Monetary Integration*, London, 1994

Coopers & Lybrand, *Economic and Monetary Union: Economic Implications and Business Impacts*, July 1997

Cottarelli, C. and Kourelis, A., *Financial Structure, Bank Lending Rates, and the Transmission Mechanism of Monetary Policy*, IMF Staff Papers 41, 1994

Craig, P. and de Burca, G., *EC Law: Text, Cases and Materials*, Oxford University Press, 2nd edn., 1998

Craig, R.S., *Who Will Join EMU? Impact of the Maastricht Convergence Criteria on Economic Policy Choice and Performance?*, Board of Governors of the Federal Reserve

System, International Finance Discussion Papers, No. 480, 1994

Crawford, M., *One Money for Europe?*, Macmillan, London, 1993

Crockett, D., 'Rules versus Discretion in Monetary Policy' in de Beaufort, Wijnholds, Eijffinger, S. and Hoogduin, L. (eds.), *A Framework for Monetary Stability*, Dordrecht, Kluwer Academic Publishers, 1994, pp.165–185

Cukierman, A., Webb, S. and Neyapti, B., 'Measuring the Independence of Central Banks and Its Effect on Policy Outcomes' in *The World Economic Journal*, September 1992, vol.6, no.3

Cukierman, A., *Central Bank Strategy, Credibility and Independence: Theory and Evidence*, Cambridge, MA, MIT University Press, 1992

Cukierman, A., 'Central Bank Independence and Monetary Control' in *The Economic Journal*, November 1994, vol.104, no.427

Currie, D. and Levine, P., *Rules, Reputation and Macroeconomic Policy Coordination*, Cambridge University Press, 1993

Currie, D., *The Pros and Cons of EMU*, HM Treasury and Economist Intelligence Unit, July 1997

Currie, D., 'EMU and Labour: Facing up to the Euro' in *Economic Outlook*, Centre for Economic Forecasting, London Business School, November 1997, vol.22, no.1

Currie, D., *Will the Euro Work: The Ins and Outs of EMU*, Economist Intelligence Unit, January 1998

Curtin, M. and O'Keeffe, D. (eds.), *Constitutional Adjudication in European Community and National Law*, Butterworth, 1992

Dale, S. and Haldane, A., 'Bank Behaviour and the Monetary Transmission Mechanism' in *Bank of England Quarterly Bulletin*, 1993, 33, pp.478–491

Dale, S. and Haldane, A., 'Interest Rates and the Channels of Monetary Transmission: Some Sectoral Estimates', in *European Economic Review*, 1995, 39, pp.1611–1626

Dale Davidson, J., *The Plague of the Black Debt: How to Survive the Coming Depression*, Agora, 1994

Davies, H., 'Averaging in a Framework of Zero Reserve Requirements: Implications for the Operation of Monetary Policy' in *Bank of England Quarterly Review*, 1998

Debelle, G., *Inflation Targeting in Practice*, IMF Working Paper No. W/97/35, Washington DC, 1997

Deutsche Bundesbank, *1997 Annual Report*, May 1998.

Deutsche Bundesbank, *Monthly Report*, May 1998.

Dornbusch, R., Favero, C. and Giavazzi, F., *Immediate Challenges for the European Central Bank* in Begg, D., von Hagen, J., Wyplosz, Ch. and Zimmermann, K. (eds.), *EMU: Prospectives and Challenges for the Euro*, Blackwell, 1998

Dowd, K., *European Monetary Reform: The Pitfalls of Central Planning*, Cato Institute, Foreign Policy Briefing No. 28, Washington DC, December 1993

Dowd, K., 'The Misguided Drive toward European Monetary Union: A Case Study in the Pitfalls of Monetary Central Planning' in Dowd, K. and Timberlake, R., *Money and the Nation State*, Oakland, CA, 1994

Dumke, R., Hermann, A., Juchens, A. and Sherman, H., *Währungsvielfalt behindert Vollendung des Europäischen Binnenmarkts*, ifo Schnelldienst 9/97, 1997

Dunnett, D., 'Legal and Institutional Issues Affecting Monetary Union' in O'Keeffe, P. and Twomey, P.M. (eds.) *Legal Issues of the Maastricht Treaty*, Chichester, Chancery Law Publishing, 1994

Dyson, K., *Elusive Union: The Progress of Economic and Monetary Union in Europe*, Longman, 1994

Eichengreen, B., *Should The Maastricht Treaty Be Saved*, Princeton Studies in International Finance No. 74, December 1992

Eichengreen, B., 'Saving Europe's Automatic Stabilisers' in *National Institute Economic Review*, 1996, 159

Eichengreen, B. and Ghironi, F., *European Monetary Unification: The Challenges Ahead*, Discussion Paper No. 1217, CEPR, 1995

Eichengreen, B. and Wyplosz, C., 'The Stability Pact: More than a Minor Nuisance', in *Economic Policy*, April 1998, no.26, pp.65–113

Eichengreen, B. and von Hagen, J., 'Fiscal Restrictions and Monetary Union: Rationales, Repercussions, Reforms' in *Empirica*, 1996, vol.23

Eijffinger, S. and Schaling, E., *Central Bank Independence: Theory and Evidence*, Centre for Economic Research, Tilburg University, Discussion Paper 9325, April 1993

Ellis, E. and Tridimas, T., *Public Law of the European Community*, Sweet & Maxwell, 1995

Enoch, C., Hilbers, P. and Kovanen, A., 'Monetary Operations in the European Economic and Monetary Union' in *Finance & Development*, June 1998

European Central Bank, *The Single Monetary Policy in Stage Three. General documentation on ESCB monetary policy instruments and procedures*, September 1998

European Commission, 'One Market, One Money: An Evaluation of the Potential Benefits and Costs of Forming and Economic and Monetary Union' in *European Economy*, No.44, Brussels, October 1990

European Commission, *Annual Economic Report for 1997*, No. 63, 1997

European Monetary Institute, *Annual Report – 1996*, April 1997

European Monetary Institute, *Annual Report – 1997*, May 1998

European Monetary Institute, *The Changeover to the Single Currency*, November 1995

European Monetary Institute, *Convergence Report – Report required by Article 109j of the Treaty establishing the European Community*, March 1998

European Monetary Institute, *Progress Towards Convergence*, May 1995

European Monetary Institute, *Role and Functions of The European Monetary Institute*, February 1996

European Monetary Institute, *The Single Monetary Policy in Stage Three – Elements of Monetary Policy Strategy of the ESCB*, February 1997

European Monetary Institute, *The Single Monetary Policy in Stage Three – General Documentation on ESCB Monetary Policy Instruments and Procedures*, September 1997

Fase, M., *On Substitutability among Domestic Money and Cross-border Deposits*, De Nederlandsche Bank, 1996, DNB-Staff Reports No 4

Fase, M., *Divisia Aggregates and the Demand for Money in Core EMU*, De Nederlandsche Bank, 1996, DNB-Staff Reports No. 5

Fase, M. and Winder, C., 'Money Demand within EMU: an Analysis with the Divisia Measure' in *De Nederlandsche Bank Quarterly Bulletin*, September 1994, pp.25–55

Fatas, A., 'Does EMU need a Fiscal Federation', in Economic Policy, April 1988, no.26, pp.163–203

Faust, J., 'Whom Can We Trust to Run the Fed? Theoretical support for the founders' views' in *Journal of Monetary Economics*, 1996, 37, pp.267–283

Faust, J. and Svensson, L., *Transparency and Credibility: Monetary Policy with Unobservable Goals*, Sveriges Riksbank Working Paper Series No. 50, December 1997

Feldstein, M., *The Costs and Benefits of Going from Low Inflation to Price Stability*, NBER Working Paper No. 5469, Cambridge, MA, 1996

Fels, J., *Is Inflation Too Low? Discuss*, Morgan Stanley Dean Witter, weekly briefing on Euro monetary policy, 30th July 1998

Fischer, S., 'Why Are Central Banks Pursuing Long-Run Price Stability?' in *Achieving Price Stability*, Federal Reserve Bank of Kansas City, 1996, pp, 7–35

Folkerts-Landau, D. and Garber, P., 'What Role for the ECB in Europe's Financial Markets?' in Steinherr, A., (ed.) *30 Years of European Monetary Integration from the Werner Plan to EMU*, Longman, 1994

Foster, N. (ed.), *Blackstone's EC Legislation*, Blackstone Press, 8th edn., 1997

de Fouloy, C., *Glossary of EC Terms*, Butterworths, 1992

Fratianni, M. and von Hagen, J., *The European Monetary System and European Monetary Union*, Oxford, Westview Press, 1992

Freedman, C., 'What Operating Procedures Should Be Adopted to Maintain Price Stability – practical issues' in *Achieving Price Stability* (op. cit.)

Frenkel, J. and Goldstein, M., *The International Role of the Deutsche Mark*, Washington, Institute for International Economics, January 1997

Frenkel, J. and Johnson, H., *The Monetary Approach to the Balance of Payments*, University of Toronto Press, 1977

Friedman, B., 'Targets and Instruments of Monetary Policy', in Friedman, B. and Hahn, F. (eds.), *Handbook of Monetary Economics*, Vol. 2, Amsterdam, North-Holland, 1990, pp.1185–1230

Friedman, M., 'The Role of Monetary Policy' in *American Economic Review*, March 1968, 58, no.1

Friedman, M., 'The Lag in the Effect of Monetary Policy' in *Journal of Political Economy*, 1961, 69, pp.447–466

Fuhrer, J., 'Central Bank Independence and Inflation Targeting: Monetary Policy Paradigms for the Next

Millennium?' in *New England Economic Review*, Federal Reserve Bank of Boston, 1997, pp.19–36

Fuhrer, J. and Madigan, B., 'Monetary Policy When Interest Rates Are Bounded at Zero' in *Review of Economics and Statistics*, 1997, 79, pp.573–585

Funke, N. and Kennedy, M., *International Implications of European Economic and Monetary Union*, OECD Economics Department Working Papers, No. 174, 1997

Gaertner, M., *Makroökonomik flexibler und fester Wechselkurse*, 2nd edn., Heidelberg, 1997

Ganley, J. and Salmon, C., 'The Industrial Impact of Monetary Policy Shocks: Some Stylised Facts' in *Bank of England Quarterly Bulletin*, 1997

Gebauer, W. (ed.), *Foundations of Economic Central Bank Policy (Studies in Contemporary Economics)*, Springer Verlag, 1993

Gebauer, W., Mueller, M., Schmidt, K., Thiel, M. and Worms A., 'Determinants of Long-Term Interest Rates in Selected Countries: Towards a European Central Bank Policy Design' in Johnson C. and Collignon S. (eds.) *The Monetary Economics of Europe: Causes of the EMS Crisis*, London, Pinter, 1994

Ghosh, A. and Masson, P., *Economic Cooperation in an Uncertain World*, Oxford, Basil Blackwell, 1994

Giovannini, A., *Central Banking in a Monetary Union: Reflections on the Proposed Statute of the European Central Bank*, Carnegie-Rochester Series of Public Policy 38, 1993

Giovannini A. and De Cecco, M. (eds.), *A European Central Bank? Perspectives on Monetary Unification after Ten Years of the EMS*, Cambridge University Press, 1989

Giovannini, A. and McKibbin, W., *The Economic Implications of Maastricht*, The Brookings Institute, June 1992

Goldman Sachs, *EMU's Excess Foreign Reserves*, EMU Briefing No. 6, London, 4th September 1996

Goldstein, M., The Asian Financial Crisis: Causes, Cures, and Systemic Implications, Institute for International Economics, Policy Analyses in International Economics 55, Washington DC, 1998

Goodfried, M., 'Acquiring and Maintaining Credibility for Low Inflation: The US Experience' in Leiderman L. and Svensson L. (eds.), *Inflation Target*, Centre for European Policy Research, 1998

Goodfried, M., 'Monetary Mystique: Secrecy and Central Banking' in *Journal of Monetary Economics*, 17, 196, pp.63–92

Goodhart, C., *The ECSB after Maastricht*, London School of Economics, Special Paper No. 44, 1992

Goodhart, C., *The Draft Statutes of the European Central Bank*, London School of Economics, Special Paper No. 37, 1992

Goodhart, C., *The External Dimension of EMU*, Recherches Economiques de Louvain, No. 59, 1993

Goodhart, C., *The Central Bank and the Financial System*, Macmillan, 1995

Goodhart, C., 'The Transition to EMU' in *Scottish Journal of Political Economy*, August 1996, vol.43, no.3

Goodhart, C., 'Why Do the Monetary Authorities Smooth Interest Rates?' in Collignon S. (ed.), *European Monetary Policy*, London, Pinter, 1996

Goodman, J., *Monetary Sovereignty – The Politics of Central Banking in Western Europe*, Ithaca, Cornell University Press, 1992

Gordon, R., 'What Is New-Keynesian Economics?' in *Journal of Economic Literature*, 1990, 27, pp.1115–1171

Gormley, L. and de Haan, J., *The Democratic Deficit of the European Central Bank*, [1996] 21 European Law Review 95.

Grant, C. (ed.), *Britain and EMU: The Case for Joining*, Centre for European Reform, 1997

Grieco, J., 'The Maastricht Treaty, Economic and Monetary Union, and the Neo-Realist Research Programme' in *Review of International Studies*, 1995, 21, pp.21-40

Grilli, V., Mascianaro, A. and Tabellini G., *Monetary Policies, Credibility and International Coordination*, 1991

Groenefeld, J., Knot, K. and Wesseling A., 'De monetaire beleidsstrategie van de ECB' in *Economisch-Statistische Berichten* 1996, 81, pp.618-621

Gros, D., *Towards a Credible Excessive Deficit Procedure*, Working Document 95, Centre for European Policy Studies, 1995

Gros, D., *Excessive Deficits and Debts*, Working Document 97, Centre for European Policy Studies, 1995

Gros, D. and Thygesen, N., *European Monetary Integration: From the European Monetary System to European Monetary Union*, London, Longmans, 2nd edn., 1998

de Grauwe P., *The Economics of Monetary Integration*, Oxford University Press, 1994

de Grauwe, P., Micossi, S. and Tullio, G., *Inflation and Wage Behaviour in Europe*, Oxford, Clarendon Press, 1996

Guitian, M., *Central Bank Independence: Issues and Diversity of Models*, paper prepared for a workshop on 'Independence and Accountability: The Role and Structure of the South African Reserve Bank' organised by the Centre for Research into Economics and Finance in Pretoria, South Africa, January 1995

de Haan, J. and Sturm, J., 'The Case for Central Bank Independence' in *Banca Nazionale del Lavoro Quarterly Review*, 1992, no.182, pp.305-327

Harden, I., 'The European Central Bank and the Role of National Central Banks in Economic & Monetary Union' in Gretschmann, K. (ed.) *Economic and Monetary Union – Implications for National Policy-Makers*, Dordrecht, 1993

Harrison, D., *The Organisation of Europe – Developing a Continental Market Order*, Routledge, 1995

Hartmann, P., *The Future of the Euro as an International Currency: A Transactions Perspective*, LSE Financial Markets Group, Special Paper No. 91, London School of Economics, November 1996

Hasse, R., *The European Central Bank – Perspectives for a Further Development of the European Monetary System*, Gütersloh, 1990

Henderson, R., *European Finance*, McGraw-Hill, 1993

Henning, C., 'Europe's Monetary Union and the United States' in *Foreign Policy*, Spring 1996, no.102

Herdegen, M., *Price Stability and Budgetary Restrains in the Economic and Monetary Union – the Law as Guardian of Economic Wisdom*, (1998), 35 CMLR 9

Hoeller, P., Louppe M.-O. and Vergriete P., *Fiscal Relations within the European Union*, OECD Economics Department Working Papers, No. 163, 1996

Hoffmann, J., *Problems of Inflation Measurement in Germany*, Deutsche Bundesbank Discussion Paper, March 1998

Holzmann, R., Hervè, Y. and Demmel, R., 'The Maastricht Fiscal Criteria: Required but Ineffective?' in *Empirica*, 1996, 23, pp.25–58

Hughes-Hallett, A. and Vines, D., *The Benefits and Costs of Currency Integration*, Centre for Economic Policy Research Discussion Paper, 1992

Huhne, C. and Forder, J., 'Both Sides of the Coin', Profile Books, 1999

Hutton, W., *The State We're In*, Vintage, 1996

Illing, G., 'Gradualism vs. Cold Turkey – How to Establish Credibility for the ECB, Working Paper No. 92, University of Frankfurt, 1998

Ilzkovietz, F., *Prospects for the Internationalization of the Euro*, European Commission Document 11/364/96-EN, DG-II, Brussels, June 1996

Isard, P., *Exchange Rate Economics*, Cambridge Surveys of Economic Literature, Cambridge, 1995

Italianer, A., 'Managing Maastricht: EMU Issues and How They Were Settled' in Gretschmann, K. (ed.), *Economic and Monetary Union: Implications for National Policy-Makers*, Dordrecht, 1993

Johnson, C., *In with the Euro, Out with the Pound*, Penguin, 1996

JP Morgan, *EMU: Impact and Opportunity*, November 1996

Judd, J. and Motley, B., 'Controlling Inflation with an Interest Rate Instrument' in *Economic Review No. 3*, Federal Reserve Bank of San Francisco, 1992, pp.3–22

Kenen, P., *EMU after Maastricht*, Washington DC, Group of Thirty, 1992

Kenen, P., *Economic and Monetary Union. Moving beyond Maastricht*, Cambridge University Press, 1995

Kenen, P., *Hazards on the Road to the Third Stage of Economic and Monetary Union*, Paper Prepared for the Forum for US-EC Legal-Economic Affairs, Session on Issues of Governance in the European Community, London, September 1995

Kennedy, E., *The Bundesbank*, London, 1991

Kenner, J. (ed.), Trends in European Social Policy, Dartmouth, 1995

Kenner, J., *Economic and Social Cohesion – The Rocky Road Ahead*, 1/94 Legal Issues of European Integration 1, 1994

Kettle, M., *The Single Currency: Should Britain Join? A Guardian Debate*, Vintage, 1997

Keynes, J.M., *A Treatise on Money, Vols. I and II*, London, Macmillan, 1930

Keynes, J.M., *The General Theory of Employment, Interest and Money*, London, Macmillan, 1933

King, M., 'The Transmission Mechanism of Monetary Policy' in *Bank of England Quarterly Bulletin*, August 1994, pp.261–267

King, M., *How Should Central Banks Reduce Inflation?– Conceptual Issues*, Federal Reserve Bank of Kansas City, 1996

Knot, K., *Fiscal Policy and Interest Rates in the European Union*, Cheltenham, Edward Elgar, 1996

KPMG, *Europe's Preparedness for EMU*, KPMG Management Consulting Research Report, 1997

Kral, F., 'Künftig Bank Ratings und Schuldnertips' in *Frankfurter Allgemeine Zeitung*, 29th July 1997

Krugman, P., 'The Confidence Game' in *The New Republic*, 5th October 1998

Kydland, F. and Prescott, E., 'Rules Rather than Discretion: The Inconsistency of the Optimal Plans' in *Journal of Political Economy*, 1977, 85, pp.473–491

Lamfalussy, A., *The Harmonisation of Monetary Policy in Europe: What Steps and When*, 1995

Lampe, O., *Die Unabhängigkeit der Deutschen Bundesbank*, München, 1972

Lannoo, K., *From 1992 to EMU: The Implications for Prudential Supervision*, Centre for European Policy Studies, Research Report No. 23, May 1998

Lasok, D. and Lasok, K., *Law and Institutions of the European Union*, Sweet & Maxwell, 6th edn., 1995

Leeper, E., Sims, C. and Zha, T., *What Does Monetary Policy Do?*, Brookings Papers on Economic Activity 2, 1996, pp.1–78

Leahy, M., 'The Dollar as an Official Reserve Currency Under EMU' in *Open Economies Review*, 1996, vol.7

Lewis, K., 'Why Doesn't Society Minimize Central Bank Secrecy' in *Economic Inquiry*, 1991, 29, pp.403–415

Lockwood, B., Miller, M. and Zhang, L., *Designing Monetary Policy when Unemployment Persists*, Department of Economics, University of Exeter, 1995

Lohmann, S., 'Optimal Commitment in Monetary Policy: Credibility versus Flexibility', in *American Economic Review*, 1992, 82, pp.273–286

Louis, J.-V., 'The Project of a European Central Bank' in Stuyck (ed.), *Financial and Monetary Integration in the European Economic Community: Legal, Institutional and Economic Aspects*, Boston, 1993

MacLean, R. (ed.), *European Community Law Textbook*, 6th edn, HLT Publications, 1994

Marsh, D., *The Bundesbank*, Mandarin, 1993

Masson, P., 'Fiscal Dimensions of EMU' in *The Economic Journal*, June 1996, vol.106, no.437

Masson, P., Symansky, S. and Meredith, G., *MULTIMOD Mark II: A Revised and Extended Model*, Occasional Paper No. 71, International Monetary Fund, Washington, July 1990

Masson, P. and Turtelboom, B., *Characteristics of the Euro, the Demand for Reserves, and Policy Coordination under EMU*, Research Department, International Monetary Fund, May 1997

Masson, P., Savastano, M. and Sharma S., 'Can Inflation Targeting Be a Framework for Monetary Policy in Developing Countries?' in *Finance & Development*, March 1998

McCallum, B., *Issues in the Design of Monetary Policy Rules*, NBER Working Paper No. 6016, 1997

McCallum, B., 'Crucial issues concerning central bank independence' in *Journal of Monetary Economics*, 1997, 39, pp.99–112

McKibbin, W., 'The New European Economy and its Economic Implication for the World Economy' in *Economic and Financial Computing*, August 1992

McKibbin, W. and Bok, T., *Which Monetary Regime for Europe?: A Quantitative Evaluation*, ESRC Macro-economic Modelling Conference on Econometric

Modelling of European Macroeconomic Integration, The Brookings Institution, May 1995

McKinnon, R., *EMU as a Device for Collective Fiscal Retrenchment*, American Economic Association Papers and Proceedings, 1997, vol.87, no.2

Melmer-Meland, R., 'Central Bank to the European Union' in *Kluwer Law International*, July 1995

Menkhoff, L., *Monetary Policy Instruments for EMU*, Springer Verlag, 1997

Middlemas, K., *Orchestrating Europe – The Informal Politics or European Union 1973–1995*, Fontana Press, 1995

Mill, J., *Principles of Political Economy*, New York, 1894

Milne, I., Maastricht: *The Case Against Economic & Monetary Union*, Oxford, Nelson & Pollard, 1993

Minford, P., Rastogi, A. and Hughes-Hallett, A., *The Price of EMU Revisited*, Centre for Economic Policy Research, Discussion Paper No. 656, London, 1992

Minikin R., *The ERM Explained*, Kogan Page, 1993

Mizen, P. and Tew, B., 'Proposals to Ensure a Smooth Transition to European Monetary Union' in *The World Economy*, July 1996, vol.19, no.4

Monticelli, C. and Papi, L., *European Integration, Monetary Co-ordination and the Demand for Money*, Oxford, Clarendon Press, 1996

Monticelli, C. and Strauss-Kahn, M.-O., 'Broad Money Aggregates and Money Demand in European Countries' in *Economies et Sociétés*, 1992 vol.26(9)

Moutot, P., *Monetary Policy in a European Union: Instruments, Strategy and Transmission Mechanism*, paper presented at the Conference on Monetary Policy in Transition, Vienna, November 1996

Mundell, R., 'Capital Mobility and Stabilization Policy Under Fixed and Flexible Exchange Rates' in *The Canadian Journal of Economics*, November 1963, 29, pp.475–485

Neumann, M.J.M., 'Central Bank Independence as a Prerequisite of Price Stability' in Commission of the EC (ed.), *The Economics of EMU*, European Economy, Special Edition 1, 1991

Neumann, M.J.M., 'Precommitment by Central Bank Independence' in *Open Economics Review*, 1991, 95

Obradovic, D., 'Policy Legitimacy and the European Union' in *Journal of Common Market Studies*, June 1996, vol.4, no.2

OECD, *Macroeconomic consequences of the move to European Monetary Union*, prepared by the European Commission, ECO/GEN 95(5), 1995

O'Keeffe, D. and Twomey, P.M. (eds.), *Legal Issues of the Maastricht Treaty*, Wiley Chancery Law Books, 1994

Panic, M., *European Monetary Union: Lessons from the Classical Gold Standard*, St. Martin's Press, 1992

Pech, H., *The Interest Rate Policy Transmission Process – The Case of Austria*, BIS, 1994, pp.31–45

Perilleux, V. and Wouters, R., The *Interest Rate Policy Transmission Process in Belgium*, BIS, 1994, pp.47–62.

Persson, T. and Tabellini G., *Designing Institutions for Monetary Stability*, Carnegie-Rochester Conference Series on Public Policy, 1993, 39, pp.53–84

Persson, T. and Tabellini, G., *Monetary and Fiscal Policy – Vol. I: Credibility*, Cambridge, MA, MIT Press, 1995

Persson, T. and Tabellini, G., *Monetary Cohabitation in Europe*, Stockholm, Institute for International Economic Studies, 1995

Pollard, D. and Ross, M., *European Community Law*, Butterworths, 1994

Prati, A. and Schinasi, G., *Financial Stability in EMU*, paper presented at a conference on the 'Monetary Policy of the ESCB: Strategic and Implementation Issues', Universita Bocconi, Milan, July 1998

Ramaswamy, R., *Monetary Frameworks: Is There a Preferred Option for the European Central Bank?*, Research Department, International Monetary Fund, Washington, January 1997

Ramaswamy, R. and Sloek, T, *The Real Effects of Monetary Policy in the European Union: What Are the Differences?*, Working Paper 97/160, Research Department, International Monetary Fund, Washington, December 1997

Redwood, J., *Our Currency, Our Country*, Penguin, 1997

Risse, T., Engelmann-Martin, D., Knopf, H-J. and Roscher, K., *To Euro or Not To Euro? The EMU and Identity Politics in the European Union*, Florence, European University Institute, Working Paper RSC No.98/9

Rogoff, K., 'The Optimal Degree of Commitment to an Intermediate Monetary Target' in *Quarterly Journal of Economics*, November 1985

Roll, E., *Independent and Accountable, A New Mandate for the Bank of England*, Centre for Economic Policy Research, London, 1993

Ross M., 'Beyond Francovich' in *Modern Law Review*, 1993, 55

Rudebusch, G. and Svensson, L., *Policy Rules for Inflation Targeting*, Sveriges Riksbank Working Paper Series No. 49, February 1998

Sachs, J., 'Global Capitalism: Making It Work' in *The Economist*, 12th September 1998

Sanderson, E., *The ECB Stirs*, EMU Supplement, Risk Publications, 1997

Sardelis, C., *Targeting a European Monetary Aggregate: Review and Current Issues*, Sveriges Riksbank, 1993, Arbetsrapport Nr.12

Schlesinger, H., *The Passage to the Euro*, Centre for European Policy Studies Working Party Report, No. 16, December 1996

Schoenmaker, D., *Banking Supervision in Stage Three of EMU*, LSE Financial Markets Group, Special Paper No. 72, 1995

Schwartz, P., *Back From the Brink: An Appeal to Fellow Europeans Over Monetary Union*, The Institute of Economic Affairs, 1997

Sievert, O., *Zur Europäischen Währungsunion – das Eigentliche und der Unrat auf dem Wege dahin*, Vortrag bei der Hamburger Sparkasse, 13th August 1997

Sijben, J., 'Monetary Policy in Game-theoretic Framework' in *Jahrbücher for Nationalökonomie und Statistik*, 1992, 210, pp.233–253

Sijben, J., '*Banken en het gewijzigde intermediatieprocess*' in *Maandschrift Economie*, 1996, 60, pp.456–477

Sims, C., 'Interpreting the Macroeconomic Time Series Facts – The Effects of Monetary Policy' in *European Economic Review*, 1992, vol.36, pp.975–1011

Smets, F., 'Central Bank Macroeconometric Models and the Monetary Policy Transmission Mechanism' in *Financial Structure and the Monetary Policy Transmission Mechanism*, Bank for International Settlements, CB 394, 1995, pp.225–266

Smets, F., *The European Central Bank: Institutional Aspects*, International Banking and Finance Law Series, Vol. 5, Kluwer Law International, July 1997

Steiner, J., *Textbook on EC Law*, 4th edn., Blackstone Press, 1994

Sturm, R., 'How Independent is the Bundesbank?' in *German Politics*, 1995, 4, pp.27–41

Summers, L., 'How Should Long-Run Monetary Policy Be Determined?' in *Journal of Money, Credit and Banking*, 1991, 23, pp.625–631

Svensson, L., 'Fixed Exchange Rates as a Means to Price Stability: What Have We Learned?' in *European Economic Review*, 1994, 38, pp.447–468

Svensson, L., *Optimal Inflation Targets, 'Conservative' Central Banks and Linear Inflation Contracts*, Institute for International Economic Studies, Stockholm University, 1995

Tanzi, V. and Zee, H., 'Consequences of the Economic and Monetary Union for the Co-ordination of Tax Systems in the European Union: Lessons from the US Experience', Fiscal Affairs Department, International Monetary Fund, August 1998

Taylor, C., *EMU 2000? Prospects for European Monetary Union*, The Royal Institute of International Affairs, 1995

Taylor, J., 'The Monetary Transmission Mechanism: An Empirical Framework' in *Journal of Economic Perspectives*, 1995, 9, pp.11–27

Taylor, J., 'How Should Monetary Policy Respond to Shocks while Maintaining Long-Run Price Stability – Conceptual Issues' in Federal Reserve Bank of Kansas City, *Achieving Price Stability*, 1996, pp.181–197.

Tietmeyer, H., *Die Auswirkungen des Euro auf die Länder innerhalb und außerhalb der Europäischen Währungsunion*, Auszüge aus Presseartikeln, No. 57, September 1998

Toedter, K.-H. and Ziebarth, G., *Preisstabilität oder geringe Inflation*, Deutsche Bundesbank, discussion paper 3/1997.

Walsh, C., 'Central Bank Independence and the Short-Run Output-Inflation Trade-Off in the European Community' in Eichengreen, B., Frieden, J. and von Hagen, J. (eds.), *Monetary and Fiscal Policy in an Integrated Europe*, Berlin, Springer, 1995

Walsh, C., 'Optimal Contracts for Central Bankers' in *American Economic Review*, March 1995, 85, pp.150–167

Weatherill, S., *Cases & Materials on EC Law*, 2nd edn., Blackstone Press, 1994

Weatherill, S. and Beaumont, P., *EC Law*, 2nd edn., Penguin Books, 1995

Weiner, S., 'The changing role of reserve requirements in monetary policy' in *Economic Review of the Federal Reserve Bank of Kansas City*, 1992, vol.77, pp.45–63.

Werner Report, *Report to the Council and the Commission on the Realisation by Stages of Economic and Monetary Union in the Community*, Supplement to Bulletin II-1970 of the European Communities, Luxembourg, 1970

Whitley, J., 'Economic Models and Policy-making' in *Bank of England Quarterly Bulletin*, 1997, 37, pp.163–173

Wise, M. and Gibb, R., *Single Market to Social Europe: The European Community in the 1990s*, Longman, 1993

Wistrich, E., *The United States of Europe*, Routledge, 1994

Wolswijk, G., 'Convergence in Europe' in *De Nederlandsche Bank Quarterly Bulletin*, March 1995

Wood, G., *Central Bank Independence in New Zealand: Analytical, Empirical And Institutional Aspects*, paper presented at the Paoli Baffi Conference on Central Bank Independence and Accountability, Milan, March 1994

Woodford, M., *Control of the Public Debt: A Requirement for Price Stability?*, NBER Working Paper, No. 5684, July 1996

Wren-Lewis, S., 'The Choice of Exchange Rate Regime' in *The Economic Journal*, July 1997, vol.107

Wyatt and Dashwood, *European Community Law*, 3rd edn., Sweet & Maxwell, 1995

Cases Referred To

Brunner v. European Union Treaty [1994] 1 CMLR 57

Opel Austria GmbH v. European Commission [1996] ECR II–39, 1 CMLR 733

Royal Hellenic Government v. Vergottis Ltd. [1945] 78 Lloyds List Rep. 292

USA v. France Air Services Agreement [1978] 54 ILR 304

Case C-146/91, KYDEP v. Council and Commission [1994] ECR I-4199

Case C-27/96, Danisco Sugar v. Allmänna Ombudet [1997]

Treaties Referred To

EC Treaty (Rome 1957)

European Economic Community Treaty *see* EC Treaty

Maastricht Treaty (Maastricht, 1992; OJ 1992 C191/1)

Protocol on certain provisions relating to the United Kingdom of Great Britain and Northern Ireland

Protocol on the convergence criteria referred to in Article 109J of the Treaty establishing the European Community

Protocol on the excessive deficit procedure

Protocol on the Statute of the European Monetary Institute

Protocol on the Statute of the European System of Central Banks and of the European Central Bank

Protocol on the transition to the third stage of Economic and Monetary Union

Single European Act (1986)

Treaty of Rome *see* European Economic Community Treaty

Treaty on European Union *see* Maastricht Treaty

Vienna Convention of the Law of Treaties

Directives, Regulations, Recommendations and Other Community Texts Referred To

European Council Decision (EC) 317/98 of 3rd May 1998 in accordance with Article 109j(4) of the EC Treaty

European Council Decision (98/345/EC) of the government of the member states of 26th May 1998 on the appointment of the President, the Vice-President and the other members of the Executive Board of the European Central Bank, OJ 1998 L154

European Council Decision (CE) 382/98 of 5th June 1998 on the statistical data to be used for the determination of the key for subscription of the capital of the European Central Bank

European Council Decision (CE) 415/98 of 29th June 1998 on the consultation of the European Central Bank by national authorities regarding draft legislative provisions

European Commission, Amended Regulation No. 260/68 laying down the conditions and procedure for applying the tax for the benefit of the EC (salaries of ECB officials)

European Commission, Amended Regulation No. 549/69 determining the categories of officials and other servants of the EC to whom the provision of Art. 12, the second paragraph of Art. 13 and Art. 14 on the Privileges and Immunities of the Communities apply

European Commission, Report to the Council and the Commission on the Realisation by Stages of Economic and Monetary Union in the Community (Werner Report), Supplement to Bulletin II-1970, Luxembourg, 1970

European Commission – Committee for the study of Economic Monetary Union (Delors Committee),

Report on Economic and Monetary Union in the European Community, Luxembourg, 1989

European Commission – Exchange Rate Relations between Participating and Non-Participating Countries in Stage Three of EMU, CSE(95) 2108

European Commission, One Currency for Europe – Green paper on the practical arrangements for the introduction of the single currency, Luxembourg, 1995

European Commission, Secondary legislation for the introduction of the Euro and some provisions relating to the introduction of the Euro, Brussels, COM(96) 499 final, 16th October 1996

European Commission, European System of National and Regional Accounts, Luxembourg, 30th November 1996, OJ No. L310 and 321

European Commission, The Community Economy in 1997–99, Autumn 1997 Economic Forecasts, 14th October 1997

European Commission, Amended proposal for a council regulation on the strengthening of the surveillance and coordination of budgetary deficits, Brussels, COM(97) 116 final, 19th March, 1997

European Commission, Amended proposal for a council regulation on speeding up and clarifying the implementation of the excessive deficit procedure, COM(97) 17 final, 19th March 1997

European Council Regulation (EC) 1103/97 on certain provisions relating to the introduction of the Euro, OJ 1997 L162

European Council Regulation 1466/97 on the strengthening of the surveillance of budgetary positions and the surveillance and co-ordination of economic policies, OJ 1997 L 209

- European Council Regulation 1467/97 on speeding up and clarifying the implementation of the excessive deficit procedure, OJ 1997 L209
- European Council Regulation (EC) 974/98 on the introduction of the Euro, OJ 1998 L139
- European Council Regulation 2531/98 on the application of minimum reserves by the ECB, OJ 1998 L356
- European Council Regulation 2532/98 concerning the powers of European Central Bank to impose sanctions, OJ 1998 L356
- European Council Regulation 2533/98 concerning the collection of statistical information by the European Central Bank, OJ 1998 L318
- European Council Regulation 2818/98 on the application of minimum reserves, OJ 1998 L356
- European Council Regulation 2819/98 concerning the consolidated balance sheet of the monetary financial institutions sectors, OJ 1998 L356
- European Council Regulation 2866/98 on the conversion rates between the Euro and the currencies of the member states adopting the Euro, OJ 1998 L359
- Regulation ECB 1998/15 on the application of minimum reserves, OJ 1998
- Regulation ECB 1998/16 concerning the consolidated balance sheet of the monetary financial institutions sector, OJ 1998 L356

Appendix I
Protocol on the Statute of the European Monetary Institute

THE HIGH CONTRACTING PARTIES
DESIRING to lay down the Statute of the European Monetary Institute,
HAVE AGREED upon the following provisions, which shall be annexed to the Treaty establishing the European Community:

Article 1 – Constitution and Name

1.1 The European Monetary Institute (EMI) shall be established in accordance with Article 109f of this Treaty; it shall perform its functions and carry out its activities in accordance with the provisions of this Treaty and of this Statute.

1.2 The members of the EMI shall be the central banks of the member states ('national central banks'). For the purposes of this Statute, the Institute Monetaire Luxembourgeois shall be regarded as the central bank of Luxembourg.

1.3 Pursuant to Article 109f of this Treaty, both the Committee of Governors and the European Monetary Co-operation Fund (EMCF) shall be dissolved. All assets and liabilities of the EMCF shall pass automatically to the EMI.

Article 2 – Objective

The EMI shall contribute to the realisation of the conditions necessary for the transition to the third stage of Economic and Monetary Union, in particular by:

- strengthening the co-ordination of monetary policies with a view to ensuring price stability;
- making the preparations required for the establishment of the European System of Central Banks (ESCB), and for the conduct of a single monetary policy and the creation of a single currency in the third stage;
- overseeing the development of the ECU.

Article 3 – General Principles

3.1 The EMI shall carry out the tasks and functions conferred upon it by this Treaty and this Statute without prejudice to the responsibility of the competent authorities for the conduct of the monetary policy within the respective member states.

3.2 The EMI shall act in accordance with the objectives stated in Article 2 of the Statute of the ESCB.

Article 4 – Primary Tasks

4.1 In accordance with Article 109f(2) of this Treaty, the EMI shall:

- strengthen co-operation between the national central banks;
- strengthen the co-ordination of the monetary policies of the member states with the aim of ensuring price stability;
- monitor the functioning of the European Monetary System (EMS);

- hold consultations concerning issues falling within the competence of the national central banks and affecting the stability of financial institutions and markets;
- take over the tasks of the EMCF; in particular it shall perform the functions, referred to in Articles 6.1, 6.2 and 6.3;
- facilitate the use of the ECU and oversee its development, including the smooth functioning of the ECU clearing system;

The EMI shall also:

- hold regular consultations concerning the course of monetary policies and the use of monetary policy instruments;
- normally be consulted by the national monetary authorities before they take decisions on the course of monetary policy in the context of the common framework for ex ante co-ordination.

4.2 At the latest by 31st December 1996, the EMI shall specify the regulatory, organisational and logistical framework necessary for the ESCB to perform its tasks in the third stage, in accordance with the principle of an open market economy with free competition. This framework shall be submitted by the Council of the EMI for decision to the ECB at the date of its establishment.

In accordance with Article 109f(3) of this Treaty, the EMI shall in particular:

- prepare the instruments and the procedures necessary for carrying out a single monetary policy in the third stage;
- promote the harmonisation, where necessary, of the rules and practices governing the collection compilation and distribution of statistics in the areas within its field of competence;
- prepare the rules for operations to be undertaken by the national central banks in the framework of the ESCB;
- promote the efficiency of cross-border payments;
- supervise the technical preparation of ECU bank notes.

Article 5 – Advisory Functions

5.1 In accordance with Article 109f(4) of this Treaty, the Council of the EMI may formulate opinions or recommendations on the overall orientation of monetary policy and exchange rate policy as well as on related measures introduced in each member state. The EMI may submit opinions or recommendations to governments and to the Council on policies which might affect the internal or external monetary situation in the Community and, in particular, the functioning of the EMS.

5.2 The Council of the EMI may also make recommendations to the monetary authorities of the member states concerning the conduct of their monetary policy.

5.3 In accordance with Article 109f(6) of this Treaty, the EMI shall be consulted by the Council regarding any proposed Community act within its field of competence.

Within the limits and under the conditions set out by the Council acting by a qualified majority on a proposal from the Commission and after consulting the European Parliament and the EMI, the EMI shall be consulted by the authorities of the member states on any draft legislative provision within its field of competence in particular with regard to Article 4.2.

5.4 In accordance with Article 109f(5) of this Treaty, the EMI may publish its opinions and its recommendations.

Article 6 – Operational and Technical Functions

6.1 The EMI shall:

- provide for the multilateralisation of positions from interventions by the national central banks in Community currencies and the multilateralisation of intra-Community settlements;
- administer the very short-term financing mechanism provided for by the Agreement of 13th March 1979 between the central banks of the member states of the European Economic Community laying down the operating procedures for the European Monetary System (hereinafter referred to as 'EMS Agreement') and the short-term monetary support mechanism provided for in the Agreement between the central banks of the member states of the European Economic Community of 9th February 1970, as amended;
- perform the functions referred to in Article 11 of Council Regulation (EEC) No. 1969/88 of 24th June 1988 establishing a single facility providing medium-term financial assistance for member states' balances of payments.

6.2 The EMI may receive monetary reserves from the national central banks and issue ECUs against such assets for the purpose of implementing the EMS Agreement. These ECUs may be used by the EMI and the national central banks as a means of settlement and for transactions between them and the EMI. The EMI shall take the necessary administrative measures for the implementation of this paragraph.

6.3. The EMI may grant to the monetary authorities of third countries and to international monetary institutions the status of 'Other Holders' of ECUs and fix the term and conditions under which such ECUs may be required, held or used by Other Holders.

6.4 The EMI shall be entitled to hold and manage foreign currency reserves as an agent for and at the request of national central banks. Profits and losses regarding these reserves shall be for the account of the national central bank depositing the reserves.

The EMI shall perform this function on the basis of bilateral contracts in accordance with rules laid down in a decision of the EMI.

These rules shall ensure that transactions with these reserves shall not interfere with the monetary policy and exchange rate policy of the competent monetary authority of any member state and shall be consistent with the objectives of the EMI and the proper functioning of the Exchange Rate Mechanism of the EMS.

Article 7 – Other Tasks

7.1 Once a year the EMI shall address a report to the Council on the state of the preparations for the third

stage. These reports shall include an assessment of the progress towards convergence on the Community and cover in particular the adoption of monetary policy instruments and the preparation of the procedures necessary for carrying out a single monetary policy in the third stage, as well as the statutory requirements to be fulfilled for national central banks to become an integral part of the ESCB.

7.2 In accordance with the Council decisions referred to in Article 109f(7) of this Treaty, the EMI may perform other tasks for the preparation of the third stage.

Article 8 – Independence

The members of the Council of the EMI who are the representatives of their institutions shall, with respect to their activities, act according to their own responsibility. In exercising the powers and performing the tasks and duties conferred upon them by this Treaty and this Statute, the Council of the EMI may not seek or take any instructions from Community institutions or bodies or governments of member states.

The Community institutions and bodies as well as the governments of the member states undertake to respect this principle and not to seek to influence the Council of the EMI in the performance of its tasks.

Article 9 – Administration

9.1 In accordance with Article 109f(1) of this Treaty, the EMI shall be directed and managed by the Council of the EMI.

9.2 The Council of the EMI shall consist of a President and the Governors of the national central banks, one

of whom shall be Vice-President. If a Governor is prevented from attending a meeting, he may nominate another representative of his institution.

9.3 The President shall be appointed by common accord of the governments of the member states at the level of Heads of State or of Government, on a recommendation from, as the case may be, the Committee of Governors or the Council of the EMI, and after consulting the European Parliament and the Council.

The President shall be selected from among persons of recognised standing and professional experience in monetary or banking matters. Only nationals of member states may be President of the EMI. The Council of the EMI shall appoint the Vice-President. The President and the Vice-President shall be appointed for a period of three years.

9.4 The President shall perform his duties on a full-time basis. He shall not engage in any occupation, whether gainful or not, unless exemption is exceptionally granted by the Council of the EMI.

9.5 The President shall:

- prepare and chair the meetings of the Council of the EMI;
- without prejudice to Article 22, present the view of the EMI externally;
- be responsible for the day-to-day management of the EMI.

In the absence of the President, his duties shall be performed by the Vice-President.

9.6. The terms and conditions of employment of the President, in particular his salary, pension and other social security benefits, shall be the subject of a contract with the EMI and shall be fixed by the Council

of the EMI on a proposal from a Committee comprising three members appointed by the Committee of Governors or the Council of the EMI, as the case may be, and three members appointed by the Council. The President shall not have the right to vote on matters referred to in this paragraph.

9.7 If the President no longer fulfils the conditions required for the performance of his duties or if he has been guilty of serious misconduct, the Court of Justice may, on application by the Council of the EMI, compulsorily retire him.

9.8 The Rules of Procedure of the EMI shall be adopted by the Council of the EMI.

Article 10 – Meetings of the Council of the EMI and Voting Procedures

10.1 The Council of the EMI shall meet at least ten times a year. The proceedings of Council meetings shall be confidential. The Council of the EMI may, acting unanimously, decide to make the outcome of its deliberations public.

10.2 Each member of the Council of the EMI or his nominee shall have one vote.

10.3 Save as otherwise provided for in this Statute, the Council of the EMI shall act by a simple majority of its members.

10.4 Decisions to be taken in the context of Articles 4.2, 5.4, 6.2 and 6.3 shall require unanimity of the members of the Council of the EMI.

The adoption of opinions and recommendations under Articles 5.1 and 5.2, the adoption of decisions under Article 6.4, 16 and 23.6 and the adoption of guidelines under Article 15.3 shall require a qualified

majority of two thirds of the members of the Council of the EMI.

Article 11 – Inter-institutional Co-operation and Reporting Requirements

11.1 The President of the Council and a member of the Commission may participate, without having the right to vote, in meetings of the Council of the EMI.

11.2 The President of the EMI shall be invited to participate in Council meetings when the Council is discussing matters relating to the objectives and tasks of the EMI.

11.3 At a date to be established in the Rules of Procedures, the EMI shall prepare an annual report, on its activities and on monetary and financial conditions in the Community. The annual report, together with the annual accounts of the EMI, shall be addressed to the European Parliament, the Council and the Commission and also to the European Council.

The President of the EMI may, at the request of the European Parliament or on his own initiative, be heard by the competent Committees of the European Parliament.

11.4 Reports published by the EMI shall be made available to interested parties free of charge.

Article 12 – Currency Denomination

The operations of the EMI shall be expressed in ECU.

Article 13 – Seat

Before the end of 1992, the decisions as to where the seat of the EMI will be established shall be taken by common

accord of the governments of the member states at the level of Heads of State or of Government.

Article 14 – Legal Capacity

The EMI, which in accordance with Article 109g(1) of this Treaty shall have legal personality, shall enjoy in each of the member states the most extensive legal capacity accorded to legal persons under their law; it may, in particular, acquire or dispose of movable or immovable property and may be a party to legal proceedings.

Article 15 – Legal Acts

15.1 In the performance of its tasks, and under the conditions laid down in this Statute, the EMI shall:

- deliver opinions;
- make recommendation;
- adopt guidelines, and take decisions which shall be addressed to the national central banks.

15.2 Opinions and recommendations of the EMI shall have no binding force.

15.3 The Council of the EMI may adopt guidelines laying down the methods for the implementation of the conditions necessary for the ESCB to perform its functions in the third stage. EMI guidelines shall have no binding force – they shall be submitted for decision to the ECB.

15.4 Without prejudice to Article 3.1, a decision of the EMI shall be binding in its entirety upon those to

whom it is addressed. Articles 190 and 191 of this Treaty shall apply to these decisions.

Article 16 – Financial Resources

16.1 The EMI shall be endowed with its own resources. The size of the resources of the EMI shall be determined by the Council of the EMI with a view to ensuring the income deemed necessary to cover the administrative expenditure incurred in the performance of the tasks and functions of the EMI.

16.2 The resources of the EMI determined in accordance with Article 16.1 shall be provided out of contributions by the national central banks in accordance with the key referred to in Article 29.1 of the statute of the ESCB and be paid up at the establishment of the EMI. For this purpose, the statistical data to be used for the determination of the key shall be provided by the Commission, in accordance with the rules adopted by the Council, acting by a qualified majority on a proposal from the Commission and after consulting the European Parliament, the Committee of Governors and the Committee referred to in Article 109c of this Treaty.

16.3 The Council of the EMI shall determine the form in which contributions shall be paid up.

Article 17 – Annual Accounts and Auditing

17.1 The financial year of the EMI shall begin on the first day of January and end on the last day of December.

17.2 The Council of the EMI shall adopt an annual budget before the beginning of each financial year.

17.3 The annual accounts shall be drawn up in accordance with the principles established by the Council of the

EMI. The annual accounts shall be approved by the Council of the EMI and shall thereafter be published.

17.4 The annual accounts shall be audited by independent external auditors approved by the Council of the EMI. The auditors shall have full power to examine all books and accounts of the EMI and to obtain full information about its transactions.

17.5 Any surplus of the EMI shall be transferred in the following order:

(a) an amount to be determined by the Council of the EMI shall be transferred to the general reserve fund of the EMI;

(b) any remaining surplus shall be distributed to the national central banks in accordance with the keys referred to in Article 16.2.

17.6 In the event of a loss incurred by the EMI, the shortfall shall be offset against the general reserve fund of the EMI. Any remaining shortfall shall be made good by contributions from the national central banks, in accordance with the keys referred to in Article 16.2.

Article 18 – Staff

18.1 The Council of the EMI shall lay down the conditions of employment of the staff of the EMI.

18.2 The Court of Justice shall have jurisdiction in any dispute between the EMI and its servants within the limits and under the conditions laid down in the conditions of employment.

Article 19 – Judicial Control and Related Matters

19.1 The acts or omissions of the EMI shall be open to review or interpretation by the Court of Justice in the cases and under the conditions laid down in this Treaty. The EMI may institute proceedings in the cases and under the conditions laid down in this Treaty.

19.2 Disputes between the EMI, on the one hand, and its creditors, debtors or any other person, on the other, shall fall within the jurisdiction of the competent national courts, save where jurisdiction has been conferred upon the Courts of Justice.

19.3 The EMI shall be subject to the liability regime provided for in Article 215 of this Treaty.

19.4 The Court of Justice shall have jurisdiction to give judgement pursuant to any arbitration clause contained in a contract concluded by or on behalf of the EMI, whether that contract be governed by public or private law.

19.5 A decision of the EMI to bring an action before the Court of Justice shall be taken by the Council of the EMI.

Article 20 – Professional Secrecy

20.1 Members of the Council of the EMI and the staff of the EMI shall be required, even after their duties have ceased, not to disclose information of the kind covered by the obligation of professional secrecy.

20.2 Persons having access to data covered by Community legislation imposing an obligation of secrecy shall be subject to such legislation.

Article 21 – Privileges and Immunities

The EMI shall enjoy in the territories of the member states such privileges and immunities as are necessary for the performance of its tasks, under the conditions laid down in the Protocol on the Privileges and Immunities of the European Communities.

Article 22 – Signatories

The EMI shall be legally binding to third parties by the President or the Vice-President or by the signatures of two members of the staff of the EMI who have been duly authorised by the President to sign on behalf of the EMI.

Article 23–Liquidation of the EMI

23.1 In accordance with Article 109f of this Treaty, the EMI shall go into liquidation on the establishment of the ECB. All assets and liabilities of the EMI shall then pass automatically to the ECB. The latter shall liquidate the EMI according to the provisions of this Article. The liquidation shall be completed by the beginning of the third stage.

23.2 The mechanism for the creation of ECUs against gold and US dollars as provided for by Article 17 of the EMS Agreement shall be unwound by the first day of the third stage in accordance with Article 20 of the said Agreement.

23.3 All claims and liabilities arising from the very short-term financing mechanism and the short-term monetary support mechanism, under the Agreements referred to in Article 6.1, shall be settled by the first day of the third stage.

23.4 All remaining assets of the EMI shall be disposed of and all remaining liabilities of the EMI shall be settled.

23.5 The proceeds of the liquidation described in Article 23.4 shall be distributed to the national central banks in accordance with the key referred to in Article 16.2.

23.6 The Council of the EMI may take the measures necessary for the application of Articles 23.4 and 23.5.

23.7 Upon the establishment of the ECB, the President of the EMI shall relinquish his office.

Appendix II
Rules of Procedure of the EMI

The Council of the European Monetary Institute, hereafter referred to as the 'Council' and the 'EMI' respectively,

- having regard to the Treaty establishing the European Community as amended by the Treaty on European Union, hereafter referred to as the 'Treaty', and in particular Article 109f thereof,
- having regard to the Protocol on the Statute of the European Monetary Institute, hereafter referred to as the 'Statute', and in particular Articles 9 and 10 thereof,

hereby adopts the following Rules of Procedure for the EMI:

Article 1 – Treaty and Statute

These Rules of Procedure shall supplement the Treaty and the Statute and the terms in these Rules of Procedure shall have the meaning which they have in the Treaty and the Statute. References to Articles are to those of the Statute, unless indicated otherwise.

Article 2 – Vice-President

The Vice-President shall be elected by the Council from among the Governors. Should the Vice-President not

complete his/her term, the Council shall elect a new Vice-President for the remainder of the term.

Article 3 – Date and Place of Council Meetings

3.1 The Council shall meet at least ten times a year. The date of the meetings shall be decided by the Council on a proposal from the President.

3.2 The President may also convene a meeting of the Council

- whenever he/she deems it necessary; or
- at the request of a member of the Council, after consulting the other members.

   The President shall convene a meeting of the Council if at least three members of the Council so request.

3.3 The Council shall in principle hold its meetings at the premises of the EMI.

3.4 In exceptional circumstances, to be determined by the President, meetings may also take place by way of teleconferences.

Article 4 – Attendance of Council Meetings

4.1 Each Governor may be accompanied at Council meetings by the respective member of the Committee of Alternates referred to in Article 7 of these Rules of Procedure and by one additional representative from his/her institution. In special circumstances, a Governor may decide that the respective member of the Committee of Alternates be replaced by another senior representative of

his/her choice of his/her central bank at the meeting or part thereof.
4.2 The President may be accompanied by the Director General, up to three Heads of Department and, as may be required by the agenda, up to three additional members of staff of the EMI.
4.3 The President of the Council of the European Union may be accompanied by the Secretary General of the Council of the European Union or his/her representative. The member of the Commission of the European Communities representing his/her institution may be accompanied by one member of the Commission's staff.
4.4 The Council may invite the Chairman of the Sub-Committees and Working Groups referred to in Article 10 of these Rules of Procedure to its meetings, if it deems it appropriate to do so.
4.5 The Council may also invite other persons to its meetings, if it deems it appropriate to do so, and in particular the Chairman of the Monetary Committee referred to in Article 109c of the Treaty.

Article 5 – Voting

5.1 If a member of the Council is prevented from attending a meeting or part thereof, he/she shall nominate another representative of his/her institution to act and vote on his/her behalf. This shall be notified to the President.
5.2 In order for the Council to vote, there shall be a quorum of two thirds of its members or of their nominees.
5.3 Decisions may also be taken by written procedure, unless at least three members of the Council object. Such decisions shall be recorded in the summary

record mentioned in Article 6.2 of these Rules of Procedure of the following meeting of the Council.

5.4 Abstentions by members of the Council or by their nominees shall not prevent the adoption by the Council of acts which require unanimity.

5.5 In those cases in which the Council adopts an opinion acting by the majority requested by the Treaty and the Statute, the dissenting minority shall have the right to have their differing view reflected in a document annexed thereto.

5.6 Secret voting may only take place in the case of matters of a personal nature.

Article 6 – Organisation of Council Meetings

6.1 The agenda for each meeting shall be adopted by the Council. A provisional agenda shall be drawn up by the President and shall be sent, together with the related documents, to the members of the Council and participants under Article 11 at least eight days before the meeting, except in emergencies, in which case the President shall act appropriately with a view to the circumstances. The Council may decide to remove items from or add items to the provisional agenda on a proposal from the President or from a member of the Council. An item shall be removed from the agenda at the request of at least three of its members if the related documents were not sent to the members in due time.

6.2 A summary of the proceedings of the Council shall be submitted to its members for approval at the next meeting.

Article 7 – Committee of Alternates

7.1 A Committee of Alternates is hereby established which shall contribute to the preparation of the meetings of the Council and draw up its agenda accordingly.

7.2 The Committee of Alternates shall be composed of senior representatives of the central banks, appointed by their respective Governors. Each member of the Committee may be accompanied at meetings of the Committee by one additional representative of his/her institution.

7.3 The Committee of Alternates shall be chaired by the Director General. He/she may be accompanied by up to three Heads of Department and, as may be required by the agenda, up to three additional members of staff of the EMI. In the absence of the Director General, the Committee of Alternates shall be chaired by the most senior Alternate.

Article 8 – Organisation of the EMI

The Council, acting on a proposal from the President based on prior consultation of its members, shall decide on:

- the department organisation of the EMI;
- the appointment of the Director General and of the Heads of Department; and
- the conditions of employment of staff of the EMI.

Article 9 – Financial Committee

9.1 A Financial Committee is hereby established consisting of the Vice-President and the two most senior members of the Council. Their term of office shall be one year. At the expiry of their term of office,

the two members of the Council ranking next in order of seniority shall become members of the Financial Committee.

9.2 Should a member of the Financial Committee not complete his/her term of office, the Council shall appoint a new member for the remainder of the term in accordance with the same rule unless the remainder of the term is less than six months. In the latter case, the new member shall serve the remainder of the term of his/her predecessor and an additional period of one year.

9.3 The Financial Committee shall be chaired by the Vice-President and shall:

- examine the President's proposals to the Council on the annual budget and the annual accounts as well as periodical statements of expenses incurred by the EMI during the financial year; and
- deliver its opinion thereon to the Council.

Article 10 – Sub-Committees and Working Groups

10.1 The Council, acting on a proposal from the President, may establish Sub-Committees and Working Groups in specific areas, lay down their mandates and appoint their Chairman.

10.2 The provision laid down in Article 10. 1 of these Rules of Procedures shall be without prejudice to the right of the President to authorise ad hoc meetings between the EMI and representatives of national central banks.

Article 11 – Confidentiality

11.1 The proceedings of the Council and of any committee or group established by the Council shall be confidential unless the Council, acting unanimously, authorises the President to make the outcome of their deliberations public.

11.2 Without prejudice to Article 11.1 and 17.3, all documents drawn up by the EMI shall be confidential unless the Council decides otherwise.

11.3 The national central banks shall ensure that their representatives are bound, with respect to their activities in the framework of the EMI, to the same obligation of secrecy as the members of staff of the EMI.

Article 12 – Annual Report

The annual report of the EMI referred to in Article 11.3 shall be adopted by the Council in the first quarter of each subsequent financial year and shall be published in the official languages of the European Community in the course of the fourth month of such financial year.

Article 13 – Final Provision

The present Rules of Procedure may be amended from time to time as and when the need arises.

Appendix III

Protocol on the Statute of the European System of Central Banks and of the European Central Bank

THE HIGH CONTRACTING PARTIES
DESIRING to lay down the Statute of the European System of Central Banks and of the European Central Bank provided for in Article 4a of the Treaty establishing the European Community,
HAVE AGREED upon the following provisions, which shall be annexed to the Treaty establishing the European Community:

CHAPTER I
CONSTITUTION OF THE ESCB

Article 1 – The European System of Central Banks

1.1 The European System of Central Banks (ESCB) and the European Central Bank (ECB) shall be established in accordance with Article 4a of this Treaty; they shall perform their tasks and carry out their activities in accordance with the provisions of this Treaty and of this Statute.

1.2 In accordance with Article 106(1) of this Treaty, the ESCB shall be composed of the ECB and of the

central banks of the member states ('national central banks'). The Institute Monetaire Luxembourgeois will be the central bank of Luxembourg.

CHAPTER II
OBJECTIVES AND TASKS OF THE ESCB

Article 2 – Objectives

In accordance with Article 105(1) of this Treaty, the primary objective of the ESCB shall be to maintain price stability. Without prejudice to the objective of price stability, it shall support the general economic policies in the Community with a view to contribution to the achievement of the objectives of the Community as laid down in Article 2 of this Treaty. The ESCB shall act in accordance with the principle of an open market economy with free competition, favouring an efficient allocation of resources, and in compliance with the principles set out in Article 3a of this Treaty.

Article 3 – Tasks

3.1 In accordance with Article 105(2) of this Treaty, the basic tasks to be carried out through the ESCB shall be:

- to define and implement the monetary policy of the Community;
- to conduct foreign exchange operations consistent with the provisions of Article 109 of this Treaty;
- to hold and manage the official foreign reserves of the member states;
- to promote the smooth operation of payment systems.

3.2 In accordance with Article 105(3) of this Treaty, the third indent of Article 3.1 shall be without prejudice to the holding and management by the governments of member states of foreign exchange working balances.

Article 4 – Advisory Functions

In accordance with Article 105(4) of this Treaty:
(a) the ECB shall be consulted:

- on any proposed Community act in its field of competence;
- by national authorities regarding any draft legislative provision in its fields of competence, but within the limits and under the conditions set out by the Council in accordance with the procedure laid down in Article 42;

(b) the ECB may submit opinions to the appropriate Community institutions or bodies or to national authorities on matters in its fields of competence.

Article 5 – Collection of Statistical Information

5.1 In order to undertake the tasks of the ESCB, the ECB, assisted by the national central banks, shall collect the necessary statistical information either from the competent national authorities or directly from economic agents. For these purposes it shall co-operate with the Community institutions or bodies and with the competent authorities of the member states or third countries and with international organisations.

5.2 The national central banks shall carry out, to the extent possible, the tasks described in Article 5.

5.3 The ECB shall contribute to the harmonisation where necessary, of the rules and practices governing the collection, compilation and distribution of statistics in the areas within its fields of competence.

5.4 The Council, in accordance with the procedure laid down in Article 42, shall define the natural and legal persons subject to reporting requirements, the confidentiality regime and the appropriate provisions for enforcement.

Article 6 – International Co-operation

6.1 In the field of international co-operation involving the tasks entrusted to the ESCB, the ECB shall decide how the ESCB shall be represented.

6.2 The ECB and, subject to its approval, the national central banks may participate in international monetary institutions.

6.3 Articles 6.1 and 6.2 shall be without prejudice to Article 109(4) of this Treaty.

CHAPTER III
ORGANISATION OF THE ESCB

Article 7 – Independence

In accordance with Article 107 of this Treaty, when exercising the powers and carrying out the tasks and duties conferred upon them by this Treaty and this Statute, neither the ECB, nor any national central bank, nor any member of their decision-making bodies shall seek or take any instructions from Community institutions or bodies, from any governments of a member state or from any other

body. The Community institutions and bodies and the governments of the member states undertake to respect this principle and not to seek to influence the members of the decision-making bodies of the ECB or of the national central banks in the performance of their tasks.

Article 8 – General Principle

The ESCB shall be governed by the decision-making of the ECB.

Article 9 – The European Central Bank

9.1 The ECB which, in accordance with Article 106(2) of this Treaty, shall have legal personality, shall enjoy in each of the member states the most extensive legal capacity accorded to legal persons under their law, it may, in particular, acquire or dispose of movable or immovable property and may be a party to legal proceedings.

9.2 The ECB shall ensure that the tasks conferred upon the ESCB under Article 105(2), (3) and (5) of this Treaty are implemented either by its own activities pursuant to this Statute or through the national central banks pursuant to Articles 12.1 and 14.

9.3 In accordance with Article 106(3) of this Treaty, the decision-making bodies of the ECB shall be the Governing Council and the Executive Board.

Article 10 – The Governing Council

10.1 In accordance with Article 109a(1) of this Treaty, the Governing Council shall comprise the members of the Executive Board of the ECB and the Governors of the national central banks.

10.2 Subject to Article 10.3, only members of the Governing Council present in person shall have the right to vote. By way of derogation from this rule, the Rules of Procedure referred to in Article 12.3 may lay down that members of the Governing Council may cast their vote by means of teleconferencing. These rules shall also provide that a member of the Governing Council who is prevented from voting for a prolonged period may appoint an alternate as a member of the Governing Council.

Subject to Article 10.3 and 11.3, each member of the Governing Council shall have one vote. Save as otherwise provided for in this Statute, the Governing Council shall act by a simple majority. In the event of a tie, the President shall have the casting vote.

In order for the Governing Council to vote, there shall be a quorum of two thirds of the members. If the quorum is not met, the President may convene an extraordinary meeting at which decisions may be taken without regard to the quorum.

10.3 For any decisions to be taken under Articles 28, 29, 30, 32, 33 and 51, the votes in the Governing Council shall be weighted according to the national central banks' shares in the subscribed capital of the ECB. The weights of the votes of the members of the Executive Board shall be zero. A decision requiring a qualified majority shall be adopted if the votes cast in favour represent at least two thirds of the subscribed capital of the ECB and represent at least half of the shareholders. If a Governor is unable to be present, he may nominate an alternate to cast his weighted vote.

10.4 The proceedings of the meetings shall be confidential. The Governing Council may decide to make the outcome of its deliberations public.

10.5 The Governing Council shall meet at least ten times a year.

Article 11 – The Executive Board

11.1 In accordance with Article 109a(2)(a) of this Treaty, the Executive Board shall comprise the President, the Vice-President and four other members.

The members shall perform their duties on a full-time basis. No member shall not engage in any occupation, whether gainful or not, unless exemption is exceptionally granted by the Governing Council.

11.2 In accordance with Article 109a(2)(b) of this Treaty, the President, the Vice-President and the other Members of the Executive Board shall be appointed from among persons of recognised standing and professional experience in monetary or banking matters by common accord of the governments of the member states at the level of Heads of State or of Government, on a recommendation from the Council after it has consulted the European Parliament and the Governing Council.

Their term of office shall be eight years and shall not be renewable. Only nationals of member states may be members of the Executive Board.

11.3 The terms and conditions of employment of the members of the Executive Board, in particular their salaries, pensions and other social security benefits shall be the subject of a contract with the ECB and shall be fixed by the Governing Council on a proposal from Committee comprising three members appointed by the Governing Council and three members appointed by the Council. The members of the Executive Board shall not have the right to vote on matters referred to in this paragraph.

11.4 If a member of the Executive Board no longer fulfils the conditions required for the performance of his duties or if he has been guilty of serious misconduct, the Court of Justice may, on application by the Governing Council or the Executive Board, compulsorily retire him.

11.5 Each member of the Executive Board present in person shall have the right to vote and shall have, for that purpose, one vote. Save as otherwise provided, the Executive Board shall act by a simple majority of the votes cast. In the event of a tie, the President shall have the casting vote. The voting arrangements shall be specified in the Rules of Procedure referred to in Article 12.3.

11.6 The Executive Board shall be responsible for the current business of the ECB.

11.7 Any vacancy on the Executive Board shall be filled by the appointment of a new member in accordance with Article 11.2.

Article 12 – Responsibilities of the Decision-making Bodies

12.1 The Governing Council shall adopt the guidelines and take the decisions necessary to ensure the performance of the tasks entrusted to the ESCB under this Treaty and this Statute. The Governing Council shall formulate the monetary policy of the Community including, as appropriate, decisions relating to intermediate monetary objectives, key interest rates and the supply of reserves in the ESCB, and shall establish the necessary guidelines for their implementation.

The Executive Board shall implement monetary policy in accordance with the guidelines and decisions laid down by the Governing Council.

In doing so the Executive Board shall give the necessary instructions to national central banks. In addition the Executive Board may have certain powers delegated to it where the Governing Council so decides.

To the extent deemed possible and appropriate and without prejudice to the provisions of this Article, the ECB shall have recourse to the national central banks to carry out operations which form part of the tasks of the ESCB.

12.2 The Executive Board shall have responsibility for the preparation of meetings of the Governing Council.

12.3 The Governing Council shall adopt Rules of Procedure which determine the internal organisation of the ECB and its decision-making bodies.

12.4 The Governing Council shall exercise the advisory functions referred to in Article 4.

12.5 The Governing Council shall take the decisions referred to in Article 6.

Article 13 – The President

13.1 The President or, in his absence, the Vice-President shall chair the Governing Council and the Executive Board of the ECB.

13.2 Without prejudice to Article 39, the President or his nominee shall represent the ECB externally.

Article 14 – National Central Banks

14.1 In accordance with Article 108 of this Treaty, each member state shall ensure, at the latest at the date of

the establishment of the ESCB, that its national legislation, including the statutes of its national central bank, is compatible with this Treaty and this Statute.

14.2 The statutes of the national central banks shall, in particular, provide that the term of office of a Governor of a national central bank shall be no less than five years.

A Governor may be relieved from office only if he no longer fulfils the conditions required for the performance of his duties or if he has been guilty of serious misconduct. A decision to this effect may be referred to the Court of Justice by the governor concerned or the Governing Council on grounds of infringement of this Treaty or of any rule of law relating to its application. Such proceedings shall be instituted within two months of the publication of the decision or of its notification to the plaintiff or, in the absence thereof, of the day on which it came to the knowledge of the latter, as the case may be.

14.3 The national central banks are an integral part of the ESCB and shall act in accordance with the guidelines and instructions of the ECB. The Governing Council shall take the necessary steps to ensure compliance with the guidelines and instructions of the ECB, and shall require that any necessary information be given to it.

14.4 National central banks may perform functions other than those specified in this Statute unless the Governing Council finds, by a majority of two thirds of the votes cast, that these interface with the objectives and tasks of the ESCB. Such functions shall be performed on the responsibility and liability of national central banks and shall not be regarded as being part of the functions of the ESCB.

Article 15 – Reporting Commitment

15.1 The ECB shall draw up and publish reports on the activities of the ESCB at least quarterly.
15.2 A consolidated financial statement of the ESCB shall be published each week.
15.3 In accordance with Article 109b(3) of this Treaty, the ECB shall address an annual report on the activities of the ESCB and on the monetary policy of both the previous and current year to the European Parliament, the Council and the Commission and also to the European Council.
15.4 The reports and statements referred to in this Article shall be made available to interested parties free of charge.

Article 16 – Bank Notes

In accordance with Article 105a(l) of this Treaty, the Governing Council shall have the exclusive right to authorise the issue of bank notes within the Community. The ECB and the national central banks may issue such notes. The bank notes issued by the ECB and the national central banks shall be the only such notes to have the status of legal tender within the Community.

The ECB shall report as far as possible existing practices regarding the issue and design of bank notes.

CHAPTER IV
MONETARY FUNCTIONS AND OPERATIONS OF THE ESCB

Article 17 – Accounts with the ECB and the National Central Banks

In order to conduct their operations, the ECB and the National central banks may open accounts for credit institutions, public entities and other market participants and accept assets, including book-entry securities, as collateral

Article 18 – Open Market and Credit Operations

18.1 In order to achieve the objectives of the ESCB and to carry out its tasks the ECB and the national central banks may:

- operate in the financial markets by buying and selling outright (spot and forward) or under re-purchase agreement and by lending or borrowing claims and marketable instruments, whether in Community or in non-Community currencies, as well as precious metal;
- conduct credit operations with credit institutions and other market participants on adequate collateral.

18.2 The ECB shall establish general principles for open market and credit operations carried out by itself or the national central banks, including for the announcement of conditions under which they stand ready to enter into such transactions.

Article 19 – Minimum Reserves

19.1 Subject to Article 2, the ECB may require credit institutions established in member states to hold minimum reserves on accounts with the ECB and national central banks in pursuance of monetary policy objectives. Regulations concerning the calculation and determination of the required minimum reserves may be established by the Governing Council. In cases of non-compliance the ECB shall be entitled to levy penalty interest and to impose other sanctions with comparable effect.

19.2 For the application of this Article, the Council shall, in accordance with the procedure laid down in Article 42, define the basis for minimum reserves and the maximum permissible ratios between those reserves and their basis, as well as the appropriate sanctions in cases of non-compliance.

Article 20 – Other Instruments of Monetary Control

The Governing Council may, by a majority of two thirds of the votes cast, decide upon the use of such other operational methods of monetary control as it sees fit, respecting Article 2.

The Council shall, in accordance with the procedure laid down in Article 42, define the scope of such methods if they impose obligations on third parties.

Article 21 – Operations with Public Entities

21.1 In accordance with Article 104 of this Treaty, overdrafts or any other type of credit facility with the ECB or with the national central banks in favour of Community institutions or bodies, central govern-

ments, regional, local or other public authorities, other bodies governed by public law or public undertakings of member states shall be prohibited, as shall the purchase directly from the by the ECB or national central bank of debt instruments.

21.2 The ECB and national central banks may act as fiscal agents for the entities referred to in Article 21.1.

21.3. The provision of this Article shall not apply to publicly-owned credit institutions which, in the context of the supply of reserves by central banks, shall be given the same treatment by national central banks and the ECB as private credit institutions.

Article 22 – Clearing and Payment Systems

The ECB and national central banks may provide facilities, and the ECB may make regulations, to ensure efficient and sound clearing and payments systems within the Community and with other countries.

Article 23 – External Operations

The ECB and national central banks may:

- establish relations with central banks and financial institutions in other countries and, where appropriate, with international organisations;
- acquire and sell spot and forward all types of foreign exchange assets and precious metals; the term 'foreign exchange asset' shall include securities and all other assets in the currency of any country or units of account and in whatever form held;
- hold and manage the assets referred to in this Article;

- conduct all types of banking transactions in relations with third countries and international organisations, including borrowing and lending operations.

Article 24 – Other Operations

In addition to operations arising from their tasks, the ECB and national central banks may enter into operations for their administrative purposes or for their staff.

CHAPTER V
PRUDENTIAL SUPERVISION

Article 25 – Prudential Supervision

25.1 The ECB may offer advice to and be consulted by the Council, the Commission and the competent authorities of the member states on the scope and implementation of Community legislation relating to the prudential supervision of credit institutions and to the stability of the financial system.

25.2 In accordance with any decision of the Council under Article 105(6) of this Treaty, the ECB may perform specific tasks concerning policies relating to the prudential supervision of credit institutions and other financial institutions with the exception of insurance undertakings.

CHAPTER VI
FINANCIAL PROVISIONS OF THE ESCB

Article 26 – Financial Accounts

26.1 The financial year of the ECB and national central banks shall begin on the first day of January and end on the last day of December.

26.2 The annual accounts of the ECB shall be drawn up by the Executive Board, in accordance with the principles established by the Governing Council. The accounts shall be approved by the Governing Council and shall thereafter be published.

26.3 For analytical and operational purposes, the Executive Board shall draw up a consolidated balance sheet of the ESCB, comprising those assets and liabilities of the national central banks that fall within the ESCB.

26.4 For the application of this Article, the Governing Council shall establish the necessary rules for standardising the accounting and reporting of operations undertaken by the national central banks.

Article 27 – Auditing

27.1 The accounts of the ECB and national central banks shall be audited by independent external auditors recommended by the Governing Council and approved by the Council. The auditors shall have full power to examine all books and accounts of the ECB and national central banks and obtain full information about their transactions.

27.2 The provisions of Article 188c of this Treaty shall only apply to an examination of the operational efficiency of the management of the ECB.

Article 28 – Capital of the ECB

28.1 The capital of the ECB, which shall become operational upon its establishment, shall be ECU 5,000 million. The capital may be decided by the Governing Council acting by the qualified majority provided for in Article 10.3, within the limits and under the condition set by the Council under the procedure laid down in Article 42.

28.2 The national central banks shall be the sole subscribers to and holders of the capital of the ECB. The subscription of capital shall be according to the key established in accordance with Article 29.

28.3 The Governing Council, acting by the qualified majority provided for in Article 10.3, shall determine the extent to which and the form in which the capital shall be paid up.

28.4 Subject to Article 28.5, the shares of the national central banks in the subscribed capital of the ECB may not be transferred, pledged or attached.

28.5 If the key referred to in Article 29 is adjusted, the national central banks shall transfer among themselves capital shares to the extent necessary to ensure that the distribution of capital shares corresponds to the adjusted key. The Governing Council shall determine the terms and conditions of such transfers.

Article 29 – Key for Capital Subscription

29.1 When in accordance with the procedure referred to in Article 1091(1) of this Treaty the ESCB and the ECB have been established, the key for subscription of the ECB's capital shall be established. Each national central bank shall be assigned a weighting in this key which shall be equal to the sum of:

- 50% of the share of its respective member state in the population of the community in the penultimate year preceding the establishment of the ESCB;
- 50% of the share of its respective member state in the gross domestic product at market prices of the Community as recorded in the last five years preceding the penultimate year before the establishment of the ESCB.

The percentage shall be rounded up to the nearest multiple of 0.05% points.

29.2 The statistical data to be used for the application of this Article shall be provided by the Commission in accordance with the rules adopted by the Council under the procedure provided for in Article 42.

29.3 The weighting assigned to the national central banks shall be adjusted every five years after the establishment of the ESCB by analogy with the provision laid down in Article 29.1. The adjusted key shall apply with effect from the first day of the following year.

29.4 The Governing Council shall take all other measures necessary for the application of this Article.

Article 30 – Transfer of Foreign Reserve Assets to the ECB

30.1 Without prejudice to Article 28, the ECB shall be provided by the national central banks with foreign reserve assets, other than member states' currencies, ECUs, IMF reserve positions and SDRs, up to an amount equivalent to ECU50,000 million. The Governing Council shall decide upon the proportion to be called up by the ECB following its establishment and the amounts called up at later dates. The

ECB shall have the full right to hold and manage the foreign reserves that are transferred to it and to use them for the purposes set out in this Statute.

30.2 The Contributions of each national central bank shall be fixed in proportion to its share in the subscribed capital of the ECB.

30.3 Each national central bank shall be credited by the ECB with the claim equivalent to its contribution. The Governing Council shall determine the denomination and remuneration of such claims.

30.4 Further calls of foreign reserve assets beyond the limit set in Article 30.1 may be effected by the ECB, in accordance with Article 30.2, within the limits and under the conditions set by the Council in accordance with the procedure laid down in Article 42.

30.5 The ECB may hold and manage IMF reserve positions and SDRs and provide for the pooling of such assets.

30.6 The Governing Council shall take all other measures necessary for the application of this Article.

Article 31 – Foreign Reserve Assets Held by National Central Banks

31.1 The national central banks shall be allowed to perform transactions in fulfilment of their obligations towards international organisations in accordance with Article 23.

31.2 All other operations in foreign reserve assets remaining with the national central banks after the transfers referred to in Article 30, and member states' transactions with their foreign exchange working balances shall, above a certain limit to be established within the framework of Article 31.3, be subject to

approval by the ECB in order to ensure consistency with the exchange rate and monetary policies of the Community.

31.3 The Governing Council shall issue guidelines with a view to facilitating such operations.

Article 32 – Allocation of Monetary Income of National Central Banks

32.1 The income accruing to the national central banks in the performance of the ESCB's monetary policy function (hereinafter referred to as 'monetary income') shall be allocated at the end of each financial year in accordance with the provisions of this Article.

32.2 Subject to Article 32.3, the amount of each national central bank's monetary income shall be equal to its annual income derived from its assets held against notes in circulation and deposit liabilities to credit institutions. These assets shall be earmarked by national central banks in accordance with guidelines to be established by the Governing Council.

32.3 If, after the start of the third stage, the balance sheet structures of the national central banks do not, in the judgement of the Governing Council, permit the application of Article 32.2, the Governing Council, acting by qualified majority, may decide that, by way of derogation from Article 32.2, monetary income shall be measured according to an alternative method for a period of not more than five years.

32.4 The amount of each national central bank's monetary income shall be reduced by an amount equivalent to any interest paid by that central bank on its deposit liabilities to credit institutions in accordance with Article 19.

The Governing Council may decide that national central banks shall be indemnified against costs incurred in connection with the issue of bank notes or in exceptional circumstances for specific losses arising from monetary policy operations undertaken for the ESCB. Indemnification shall be in a form deemed appropriate in the judgement of the Governing Council; these amounts may be offset against the national central banks' monetary income.

32.5 The sum of the national central banks' monetary income shall be allocated to the national central bank in proportion to their paid-up shares in the capital the ECB subject to any decision taken by the Governing Council pursuant to Article 33.2.

32.6 The clearing and settlement of the balances arising from the allocation of monetary income shall be carried out by the ECB in accordance with guidelines established by the Governing Council.

32.7 The Governing Council shall take all other measures necessary for the application of this Article.

Article 33 – Allocation of Net Profits and Losses of the ECB

33.1 The net profit of the ECB shall be transferred in the following order:

(a) an amount to be determined by the Governing Council, which may not exceed 20% of the net profit, shall be transferred to the general reserve fund subject to a limit equal to 100% of the capital;

(b) the remaining net profits shall be distributed to the shareholders of the ECB in proportion to their paid-up shares.

33.2 In the event of a loss incurred by the ECB, the shortfall may be offset against the general reserve fund of the ECB and, if necessary, following a decision by the Governing Council, against the monetary income of the relevant financial year in proportion and up to the amounts allocated to the national central banks in accordance with Article 32.5.

CHAPTER VII
GENERAL PROVISIONS

Article 34 – Legal Acts

34.1 In accordance with Article 108a of this Treaty, the ECB shall:

- make regulations to the extent necessary to implement the tasks defined in Article 3.1, first indent, Articles 19.1, 22 or 25.2 and in cases which shall be laid down in the acts of the Council referred to in Article 42
- take decisions necessary for carrying out the tasks entrusted to the ESCB under this Treaty and this Statute;
- make recommendations and deliver opinions.

34.2 A regulation shall have general application. It shall be binding in its entirety and directly applicable in all member states.

Recommendations and opinions shall have no binding force.
A decision shall be binding in its entirety upon those to whom it is addressed.

Article 190 to 192 of this Treaty shall apply to regulations and decisions adopted by the ECB.

The ECB may decide to publish its decision, recommendations and opinions.

34.3 Within the limits and under the conditions adopted by the Council under the procedure laid down in Article 42, the ECB shall be entitled to impose fines or periodic penalty payments on undertakings for failure to comply with obligations under its regulations and decisions.

Article 35 – Judicial Control and Related Matters

35.1 The acts or omissions of the ECB shall be open to review or interpretation by the Court of Justice in the cases and under the conditions laid down in this Treaty. The ECB may institute proceedings in the cases and under the conditions laid down in this Treaty.

35.2 Disputes between the ECB, on the one hand, and its creditors, debtors or any other person, on the other, shall fall within the jurisdiction of the competent national courts, save where jurisdiction has been conferred upon the Courts of Justice.

35.3 The ECB shall be subject to the liability regime provided for in Article 215 of this Treaty. The national central banks shall be liable according to their respective national laws.

35.4 The Court of Justice shall have jurisdiction to give judgement pursuant to any arbitration clause contained in a contract concluded by or on behalf of the ECB, whether that contract be governed by public or private law.

35.5 A decision of the ECB to bring an action before the Court of Justice shall be taken by the Governing Council.

35.6 The Court of Justice shall have jurisdiction in disputes concerning the fulfilment by a national central bank of obligations under this Statute. If the ECB considers that a national central bank has failed to fulfil an obligation under this Statute, it shall deliver a reasoned opinion on the matter after giving the national central bank concerned the opportunity to submit its observations. If the national central bank concerned does not comply with the opinion within the period laid down by the ECB, the latter may bring the matter before the Court of Justice.

Article 36 – Staff

36.1 The Governing Council, on a proposal from the Executive Board, shall lay down the conditions of employment of the staff of the ECB.

36.2 The Court of Justice shall have jurisdiction in any dispute between the ECB and its servants within the limits and under the conditions laid down in the conditions of employment.

Article 37 – Seat

Before the end of 1992, the decisions as to where the seat of the ECB will be established shall be taken by common accord of the governments of the member states at the level of Heads of State or of Government.

Article 38 – Professional Secrecy

38.1 Member of the governing bodies and the staff of the ECB and the national central banks shall be required,

even after their duties have ceased, not to disclose information of the kind covered by the obligation of professional secrecy.

38.2 Persons having access to data covered by Community legislation imposing an obligation of secrecy shall be subject to such legislation.

Article 39 – Signatories

39.1 The ECB shall be legally binding to third parties by the President or two members of the Executive Board or by the signatories of two members of the staff of the ECB who have been duly authorised by the President to sign on behalf of the ECB.

Article 40 – Privileges and Immunities

The ECB shall enjoy in the territories of the member states such privileges and immunities as are necessary for the performance of its tasks, under the conditions laid down in the Protocol on the Privileges and Immunities of the European Communities.

CHAPTER VIII
AMENDMENT OF THE STATUTES AND COMPLEMENTARY LEGISLATION

Article 41 – Simplified Amendment Procedure

41.1 In accordance with Article 106(5) of this Treaty, Articles 5.1, 5.2, 5.3, 17, 18, 19.1, 22, 23, 24, 26, 32.2, 32.3, 32.4, 32.6, 33.1(a) and 36 of this Statute may be amended by the Council, acting either by a qualified majority on a recommendation from the ECB and

after consulting the Commission, or unanimously on a proposal from the Commission and after consulting the ECB. In either case the assent of the European Parliament shall be required.

41.2 A recommendation made by the ECB under this Article shall require a unanimous decision by the Governing Council.

Article 42 – Complementary Legislation

In accordance with Article 106(6) of this Treaty, immediately after the decision on the date for the beginning of the third stage, the Council, acting by a qualified majority either on a proposal from the Commission and after consulting the European Parliament and the ECB, or on a recommendation from the ECB and after consulting the European Parliament and the Commission, shall adopt the provisions referred to in Articles 4, 5.4, 19.2, 20, 28.1, 29.2, 30.4 and 34.3 of this Statute.

CHAPTER IX
TRANSITIONAL AND OTHER PROVISIONS FOR THE ESCB

Article 43 – General Provisions

43.1 A derogation as referred to in Article 109k(l) of this Treaty shall entail that the following Articles of this Statute shall not confer any rights or impose any obligations on the member state concerned: 3, 6, 9.2, 12.1, 14.3, 16, 18, 19, 20, 22, 23, 26.2, 27, 30, 31, 32, 33, 34, 50 and 52.

43.2 The central banks of member states with a derogation as specified in Article 109k(l) of this Treaty shall

retain their powers in the field of monetary policy according to national law.

43.3 In accordance with Article 109k(4) of this Treaty, 'member states' shall be read as 'member states without a derogation' in the following Articles of this Statute: 3, 11.2, 19, 34.2 and 50.

43.4 'National central banks' shall be read as 'central banks of member states without derogation' in the following Articles of this Statute: 9.2, 10.1, 10.3, 12.1, 16, 17, 18, 22, 23, 27, 30, 31, 32, 33.2 and 52.

43.5 'Shareholders' shall be read as 'central banks of member states without a derogation' in Articles 10.3 and 33.1.

43.6 'Subscribed capital of the ECB' shall be read as 'capital of the ECB subscribed by the central banks of member states without a derogation' in Articles 10.3 and 30.2.

Article 44 – Transitional Tasks of the ECB

The ECB shall take over those tasks of the EMI which, because of the derogation of one or more member states, still have to be performed in the third stage.

The ECB shall give advice in the preparation for the abrogation of the derogations specified in Article 109k of this Treaty.

Article 45 – The General Council of the ECB

45.1 Without prejudice to Article 106(3) of this Treaty, the General Council shall be constituted as a third decision-making body of the ECB.

45.2 The General Council shall comprise the President and Vice-President of the ECB and the Governors of the national central banks. The other members of the

Executive Board may participate, without having the right to vote, in meetings of the General Council.

45.3 The responsibilities of the General Council are listed in full in Article 47 of this Statute.

Article 46 – Rules of Procedure of the General Council

46.1 The President or in his absence the Vice-President of the ECB shall chair the General Council of the ECB.

46.2 The President of the Council and a member of the Commission may participate, without having the right to vote, in meetings of the General Council.

46.3 The President shall prepare the meetings of the General Council.

46.4 By way of derogation from Article 12.3, the General Council shall adopt its Rules of Procedure.

46.5 The Secretariat of the General Council shall be provided by the ECB.

Article 47 – Responsibilities of the General Council

47.1 The General Council shall:

- perform the tasks referred to in Article 44;
- contribute to the advisory functions referred to in Articles 4 and 25.1.

47.2 The General Council shall contribute to:

- the collection of statistical information as referred to in Article 5;
- the reporting activities of the ECB as referred to in Article 15;

- the establishment of the necessary rules for the application of Article 26 as referred to in Article 26.4,
- the taking of all other measures necessary for the application of Article 29 as referred to in Article 29.4;
- the laying down of the conditions of employment of the staff of the ECB as referred to in Article 36.

47.3 The General Council shall contribute to the necessary preparations for irrevocably fixing the exchange rates of the currencies of member states with a derogation against the currencies, or the single currency, of the member states without a derogation, as referred to in Article 1091(5) of this Treaty.

47.4 The General Council shall be informed by the President of the ECB of decisions of the Governing Council.

Article 48 – Transitional Provisions for the Capital of the ECB

In accordance with Article 29.1 each national central bank shall be assigned a weighting in the key for subscription of the ECB's capital. By way of derogation from Article 28.3, central banks of member states with a derogation shall not pay up their subscribed capital unless the General Council, acting by a majority representing at least two thirds of the subscribed capital of the ECB and at least half of the shareholders, decides that a minimal percentage has to be paid up as a contribution to the operational costs of the ECB.

Article 49 – Deferred Payment of Capital, Reserves and Provisions of the ECB

49.1 The central bank of a member state whose derogation has been abrogated shall pay up its subscribed share of the capital of the ECB to the same extent as the central banks of other member states without a derogation, and shall transfer to the ECB foreign reserve assets in accordance with Article 30.1. The sum to be transferred shall be determined by multiplying the ECU value at current exchange rates of the foreign reserve assets which have already been transferred to the ECB in accordance with Article 30.1, by the ratio between the number of shares subscribed by the national central bank concerned and the number of shares already paid up by the other national central banks.

49.2 In addition to the payment to be made in accordance with Article 49.1, the central bank concerned shall contribute to the reserves of the ECB, to those provisions equivalent to reserves, and to the amount still to be appropriated to the reserves and provisions corresponding to the balance of the profit and loss account as at 31st December of the year prior to the abrogation of the derogation. The sum to be contributed shall be determined by multiplying the amount of the reserves, as defined above and as stated in the approved balance sheet of the ECB, by the ratio between the number of shares subscribed by the central bank concerned and the number of shares already paid up by the other central banks.

Article 50 – Initial Appointment of the Members of the Executive Board

When the Executive Board of the ECB is being established, the President, the Vice-President and the other members of the Executive Board shall be appointed by common accord of the governments of the member states at the level of Heads of State or of Government, on a recommendation from the Council after consulting the European Parliament and the Council of the EMI. The President of the Executive Board shall be appointed for eight years. By way of derogation from Article 11.2, the Vice-President shall be appointed for four years and the other members of the Executive Board for terms of office between five and eight years. No term of office shall be renewable. The number of member of the Executive Board may be smaller than provided for in Article 11.1, but in no circumstances shall it be less than four.

Article 51 – Derogation from Article 32

51.1 If, after the start of the third stage, the Governing Council decides that the application of Article 32 results in significant changes in national central banks' relative income positions, the amount of income to be allocated pursuant to Article 32 shall be reduced by a uniform percentage which shall not exceed 60% in the first financial year after the start of the third stage and which shall decrease by at least 12 percentage points in each subsequent financial year.

51.2 Article 51.1 shall be applicable for not more than five financial years after the start of the third stage.

Article 52 – Exchange of Bank Notes in Community Currencies

Following the irrevocable fixing of exchange rates, the Governing Council shall take the necessary measures to ensure that bank notes denominated in currencies with irrevocably fixed exchange rates are exchanged by the national central banks at their respective par value.

Article 53 – Applicability of the Transitional Provisions

If and as long as there are member states with a derogation Articles 43 and 48 shall be applicable.

Appendix IV
Rules of Procedure of the Governing Council of the European Central Bank

Having regard to the Protocol on the Statute of the European System of Central Banks and of the European Central Bank (hereinafter referred to as the 'Statute') and in particular to Article 12.3 thereof;

HAS DECIDED TO ADOPT THESE RULES OF PROCEDURE:

PRELIMINARY CHAPTER

Article 1 – Treaty and Statute

These Rules of Procedure shall supplement the Treaty establishing the European Community (hereinafter referred to as the 'Treaty') and the Statute. The terms in these Rules of Procedure shall have the meaning which they have in the Treaty and the Statute.

CHAPTER I
THE GOVERNING COUNCIL

Article 2 – Date and Place of Governing Council Meetings

2.1 The date of the meetings shall be decided by the Governing Council on a proposal from the President. The Council shall, in principle, meet regularly following a schedule determined by the Governing Council in good time before the start of each calendar year.

2.2 The President shall convene a meeting of the Governing Council if a request for a meeting is submitted by at least three members of the Governing Council.

2.3 The President may also convene meetings of the Governing Council whenever he/she deems it necessary.

2.4 The Governing Council shall normally hold its meetings on the premises of the European Central Bank (hereinafter referred to as the 'ECB').

2.5 Meetings may also be held by means of teleconferencing, unless at least three Governors object.

Article 3 – Attendance at Governing Council Meetings

3.1 Except as provided hereto, attendance at meetings of the Governing Council shall be restricted to its members, the President of the Council of the European Union, and a member of the Commission of the European Communities.

3.2 Each Governor may normally be accompanied by one person for those parts of the meetings which are not related to monetary policy deliberations.

3.3 If a Governor is unable to attend, he/she may appoint, in writing, an alternate without prejudice to Article 4. This written communication shall be sent to the President in due time before the meeting.

3.4 The Governing Council may also invite other persons to attend its meetings if it deems it appropriate to do so.

Article 4 – Voting

4.1 In order for the Governing Council to vote, there shall be a quorum of two thirds of the members. If the quorum is not met, the President may convene an extraordinary meeting at which decisions may be taken without regard to the quorum.

4.2 The Governing Council shall proceed to vote at the request of the President. The President shall also initiate a voting procedure if any member requests him/her to do so.

4.3 Abstentions shall not prevent the adoption by the Governing Council of decisions under Article 41.2 of the Statute.

4.4 If a member of the Governing Council is prevented from voting for a prolonged period (of more than one month), he/she may appoint an alternate as a member of the Governing Council.

4.5 In accordance with Article 10.3 of the Statute, if a Governor is unable to vote on a decision to be taken under Articles 28, 29, 30, 32, 33 and 51 of the Statute, his/her appointed alternate may cast his/her weighted vote.

4.6 The President may initiate a secret ballot if requested to do so by three members of the Governing Council. If members of the Governing Council are personally affected by a prospective decision under Articles 11.1, 11.3 or 11.4 of the Statute, there shall always be secret balloting. In such cases the members concerned shall not participate in the vote.

4.7 Decisions may also be taken by written procedure, unless at least three members of the Governing Council object. A written procedure shall require:

(i) normally not less than five working days for consideration by every member of the Governing Council;

(ii) the personal signature of each member of the Governing Council (or his/her alternate in accordance with Article 4.4); and

(iii) a record of any such decision to be made in the minutes of the next meeting of the Governing Council.

Article 5 – Organisation of Governing Council Meetings

5.1 The agenda for each meeting shall be adopted by the Governing Council. A provisional agenda shall be drawn up by the Executive Board and shall be sent, together with the related documents, to the members of the Governing Council and other authorised participants at least eight days before the relevant meeting, except in emergencies, in which case the Executive Board shall act appropriately with a view to the circumstances. The Governing Council may decide to remove items from or add items to the provisional agenda on a proposal from the President

or from a member of the Governing Council. An item shall be removed from the agenda at the request of at least three of its members if the related documents were not sent to the members in due time.

5.2 The minutes of the proceedings of the Governing Council shall be submitted to its members for approval at the next meeting (or earlier, if necessary, by written procedure) and shall be signed by the President.

CHAPTER II
THE EXECUTIVE BOARD

Article 6 – Date and Place of Executive Board Meetings

6.1 The date of the meetings shall be decided by the Executive Board on a proposal from the President.

6.2 The President may also convene meetings of the Executive Board whenever he/she deems it necessary.

Article 7 – Voting

7.1 In order for the Executive Board to vote, in accordance with Article 11.5 of the Statute, there shall be a quorum of two thirds of the members. If the quorum is not met, the President may convene an extraordinary meeting at which decisions may be taken without regard to the quorum.

7.2 Decisions may also be taken by written procedure, unless at least two members of the Executive Board object.

7.3 Members of the Executive Board personally affected by a prospective decision under Articles 11.1, 11.3 or 11.4 of the Statute shall not participate in the vote.

Article 8 – Organisation of Executive Board Meetings

The Executive Board shall decide on the organisation of its meetings.

CHAPTER III
THE ORGANISATION OF THE EUROPEAN CENTRAL BANK

Article 9 – Committees of the European System of Central Banks

9.1 Committees of the European System of Central Banks (hereinafter referred to as 'ESCB Committees'), composed of representatives of the ECB and of the national central bank of each participating Member State, will be formed to assist in the work of the European System of Central Banks (hereinafter referred to as the 'ESCB').

9.2 The Governing Council shall lay down the mandates of the ESCB Committees and appoint their chairpersons. As a rule, the chairperson shall be a representative of the ECB. Both the Governing Council and the Executive Board shall have the right to request studies of specific topics by ESCB Committees.

9.3 ESCB Committees shall report to the Governing Council via the Executive Board. The Banking Supervisory Committee shall not be obliged to report via the Executive Board whenever it acts as a forum for consultation on issues which are not related to the supervisory functions of the ESCB as defined in the Treaty and in the Statute.

9.4 The national central bank of each non-participating Member State may also appoint a representative to take part in the meetings of an ESCB Committee whenever it deals with matters which fall within the field of competence of the General Council. The representatives may also be invited to take part in meetings whenever this is deemed appropriate by the chairperson of a Committee and the Executive Board.

9.5 For specific matters of direct interest to the Commission of the European Communities, representatives of the Commission services may be invited to attend meetings of ESCB Committees. Representatives of other Community bodies and of third parties may also be invited if and where deemed appropriate.

9.6 The ECB shall provide secretarial assistance to the ESCB Committees.

Article 10 – Internal Structure

10.1 Having consulted the Governing Council, the Executive Board shall decide upon the number, name and respective competence of each of the work units of the ECB. This decision shall be made public.

10.2 All work units of the ECB shall be placed under the managing direction of the Executive Board. The Executive Board shall decide upon the individual responsibilities of its members with respect to the work units of the ECB, and shall inform the Governing Council, the General Council and the staff of the ECB thereof. Any such decision shall be taken only in the presence of all the members of the Executive Board, and may not be taken against the vote of the President.

Article 11 – Staff of the ECB

11.1 Each member of the staff of the ECB shall be informed of his/her position within the structure of the ECB, his/her reporting line and his/her professional responsibilities.

11.2 Without prejudice to Articles 36 and 47 of the Statute, the Executive Board shall enact organisational rules (hereinafter referred to as 'Administrative Circulars'). Such rules shall be obligatory for the staff of the ECB.

11.3 The Executive Board shall enact and update a Code of Conduct for the guidance of its members and of members of its staff.

CHAPTER IV
INVOLVEMENT OF THE GENERAL COUNCIL IN THE TASKS OF THE EUROPEAN SYSTEM OF CENTRAL BANKS

Article 12 – Relationship between the Governing Council and the General Council

12.1 The General Council of the ECB shall be given the opportunity to submit observations before the Governing Council adopts:

- opinions under Articles 4 and 25.1 of the Statute;
- ECB Recommendations in the statistical field, under Article 42 of the Statute;
- the rules on the standardisation of accounting rules and reporting of operations;

- the measures for the application of Article 29 of the Statute;
- the conditions of employment of the staff of the ECB;
- in the context of the preparations for the irrevocable fixing of exchange rates, an ECB opinion either under Article 109l (5) of the Treaty or concerning EC legal acts to be adopted when a derogation is abrogated.

12.2 Whenever the General Council is requested to submit observations under the above paragraph, it shall be given a reasonable period of time within which to do so, which may not be less than ten working days. In a case of urgency (which must be justified in the request), the period may be reduced to five working days. The President may decide to use written procedure.

12.3 The President shall inform the General Council, in accordance with Article 47.4 of the Statute, of decisions adopted by the Governing Council.

Article 13 – Relationship between the Executive Board and the General Council

13.1 The General Council of the ECB shall be given the opportunity to submit observations before the Executive Board:

- implements legal acts of the Governing Council for which, in accordance with Article 12.1 above, the contribution of the General Council is required;
- adopts, by virtue of powers delegated by the Governing Council in accordance with Article 12.1 of the Statute, legal acts for which, in accordance

with Article 12.1 of these Rules, the contribution of the General Council is required.

13.2 Whenever the General Council is requested to submit observations under the above paragraph, it shall be given a reasonable period of time within which to do so, which may not be less than ten working days. In a case of urgency (which must be justified in the request), the period may be reduced to five working days. The President may decide to use written procedure.

CHAPTER V
SPECIFIC PROCEDURAL PROVISIONS

Article 14 – Delegation of Powers

14.1 The delegation of powers of the Governing Council to the Executive Board under Article 12.1, second paragraph, last sentence, of the Statute shall be notified to the parties concerned, or published if appropriate, in matters having legal effects on third parties. Acts adopted by way of delegation shall be promptly notified to the Governing Council.

14.2 The Book of Authorised Signatories of the ECB, established pursuant to decisions adopted under Article 39 of the Statute, shall be circulated to interested parties.

Article 15 – Budgetary Procedure

15.1 The Governing Council, acting upon a proposal from the Executive Board in accordance with any principles laid down by the former, shall adopt, before the

end of each financial year, the budget of the ECB for the subsequent financial year.

15.2 For assistance in matters related to the budget of the ECB, the Governing Council shall establish a Budget Committee and lay down its mandate and composition.

Article 16 – Reporting and Annual Accounts

16.1 The competence to adopt the annual report required under Article 15.3 of the Statute shall pertain to the Governing Council.

16.2 The competence to adopt and publish the quarterly reports under Article 15.1 of the Statute, the weekly consolidated financial statements under Article 15.2 of the Statute, the consolidated balance sheets under Article 26.3 of the Statute and other reports shall be delegated to the Executive Board.

16.3 The Executive Board shall, in accordance with the principles established by the Governing Council, prepare the annual accounts of the ECB within the first month of the subsequent financial year. These shall be submitted to the external auditor.

16.4 The Governing Council shall adopt the annual accounts of the ECB within the first quarter of the subsequent year. The external auditor's report shall be submitted to the Governing Council before their adoption.

Article 17 – Legal Instruments of the ECB

17.1 ECB Regulations shall be adopted by the Governing Council and signed on its behalf by the President.

17.2 ECB Guidelines shall be adopted by the Governing Council and signed on its behalf by the President.

They shall state the reasons on which they are based. Notification of the national central banks may take place by means of telefax, electronic mail or telex or in paper form.

17.3 The Governing Council may delegate its normative powers to the Executive Board for the purpose of implementing its regulations and guidelines. The regulation or guideline concerned shall specify the issues to be implemented as well as the limits and scope of the delegated powers.

17.4 ECB Decisions and Recommendations shall be adopted by the Governing Council or the Executive Board in their respective domain of competence, and shall be signed by the President. They shall state the reasons on which they are based. The Recommendations for secondary Community legislation under Article 42 of the Statute shall be adopted by the Governing Council.

17.5 Without prejudice to Article 44, second paragraph, and Article 47.1, first indent, of the Statute, ECB Opinions shall be adopted by the Governing Council. However, in exceptional circumstances and unless not less than three Governors state their wish to retain the competence of the Governing Council for the adoption of specific opinions, ECB Opinions may be adopted by the Executive Board, in line with comments provided by the Governing Council and taking into account the contribution of the General Council. ECB Opinions shall be signed by the President.

17.6 ECB Instructions shall be adopted by the Executive Board and signed on its behalf by the President or any two Executive Board members. Notification of the national central banks may take place by means of telefax, electronic mail or telex or in paper form.

17.7 All ECB legal instruments shall be numbered sequentially for ease of identification. The Executive Board shall ensure the safe custody of the originals, the notification of the addressees or consulting authorities, and the immediate publication in all the official EU languages in the Official Journal of the European Communities in the case of ECB Regulations, ECB Opinions on draft Community legislation and those ECB legal instruments whose publication has been expressly decided.

Article 18 – Procedure under Article 105a (2) of the Treaty

The approval provided for in Article 105a (2) of the Treaty shall be adopted by the Governing Council in a single decision for all participating Member States within the last quarter of every year and for the following year.

Article 19 – Procurement

19.1 In the procurement of goods and services for the ECB due regard shall be given to the principles of publicity, transparency, equal access, non-discrimination and efficient administration.

19.2 Without derogation to the principle of efficient administration, exceptions may be made to the above principles in cases of urgency; for reasons of security or secrecy; where there is a sole supplier; for supplies from the national central banks to the ECB; to ensure the continuity of a supplier; and for assets acquired from the European Monetary Institute (hereinafter referred to as the 'EMI').

Article 20 – Selection, Appointment and Promotion of Staff

20.1 All members of staff shall be selected, appointed and promoted by the Executive Board.
20.2 Members of staff shall be selected, appointed and promoted with due regard to the principles of professional qualification, publicity, transparency, equal access and non-discrimination. An Administrative Circular shall further specify the rules and procedures for recruitment and for internal promotion.
20.3 The Executive Board may recruit for the ECB members of the staff of the EMI (under liquidation) without specific recruitment rules and procedures.

Article 21 – Conditions of Employment

21.1 The employment relationship between the ECB and its staff shall be determined by the Conditions of Employment and the Staff Rules.
21.2 The Conditions of Employment shall be approved and amended by the Governing Council upon a proposal from the Executive Board. The General Council shall be consulted under the procedure laid down in these Rules of Procedure.
21.3 The Conditions of Employment shall be implemented by Staff Rules, which shall be adopted and amended by the Executive Board.
21.4 The Staff Committee shall be consulted before the adoption of new Conditions of Employment or Staff Rules. Its opinion shall be submitted, respectively, to the Governing Council or the Executive Board.

Article 22 – Communications and Announcements

General communications and announcements of decisions taken by the decision-making bodies of the ECB may be effected through the Official Journal of the European Communities and by means of wire services common to financial markets.

Article 23 – Confidentiality of and Access to ECB Documents and Archives

23.1 The proceedings of the decision-making bodies of the ECB and of any committee or group established by them shall be confidential unless the Governing Council authorises the President to make the outcome of their deliberations public.

23.2 All documents drawn up by the ECB shall be confidential unless the Governing Council decides otherwise. The Governing Council shall specify the access criteria applicable to ECB documentation and archives. Such a decision shall be published in the Official Journal of the European Communities.

23.3 Access to documents held in the archives of the EMI shall be governed by Decision No. 9/97 of the Council of the EMI until this is replaced by a Decision of the Governing Council. In view of the liquidation of the EMI:

- all responsibilities of the EMI Council under this decision shall be transferred to the Governing Council;
- all responsibilities of the Secretary General of the EMI shall be transferred to the Executive Board.

23.4 Documents held in the archives of the Committee of Governors of the Central Banks of the Member States of the European Economic Community, of the EMI and of the ECB shall be freely accessible after thirty years. In special cases the Governing Council may shorten this period.

CHAPTER VI
FINAL PROVISIONS

Article 24 – Amendments to these Rules of Procedure

The Governing Council may amend these Rules of Procedure. The General Council may propose amendments and the Executive Board may adopt supplementary rules within its field of competence.

Article 25 – Publication

These Rules of Procedure shall be published in the Official Journal of the European Communities.

Done at Frankfurt am Main on 7 July 1998.
For and on behalf of the Governing Council
The President
[signed]
Willem F. Duisenberg

Appendix V
Statutes of the Economic and Financial Committee

Article 1.

The Economic and Financial Committee shall carry out the tasks described in Article 109c(2) of the Treaty establishing the European Community.

Article 2.

The Economic and Financial Committee may, *inter alia*:

- be consulted in the procedure leading to decisions relating to the exchange-rate mechanism of the third stage of economic and monetary union (ERM II),
- without prejudice to Article 151 of the Treaty, prepare the Council's reviews of the development of the exchange rate of the euro,
- provide the framework within which the dialogue between the Council and the European Central Bank (ECB) can be prepared and continued at the level of senior officials from ministries, national central banks, the Commission and the ECB.

Article 3.

Members of the Committee and alternates shall be guided, in the performance of their duties, by the general interests of the Community.

Article 4.

Opinions, reports or communications shall be adopted by a majority of the members if a vote is requested. Each member of the Committee shall have one vote. However, when advice or an opinion is given on questions on which the Council may subsequently take a decision, members from central banks and the Commission may participate fully in the discussions but shall not participate in a vote. The Committee shall also report on minority or dissenting views expressed in the course of the discussion.

Article 5.

The Committee shall elect from among its members, by a majority of its members, a President for a period of two years. The two-year term shall be renewable. The President shall be elected from among members who are senior officials in the national administrations. The President shall delegate his/her voting right to his/her alternate.

Article 6.

In the event of being prevented from fulfilling his/her duties, the President shall be replaced by the Vice-President of the Committee who shall be elected according to the same rules.

Article 7.

Unless the Committee decides otherwise, alternates may attend meetings of the Committee. They shall not vote. Unless the Committee decides otherwise they shall not take part in the discussions.

A member who is unable to attend a meeting of the Committee may delegate his/her functions to one of the alternates. He/she may also delegate them to another member. The Chairman and the Secretary should be informed in writing before a meeting. In exceptional circumstances the President may agree to alternative arrangements.

Article 8.

The Committee may entrust the study of specific questions to its alternate members, to sub-committees or to working parties. In these cases, the presidency shall be assumed by a member or an alternate member of the Committee, appointed by the Committee. The members of the Committee, its alternates, and its sub-committees or working parties may call upon experts to assist them.

Article 9.

The Committee shall be convened by the President on his/her own initiative, or at the request of the Council, of the Commission or of at least two members of the Committee.

Article 10.

As a rule the President represents the Committee; in particular the President may be authorised by the Committee to report on discussions and deliver oral comments

on opinions and communications prepared by the Committee. The President of the Committee shall have the responsibility of maintaining the Committee's relations with the European Parliament.

Article 11.

The proceedings of the Committee are confidential. The same rule shall apply to the proceedings of its alternates, sub-committees or working parties.

Article 12.

The Committee shall be assisted by a secretariat under the direction of a Secretary. The Secretary and the staff needed for the secretariat shall be supplied by the Commission. The Secretary shall be appointed by the Commission after consultation of the Committee. The Secretary and his/her staff shall act on the instructions of the Committee when carrying out their responsibilities to the Committee.

The expenses of the Committee shall be included in the estimates of the Commission.

Article 13.

The Committee shall adopt its own procedural arrangements.

Appendix VI
The Key Players

Willem Frederik Duisenberg

Date of birth: 9th July 1935
Place of birth: Heerenveen, the Netherlands

EDUCATION:

1954 Grammar school leaving certificate
1961 Degree in Economics (*cum laude*), University of Groningen, the Netherlands
Subject: Econometrics
Specialisation: International economic relations
1965 PhD, University of Groningen, the Netherlands; Doctoral thesis: Economic consequences of disarmament

PROFESSIONAL CAREER:

1961–1965 Teaching assistant, University of Groningen
1965–1969 Staff member of the International Monetary Fund, Washington, DC
1969–1970 Adviser to the Governing Board of De Nederlandsche Bank
1970–1973 Professor of Macroeconomics, University of Amsterdam
1973–1977 Minister of Finance, the Netherlands
1977–1978 Member of Parliament for the Partij van de Arbeid (Socialist Party)

1978–1981 Member and Vice-Chairman of the Executive Board of Rabobank Nederland
1981–1982 Executive Director of De Nederlandsche Bank
1982–1997 President of De Nederlandsche Bank
1997–1998 President of the European Monetary Institute
since 1st June 1998 President of the European Central Bank (ECB)

OTHER POSTS:

- Chairman of the Board and President of the Bank for International Settlements, Basle (January 1988 – December 1990, and January 1994 – June 1997)
- Member of the Board of Patrons of the European Association for Banking History, Frankfurt (since 1990)
- Member of the Board of Directors of the Bank for International Settlements, Basle (January 1982 – June 1997)
- Chairman of the Committee of the Governors of the Central Banks of the Member States of the EEC (January–December 1993)
- Member of the Council of the European Monetary Institute (January 1994 – June 1997)
- Governor of the International Monetary Fund, Washington, DC (January 1992 – June 1997)
- Chairman of the Netherlands Cancer Institute (since June 1997)

DECORATIONS

- The Netherlands: Knight of the Order of the Netherlands Lion
- The Netherlands: Commander of the Order of Orange-Nassau

- The Netherlands: Commander of the Order of the Netherlands Lion
- Luxembourg: Grand Cross of the Order of Merit
- Sweden: Knight Grand Cross of the Royal Order of the Star of the North
- Senegal: Grand Cross of tile Order of Merit
- Belgium: Grand Cross of the Order of the Crown
- Portugal: Honorary doctorate from the New University of Lisbon
- France: Commander of the *Légion d'Honneur*

Christian Noyer

Date of birth: 6th October 1950
Place of birth: Soisy, France

EDUCATION:

1971   University of Rennes: degree in Law
1972   University of Paris: higher degree in Law
1972   Institute of Political Science: diploma
1974–1976 Ecole Nationale d'Administration

PROFESSIONAL CAREER:

1976   Joined the French Treasury
1980–1982 Financial Attaché, French delegation to the EC in Brussels
1982–1985 Chief of the Banking Office and subsequently of the Export Credit Office of the French Treasury
1986–1988 Technical Adviser and subsequently Senior Adviser to the Minister for Economic Affairs, Finance and Privatisation (E. Balladur)
1988–1990 Deputy Director in charge of International Multilateral Issues at the Treasury
1990–1992 Deputy Director in charge of the Treasury's debt management, monetary and banking issues
1992–1993 Director of the Department responsible for public holdings and public financing
1993 Chief of Staff of the Minister for Economic Affairs (R. Alphandéry)
1993–1995 Director of the Treasury
1995–1997 Chief of Staff of the Minister for Economic Affairs and Finance (J. Arthuis)
1997–1998 Director of the Ministry for Economic Affairs, Finance and Industry, working on various assignments related to the banking reform

since 1st June 1998 Vice-President of the European Central Bank (ECB)

OTHER POSTS:

- Alternate member of the European Monetary Committee (1988–1990)
- Member of the European Monetary Committee (1993–1995 and since June 1998)
- Alternate Governor of the International Monetary Fund and of the World Bank (1993–1995)
- Alternate member of the G7 and G10 (1993–1995)
- Member of Working Party No. 3 of the OECD (1993–1995)
- Chairman of the Paris Club (1993–1997)

DECORATIONS:

- France: Knight of the *Légion d'Honneur*
- France: Knight of the National Order of Merit
- Senegal: Commander of the Order of the Lion

PUBLICATIONS:

- Author of *Banks, the rules of the game* (1990) and various articles

Eugenio Domingo Solans

Date of birth: 26th November 1945
Place of birth: Barcelona, Spain

EDUCATION:

French Lycée of Barcelona
1968 University of Barcelona, Spain: degree in Economics
Graduation prize awarded by the Caja de Ahoirros Provincial de la Diputación de Barcelona (currently Caixa de Catalunya)
1975 Autonomous University of Madrid, Spain: Doctorate in Economics

PROFESSIONAL CAREER:

1968–1970 Professor of Public Finance in the Faculty of Economics, University of Barcelona
1969 Visiting professor at York University (United Kingdom), invited by the Institute for Social and Economic Research
1970 to date: Professor of Public Finance, Autonomous University of Madrid
1970 Economist at the Banco Atlántico (Research Department, Planning and Finance Division)
1970–1973 Economist in the Research Group of the Economic and Social Development Plan Department (Presidency of the Spanish Government)
1973–1977 Economist at the Banco Atlántico
1977–1978 Economic Adviser to the Secretariat of State for Economic Co-ordination and Planning of the Ministry of Economy
1978–1979 Economist at the Banco Atlántico
1979–1986 Manager of the Research Department at the Institute of Economic Studies (IEE) and of the IEE's Review

1986–1994 Assistant President of Banco Zaragozano
1987–1991 Member of the Board of BZ Gestión
1988-1994 Member of the Board of Banco Zaragozano and of its Executive Commission
1988-1994 Member of the Board of Banco de Toledo
1994-1998 Member of the Governing Council of the Executive Commission of the Banco de España
1996 to date Professor of Monetary Policy and the Spanish Tax System, University College of Financial Studies (CUNEF) attached to the Complutense University of Madrid
since 1st June 1998 Member of the Executive Board of the European Central Bank

OTHER TEACHING ACTIVITIES:

- Classes given at the National School of Local Administration, the United Nations
- International Environmental Sciences Training Center for Spanish-speaking students (CIFCA)
- The National School of Public Administration
- The School of Industrial Organisation

THE INTERNATIONAL CHARLES V CENTRE OTHER POSTS:

- Member of the Advisory Board to *Gaceta Fiscal* and of the Editorial Board of *Presupuesto y Gasto Público*
- Joined the body of Assistant University Professors after taking first place in a competitive examination (1979)
- Member of the Tax, Financing and Economic Situation Committees of the Spanish Confederation of Business Organisations (CEOE) (1979–1994)

- Joined the Body of Associate University Professors after taking first place in a competitive examination (1981)
- Joined the Body of University Professors when the Associate Professorship was converted into a Chair (1983)
- Chair of Applied Economics at the Faculty of Economics, Autonomous University of Madrid (currently held)
- Rapporteur of the Kieler Konjunkturgespräch of the Institut für Weltwirtschaft, Kiel, Germany (1985–1994)
- Vice-President of the Economy and Finance Commission of the Union des Confédérations des Employeurs d'Europe (UNICE), Brussels (1986–1994)
- Member and subsequently Chairman of the Working Group on Economic Policy of the Economy and Finance Commission (1986–1994)
- Member of the Commission for the study and proposed measures for the reform of the personal income tax (1997–1998)

DECORATIONS:

- Spain: Member of the Qualification Commission for King Juan Carlos International Economy Prizes (1981 and 1993)
- Spain: Businessmen's Society Award (1994)
- Spain: Member of the Jury for the Prince of Asturias Social Sciences Prize (1997)

PUBLICATIONS:

- Author of publications in the area of applied economics, particularly public economics

Sirkka Aune-Marjatta Hämäläinen

Date of birth: 8th May 1939
Place of birth: Riihimäki, Finland

EDUCATION:

1961 Bachelor of Science (Economics)
1964 Master of Science (Economics)
1979 Licentiate of Science (Economics)
1981 Doctor of Science (Economics), Helsinki School of Economics and Business Administration; Doctoral thesis: 'The Savings Behaviour of Finnish Households: A Cross-Section Analysis of Factors Affecting the Rate of Saving'

PROFESSIONAL CAREER:

1961–1972 Economist, Economics Department, Bank of Finland
1972–1979 Head of Office, Economics Department, Bank of Finland
1979–1981 Acting Head of the Economics Department, Bank of Finland
1981–1982 Director of the Economics Department, Finnish Ministry of Finance
1982–1991 Director of the Bank of Finland, responsible for macroeconomic analysis and monetary and exchange rate policy
1991–1992 Member of the Board of the Bank of Finland
1992–1998 Governor and Chairman of the Board of the Bank of Finland
1992–1998 Member of the Council of the European Monetary Institute
1992–1998 Governor of the International Monetary Fund for Finland

1992–1998 Member of the Economic Council of Finland

1992–1998 Member of the National Board of Economic Defence

1990–1997 Chairman of the Board of the Financial Supervision Authority

since 1st June 1998 Member of the Executive Board of the European Central Bank

ACADEMIC POSITION:

1991–1992 Docent and lecturer in Economics at the Helsinki School of Economics and Business Administration

OTHER POSTS:

- Member of the Board of the Finnish National Theatre (1992–1998)
- Member of the Board of Trustees, Savonlinna Opera Festival Patrons' Association (since 1993)
- Member of CEPS International Advisory Council (1993–1998)
- Member of the Delegation of Åbo Akademi University (since 1995)
- Member of the Trilateral Commission (Europe) (since 1995)
- Member of the Board of the Foundation for Economic Education (since 1996)
- Member of the Supervisory Board of Finnish Cultural Foundation (since 1996)
- Member of the Central Bank Governance Steering Committee of the Bank for International Settlements (1996–1998)
- Member of the Development Programme of National Strategy (1996–1998)

- Chairman of the Board of the theatre group 'The Raging Roses' (since 1997)
- Member of the Finnish Public R&D Financing Evaluation Group (1998)

DECORATIONS:

- Finland: Commander, 1st Class of the Order of the White Rose of Finland
- Finland: Honorary doctorate awarded by the University of Turku (1995)
- Estonia: Merit Medal, 1st Class of the Order of the White Star

PUBLICATIONS:

- Author of numerous publications and articles in the areas of economics and monetary policy

Otmar Issing

Date of birth: 27th March 1936
Place of birth: Würzburg, Germany

EDUCATION:

1954 Grammar school leaving certificate (Abitur) from the Humanistisches Gymnasium, Würzburg
1954–1960 University of Würzburg: Classical Philology (one year), then Economics (including temporary studentships in London and Paris)
1960 University degree in Economics
1960–1966 Research assistant at the Institute of Economics and Social Sciences, University of Würzburg
1961 Doctorate, Faculty of Law and Political Sciences, University of Würzburg; Doctoral thesis: '*Probleme der Konjunkturpolitik bei festen Devisenkursen und freier Konvertibilität der Währungen. Dargestellt am Beispiel der EWG*' ('Problems of business cycle policy, given fixed exchange rates and free convertibility of currencies, using the EEC as an example')
1965 Qualification at the Faculty of Law and Political Sciences as a University lecturer; thesis: '*Leitwährung und internationale Währungsordnung*' ('Key currencies and the international monetary system'); *venia legendi* for economic theory and economic policy

PROFESSIONAL CAREER:

1965–1967 Lecturer, University of Würzburg; Temporary professor, University of Marburg (1965–1966) and at the Faculty of Economics and Social Sciences, University of Erlangen-Nuremberg (1966–1967)
1967–1973 Professor in the Faculty of Economics and Social Sciences, University of Erlangen-Nuremberg (temporary holder of this Chair: 1973–1975); Director

of the Institute for International Economic Relations (within the Faculty of Economics and Social Sciences), University of Erlangen-Nuremberg

1969–1970 Dean of the Nuremberg Faculty

1973–1990 Professor of Economics and Chair of Economics, Monetary Affairs and International Economic Relations, University of Würzburg

1985–1987 Dean of the Würzburg Faculty

1990–1998 Member of the Directorate of the Deutsche Bundesbank

since 1st June 1998, Member of the Executive Board of the European Central Bank

OTHER POSTS:

- Co-founder (1972) and co-editor of the journal 'WiSt' ('Wirtschaftswissenschaftliches Studium, Zeitschrift für Ausbildung und Hochschulkontakt' – 'Economic Studies, Journal for Education and University Contacts')
- Member of the Law and Economics Appointments Committee of the newly founded University of Bayreuth (1975–1977)
- Chairman of the Economic Policy Committee of the Verein für Socialpolitik (Association for Economic and Social Sciences) (1975–1979)
- Chairman of the Academic Preparations Committee for the 1980 Annual Meeting of the Verein für Socialpolitik (1979–1980)
- Visiting scholar at the University of Michigan, United States (February to March 1981)
- Called to take the Chair of International Economics at the University of Constance (1983)

- Member of the joint working group of the Council of the German Protestant Church and the German Episcopal Conference for the elaboration of a joint statement on 'How can we nurture Creation responsibly?' (1983–1985)
- Specialist adviser to the Deutsche Forschungsgemeinschaft (German Research Association) in the area of economic policy (1983–1987)
- Academic Director of the Second Colloquium of the Confederation of European Economic Associations on the subject of 'disinflation' (since 1984)
- Member of the Senate of the University of Würzburg (1984–1988)
- Visiting scholar at the International Monetary Fund, Washington DC (September to October 1985)
- Member of the Economic Advisory Council at the Federal Ministry of Economics (since 1980, currently dormant); Deputy Chairman (1987–1988)
- Member of the 'Kronberger Kreis' (1987–1990)
- Member of the German Council of Economic Experts (1988–1990)
- Full member of the Akademie der Wissenschaften und der Literatur (Academy of Sciences and Literature) (since 1991)
- Member of the Academia Scientarium et Artium Europaea (European Academy of Sciences and Arts) (since 1991)
- Member of the CEPS International Advisory Council (since 1992)
- Member of the CEPR Executive Committee (1992–1996)
- Member of the Board of the Ludwig Börne Foundation (1992–1998)

- Member of the Inner Board of the Verein für Socialpolitik (Treasurer) (since 1993)
- Member of the Supervisory Board of the Institute for Bank Historical Research (since 1993)
- Member of the Foundation Board of the International Centre for Monetary and Banking Studies, Geneva (since 1993)
- Member of the Academic Advisory Council at the Institute for the World Economy at the University of Kiel (since 1994)
- Founder member of the Advisory Board of International Finance (since 1997)
- Member of the American Economic Association
- Member of the List Gesellschaft (List Society)
- Member of the Arbeitskreis Europäische Integration (Working Party on European Integration)

DECORATIONS:

- Honorary Professorship at the University of Würzburg (since 1991)
- Honorary doctorate awarded by the Faculty of Law and Economic Sciences of the University of Bayreuth (1996)

Tommaso Padoa-Schioppa

Date of birth: 23rd July 1940
Place of birth: Belluno, Italy

EDUCATION:

1966 Graduated from the Luigi Bocconi University, Milan, Italy

1970 Master of Science from the Massachusetts Institute of Technology (returning in 1978 to spend one semester as a visiting scholar)

PROFESSIONAL CAREER:

1964–1965 Military Service: Artillery Officer

1966–1968 Worked for C & A Brenninkmeyer in Germany, Italy and other countries

1968 Joined the Milan branch of the Banca d'Italia

1970–1979 Worked in and was subsequently appointed Head of the Money Market Division of the Research Department (contributed to the policies and reforms concerning monetary policy, the money market and the banking system in Italy)

1979 Director-General for Economic and Financial Affairs at the Commission of the European Communities, Brussels (involved in launching the European Monetary System and in international co-operation on economic and monetary issues)

1983 Central Director for Economic Research at the Banca d'Italia

1984–1997 Deputy Director General of the Banca d'Italia

1997–1998 Chairman of CONSOB (Commissione Nazionale per le Società e la Borsa)

since 1st June 1998, Member of the Executive Board of the European Central Bank

POSITIONS HELD:

- 1988–1989 Joint Secretary to the Delors Committee for the study of European Economic and Monetary Union
- 1988–1991 Chairman of the Banking Advisory Committee of the Commission of the European Communities
- 1991–1995 Chairman of the Working Group on Payment Systems of the Central Banks of the European Community (European Monetary Institute)
- 1993–1997 Chairman of the Basle Committee on Banking Supervision
- 1997–1998 Chairman of the European Regional Committee of IOSCO, which comprises thirty-four countries
- 1997–1998 Chairman of the FESCO (Forum of the European Securities Commissions)
- Other posts:
- Member of the Group of Thirty (since 1979)
- Member of the Monetary Committee (1979–1983)
- Participant in the Committee of Governors and in the Group of Ten (1979–1983)
- Member of the Board of Directors of the European Investment Bank (1979–1983)
- Member of Working Party 3 of the Economic Policy Committee of the OECD (1984–1997)
- Alternate Member of the Council of the European Monetary Institute (1995–1997)
- Member of the G10 Deputies (1996–1997)
- Member of the Advisory Board of the Institute for International Economics (IIE)
- Member of the Advisory Board of the European University Institute (EUI)

- Member of the General Council of the Aspen Institute Italia

DECORATIONS:
- Italy: Grande Ufficiale al Merito della Repubblica Italiana (1989)

PUBLICATIONS:

Author of numerous essays and articles, including:
- *The Management of an Open Economy with 100% Plus Wage Indexation*, with Franco Modigliani, Princeton University, 1978
- *Agenda e Non-Agenda – limiti o crisi della politica ecomomica?* (with Fiorella Padoa-Schioppa), Milan, 1984
- *Money, Economic Policy and Europe*, Luxembourg, Office for Official Publications of the European Communities, 1985
- *Efficiency, Stability and Equity: a Strategy for the Evolution of the Economic System of the European Community*, Oxford University Press, 1987
- *La moneta e il sistema dei pagamenti*, Bologna, 1992
- *The Road to Monetary Union in Europe: the Emperor, the Kings and the Genies*', Oxford University Press, 1994
- *Europe, The Impossible Status Quo*, Club of Florence, London, MacMillan Press,1997
- *Il governo dell'economia*, Il Mulino, Bologna, 1997

Appendix VII
Tables and Diagrams

Table I: *European Central Bank*

Executive Board President Willem F. Duisenberg			Executive Board Vice-President Christian Noyer		
Counsel to the Executive Board Co-ordinator: L. Hoogduin			Directorate General Administration and Personnel H. K. Scheller		Directorate General Legal Services A. Sáint de Vicuña
Directorate External Relations M. J. Körber	Directorate Secretariat, Protocol and Conferences F. Moss	Directorate Internal Audit M. Caparello	Directorate Internal Finance I. Ingram	Directorate Personnel B. van Baak	
Division Official Publications Archives and Library	Division Secretariat			Division Personnel Development	Division Financial Law
Division Press	Division Protocol and Conferences			Division Personnel Policy	Division Institutional Law
Division Translation				Division Office Services and Security	Division Middle Office
				Division Premises	

Table I: *European Central Bank*

Executive Board Eugenio Domingo Solans			Executive Board Sirkka Hämäläinen	
Directorate General Information Systems J. Etherington			Directorate General Operations F. Papadia	
	Directorate Statistics P. Bull	Directorate Banknotes A. Heinonen		Directorate Controlling and Organisation K. Gressenbauer
Division IT Business Development	Division Balance of Payments Statistics and External Reserves		Division Front Office	
Division IT Operations and Customer Service	Division General Economic and Financial Statistics		Division Operations Analysis	
Division IT Infrastructure and Systems Support	Division Money and Banking Statistics		Division Back Office	
Division Central IT Services				

Table I: *European Central Bank*

Executive Board Otmar Issing		Executive Board Tommaso Padoa-Schioppa		

| Directorate General
Economics
G. J. Hogeweg | Directorate General
Research
V. Gaspar | Directorate General
International
and European
Relations
B. Goos | Directorate General
Payment
Systems
J.-M. Godeffroy | |

| Division Economic
Developments | Division Econometric
Modelling | Division
European
Relations | Division
Payment
Systems
Policy | Division
Prudential
Supervision |

| Division Fiscal Policies | Adviser | | Division
Securities
Settlement
Systems
Policy | |

Table II: *ESCB Committees and their Chairpersons*

Accounting and Monetary Income Committee (AMICO) Hanspeter K. Scheller
Banking Supervision Committee (BSC) Edgar Meister
Banknote Committee (BANCO) Antti Heinonen
Budget Committee (BUCO) Liam Barron
External Communications Committee (ECCO) Manfred J. Körber
Information Technology Committee (ITC) Jim Etherington
Internal Auditors Committee (IAC) Michèle Caparello
International Relations Committee (IRC) Hervè Hannoun

Table II: *ESCB Committees and their Chairpersons*

Legal Committee (LEGCO) Antonio Sáinz de Vicuña
Market Operations Committee (MOC) Francesco Papadia
Monetary Policy Committee (MPC) Gert Jan Hogeweg
Payment and Settlement Systems Committee (PSSC) Wendelin Hartman
Statistics Committee (STC) Peter Bull

Table III: *ECB Executive Board*

Otmar Issing	
Directorate General Economics G. J. Hogeweg Deputies: P. Moutot, W. Schill	Directorate General Research V. Gaspar Deputy: I. Angeloni
Division Economic Developments W. Schill	Division Economic Modelling G. Fagan
Division Monetary Policy H.-J. Klöckers	Division General Economic Research I. Angeloni
Division Fiscal Policies J. Marin	F. Browne Adviser

Tommaso Padoa-Schioppa		
Directorate General International and European Relations B. Goos Deputy G. Pineau	Directorate General Payment Systems J.-M. Godeffroy	Representative Office Washington R. Raymond
Division European Relations J. Durán	Division Payment Systems Policy K. de Geest	Division Prudential Supervision M. Grande
Division International Relations G. Pineau	Division TARGET and Payment Processing H.-D. Becker	
	Division Securities Settlement Systems Policy D. Russo	

Table III: *ECB Executive Board*

Vice-President Christian Noyer

Directorate General Administration and Personnel H. K. Scheller	Directorate General Legal Services A. Sáinz de Vicuña

Directorate Internal Finance I. Ingram	Directorate Personnel B. van Baak	
	Division Personnel Development K. Riemke	Division Financial Law E. Nierop
	Division Personnel Policy M. Carroll	Division Institutional Law C. Zilioli
	Division Office Services and Security W. Schuster	Division Middle Office C. Bernadell
	Division Premises T. Rinderspacher	

President Willem F. Duisenberg

Counsel to the Executive Board Coordinator: L. Hoogduin		

Directorate External Relations M. Körber	Directorate Secretariat, Protocol and Conferences F. Moss	Directorate Internal Audit M. Caparello
Division Official Publications, Archives and Library D. Freytag	Division Secretariat C. Stone	
Division Press M. Almeida	Division Protocol and Conferences H. Meister	
Division Translation S. Johns		

Table III: *ECB Executive Board*

Eugenio Domingo Solans		

Directorate General Information Systems J. Etherington Deputy: C. Boersch		
	Directorate Statistics P. Bull	Directorate Banknotes A. Heinonen
Division IT Business Development F. Laurent	Division Balance of Payments Statistics and External Reserves J.-M. Israel	
Division IT Operations and Customer Service M. Lapper	Division General Economic and Financial Statistics W. Bier	
Division IT Infrastructure and Systems Support P. Dickman	Division Money and Banking Statistics M. Stubbe	
Division Central IT Services C. Boersch		

Sirkka Hämäläinen		

Directorate General Operations F. Papadia Deputies: P. Mercier, W. Studener		
		Directorate Controlling and Organisation K. Gressenbauer
Division Front Office R. Schiavi		
Division Operations Analysis D. Blenck		
Division Back Office E. Vermeir		

Convergence Criteria: *EU Member States*

B	Belgium
FIN	Finland
D	Germany
P	Portugal
E	Spain
F	France
IRL	Ireland
I	Italy
L	Luxembourg
NL	Netherlands
A	Austria
GR	Greece
S	Sweden
DK	Denmark
UK	United Kingdom
EU11	EU Member States (excluding GR, S, DK &UK)
EU15	EU Member States

With the
wishes of
the author.

Chris Schweiger
12.VI.2000